Barrie Mahoney worked as a teacher and head teacher in the south west of England, and then became a school inspector in England and Wales. A new life and career as a newspaper reporter in Spain's Costa Blanca led to him launching and editing an English language newspaper in the Canary Islands. Following the successful publication of his novels, 'Journeys and Jigsaws' and 'Threads and Threats', and then 'Letters from the Atlantic', 'Living the Dream', 'Expat Survival' and 'Message in a Bottle' that give an amusing and reflective view of life abroad, he is still enjoying life in the sun and writes regular columns for newspapers and magazines in Spain, Portugal, Ireland, Australia, South Africa, Canada and the USA.

Visit the author's websites:

www.barriemahoney.com
www.thecanaryislander.com
www.twittersfromtheatlantic.com

Other books by Barrie Mahoney

Journeys and Jigsaws (Vanguard Press) 2009 ISBN: 978 184386 538 4 (Paperback and Kindle)

Threads and Threats (Vanguard Press) 2011 ISBN: 978 184386 646 6 (Paperback and Kindle)

Letters from the Atlantic (Vanguard Press) 2011 ISBN: 978 184386 645 9 (Paperback and Kindle)

Living the Dream (The Canary Islander Publishing) 2011
ISBN: 978 145076 704 0 (Paperback and Kindle)

Expat Survival (The Canary Islander Publishing) 2012
ISBN: 978-1479130481 (Paperback and Kindle)

Message in a Bottle (The Canary Islander Publishing) 2012
ISBN: 978-1480031005 (Paperback and Kindle)

Other publications by Barrie Mahoney

News from the Canary Islands (Kindle) 2011

Twitters from the Atlantic (Kindle) 2011

TWITTERS FROM THE ATLANTIC

BARRIE MAHONEY

The Canary Islander Publishing

© Copyright 2012

Barrie Mahoney

The right of Barrie Mahoney to be identified as author of this work has been asserted by him in accordance with the Copyright, Designs and Patents Act 1988.

All Rights Reserved

No reproduction, copy or transmission of this publication may be made without written permission. No paragraph of this publication may be reproduced, copied or transmitted save with the written permission of the author, or in accordance with the provisions of the Copyright Act 1956 (as amended). Any person who commits any unauthorised act in relation to this publication may be liable to criminal prosecution and civil claims for damages.
A CIP catalogue record for this title is available from the British Library.

ISBN 978-1480033986
www.barriemahoney.com

First Published in 2012
The Canary Islander Publishing

DEDICATION

To my life partner, David, for his love and support and for travelling the journey together.

Acknowledgements

I would like to thank all those people that I have met on my journey to where I am now.

To supportive friends who helped me to overcome the many problems and frustrations that I faced and taught me much about learning to adapt to a new culture. Also, to friends in the UK, or scattered around the world, who kept in touch despite being so far away.

To people that I met through working as a newspaper reporter and editor in Spain and the Canary Islands and the privilege of sharing their successes and challenges in life.

Disclaimer

This is a book about real people, real places and real events, but names of people and companies have been changed to avoid any embarrassment.

CONTENTS	
Preface – It began with a dream	21
LIVING THE DREAM	27
Living the Dream	29
Airports and Travel	32
A Bit of a Wrench	33
A Pair of Shorts and a Toothbrush	37
Holiday Souvenirs	41
Airport Security	44
What Does a Scotsman Wear Beneath His Kilt?	47
Post, Phone and Email	50
A Drag Queen at the Correos	51
Keeping in Touch	54
"Lots of Love" or "Laugh Out Loud"?	57
Postal Express?	60
Tomorrow, Tomorrow...!	63
Food and Drink	66
A Recession Busting Breakfast	67
Marmite Soldier, Anyone?	70
Tortillas Are Not Always What They Seem	72

A Drop of the Hard Stuff	75
Environmental	78
Saving the Planet with a Plastic Bag	79
Scotch and Oestrogen, Sir?	82
The Canarian Calima	85
The Magic Blue Ball	88
The Week the Planes Stopped Flying	91
Water from Wind	95
Cars from Bananas	97
Seaside Burps	100
Language and Culture	103
Fax Machines and Bureaucrats	104
Love thy Neighbour - Canaries style	107
The Sunday Slowdown	110
'The Big Sleep'	113
The End of The Siesta?	116
The Spanish Mistress and the Gym Master	118
Not Exactly Cool...!	121
Historical	123
Greenwich Mean Time and the Canary Islands	124
World War Heroes	127
The Virgin and the Pines	130
Health	132
The Boob Job	133
A Playground for the Wrinklies	135
A Question of Convenience (Health)	138

"We Love The NHS!"	141
Legal and Financial	144
Whack a Banker!	145
Until Death Do Us Part (or until someone better comes along)	148
The Telemarketing Plague	152
The Parking Ticket	155
Police Crackdown on Speeding Infants	158
Attitudes	**161**
Build 'Em Up and Knock 'Em Down	162
The UK Election and the Euro Brit	165
The Beautiful Game?	168
Fancy a Change of Career?	171
Boot-camps, (Arch)Bishops and Blogs	173
People, Pets and Places	175
'From Teacher to Drag Queen'	176
A Canarian Garden	178
Walking the Dog	181
A Cat and Dog Story	184
The Uniqueness of Gran Canaria	187
EXPAT SURVIVAL	191
Celebration	192
Canary Island's Day	193
"Your hat looks wonderful, my dear"	195
The Twelve Grapes	199
The South American Factor	202

"It makes me feel alive"	206
"It's hot up my barranco!"	209
Cultural and Heritage	213
Agatha Christie and the Canary Islands	214
The Whistle Language	218
"Is anyone here called Juan?"	221
An Explosive Island	224
Gadgets and Gizmos	227
Technology for Expats - Voip phones	228
Rediscovering Radio	231
Expats and Ebooks	234
Expat Television	237
Go Virtual	241
A Connection at the Mortuary	244
Food and Drink	247
The Vegetarian Expat	248
Fit to drink?	251
Just a Trifle	254
A Mince Pie for Christmas	256
Baking Bread	259
Fancy a Cup of Coffee?	262
Marmite and Mosquitoes	265
Political	268
Voting in Spain	269
Flamenco - the latest weapon!	272
Getting into hot water	274
The European Family	277

Fluffy Tales	281
A Kitten in the Canaries	282
Vets and Pets	285
Vets at home	288

How to do it	291
Debit cards for Expats	292
Complaining in Spain	297
Paternity leave	299
"What's your address?"	302
Learning the Language	305
"You need new track rod ends, Sir"	309

Complaining	313
"I just wanna be OK, be OK, be OK..."	314
A Tortoise called Aduana	318
How big is your gnome?	321
The Sunshine Expat	324

Expat Life	327
Beware of Submarines and Drug Smuggling Grannies	328
Weather influences walking	330
Mowing the lawn	333
The Lollipop People	336
Collapse of the Euro?	339

"Maybe I want to go home?"	343
No doors or windows	344
Lightning Strike	347
Too much of a good thing	350
Hypertension in the Canary Islands	353

Embalming anyone?	356
Expats and Recession	359
'The Seven Year Itch'	362
The beginning of the end, or is it the end of the beginning?	366
MESSAGE IN A BOTTLE	371
History and Culture	372
A Queen Calls...	373
Size Does Matter	376
The Baby Sellers	379
Lighthouses and Lime Kilns	382
The Ship that died	385
Camels and Cauliflowers	388
Admiral Nelson and the Canary Islands	391
Slavery in the Canary Islands	394
Wear White and Throw Talcum Powder	397
Living on a volcano	400
Live and Let Live	403
Mystery, Awe and Wonder	406
Do you suffer from Paraskavedekatriaphobia?	407
Imaginary noises?	410
"The Stars Smile Down on You"	413
Environmental	416
Energy Island	417
Lizards Prefer Islands	420

Daring to dream the impossible	423
Solar Rubbish Bins	426
Are we bothered?	429
A Prickly Issue	433
What a load of old rubbish!	436
Cleaning the floors	439
Places to Visit	442
Head for the Mountains!	443
Just 27 Crossings	446
Small, but beautifully formed	450
Reminders of Home	453
A Mini in the Canaries	454
The Grandfather Clock	456
Reclaiming the flag	459
Something for the weekend, Sir?	462
You Look Well	465
It's an Island thing	468
Tulip Heads and Cabbage Fields	472
Faith, Politics and Beliefs	476
The Euro Game	477
Does one size fit all?	479
Bankers go bananas	483
Quakers in the Canaries	487
The Conservatory Government	493
Food, Drink and Health	496
A decent cup of coffee	497
The World Cradle of Rum	500
Pie in the Sky	503

17

Don't do as I do, do as I say	507
Dentists and Sweets	510
Expat life, Sport and Community	512
Helping Hands	513
A letter from George	516
Blisters and sore bums	520
Extreme Sport or Natural Selection?	523
Look no lights!	526
Where should I move to?	529
Christmas	533
The Poinsettia	534
Sandcastles at Christmas	537
Roundabouts, Girls and Prickly Cactus	540
Final Thought	543

Preface

It began with a dream

When we sleep we sometimes have dreams that come and go in our unconscious state; some dreams are just a little bit of nonsense, whilst others stay with us. Sometimes these dreams become something new for us to achieve or maybe to do something different or better. Maybe it is a dream of a better life, more money, less pressure at work, sunshine, beaches, blue skies, mountains, lakes, quiet places and noisy and exciting places. Dreams are unique, yet there are themes in dreams that bring many people with a common interest together.

For me the dream has often been about islands. From a small boy seeing Brownsea Island in Poole Harbour for the very first time, I have always wanted to live on one. Maybe it would be the Isle of Wight, the Scilly Islands, the Isle of Skye or maybe even further afield?

Maybe the dream will lead to living in another country, working in a different culture, meeting new people, learning more about the world, widening horizons, improving future job prospects, making more money, making new friends and probably learning a new language. For many, the thought of moving to live for a time or forever in another country may remain a dream or a fantasy; a plan for next year, when the kids grow up, after retirement or when there is a big win on the lottery. However, many others actually do live their dream. So how do they live the dream? What did they do? Were they just lucky? Can only some people live their dream?

Another climate will not appeal to all dreamers, as many enjoy the patterns of seasonal weather. The cycle of spring signalling the beginnings of new life and also signalling the end of the cold, wet, winter weather, also has a spiritual uplift for many people around the world. Summer for most people brings time for holidays or more time for relaxation and outdoor activities that can be so miserable in winter weather conditions. Of course, this all depends where you live in the world, as some countries see greater differences in seasons than others, but the security of weather patterns becomes part of growing up and living and who we are.

Despite feelings of contentment with seasons, many people just want to live in a climate where it is not too cold or too wet, and where it is possible to swim in the sea without freezing or to lie on a sun terrace with a cool glass of wine. People who move abroad for a better climate are often called expats and will certainly be foreigners in another country, but they are not lucky or different. They just decided to live their dream, maybe for just part of the year or maybe to stay for longer. If they were not just lucky, what did they do to achieve this? How can we live our dreams?

Another lifestyle will appeal when the pressures of money, families, relationships, jobs and pressure to conform to society's expectations of what people should do and how to behave become too much to bear. Many people will have a lifestyle with which they are content and happy, and can cope easily with the ups and downs of life; the rollercoaster ride that at times takes your breath away and at other times threatens your sanity and stability.

Society expects people to fit in, but there are many people who simply cannot for many reasons, and often for reasons that they cannot explain to others or perhaps even to themselves. So moving somewhere new to follow a different lifestyle is very appealing, especially if the new lifestyle gives less personal pressure, a job without unrealistic demands, a different type of relationship, breathing space away from claustrophobic families, to earn more money or maybe to live where the cost of living is lower. How about a new lifestyle? How did others achieve a better lifestyle? Can I live my dream?

I have learned many things in life, but one lesson that I learned many years ago was that whatever you plan it will change and be better or worse than the original plan; however, it will be different. Life experiences are sometimes good, but they can also be sad, threatening, unhappy and very dark.

However, a dream remains with you throughout your life; it starts as a want and then becomes a need. So, to live your dream you need to believe in the dream, and begin to open a new chapter in your life; this chapter is blank yet you are going to write it.

I grew up in a rural part of Lincolnshire in the UK and then moved to a large town on the south coast to work as a civil servant, and then a new chapter opened and I trained to be a teacher, and eventually became a head teacher of two schools. Throughout this time I had a dream to live on an island, and spent many holidays exploring different islands around the UK and Europe. Only one island offered the perfect appeal for me, but it was not in the UK, and is the subject of another book.

For me life is like a jigsaw, with me trying to fit pieces into spaces that do not always seem to be right. The easiest part of a jigsaw is seeing the final picture that you have made, but the jigsaw of life only becomes clear when we near the end of our lives; maybe just a little late! Journeys are also an important part of our lives as we travel to school, to work, to other places for work or holidays, or just travelling through life; learning and growing from our achievements, as well as from our mistakes.

Journeys and Jigsaws became part of the dream of finding this elusive island, but I could not explain what directions the journey would take or how the parts could fit into the jigsaw, but 'Journeys and Jigsaws' did become part of fulfilling the dream as the title for my first novel.

A new direction began when I became a school inspector for schools in England and Wales, and made many journeys to visit some amazing and wonderful schools where teachers were educating young children and giving them dreams for their future. This job was a privilege and a wonderful experience, but I always believed that we need to know our own sell-by-date, and I sensed that my own was approaching. So it was time to move on, but where?

My move from the UK to the Costa Blanca in Spain and then the Canary Islands in the middle of the Atlantic and just off the west coast of Africa led me to experience incidents that were hilarious, frustrating, unbelievable and heart warming. These reflections (or Twitters as I call them in my magazine and newspaper columns) are about living as an expat or foreigner in another country, and I am happy to share these with the reader if, like me, you have a desire to live the dream and want to learn more from those that have begun to write a new chapter in their lives.

This book is a collection of my three earlier books, 'Living the Dream', 'Expat Survival' and Message in a Bottle, and are published at the request of regular readers of my 'Twitters' who requested a compilation.

All are meant to entertain and amuse, as well as to encourage and support you to live your dream - whatever and wherever that is! What was the name of the island where I had wanted to live so many years ago? It was Gran Canaria.

Living the Dream

Living the Dream

Living the Dream

When I moved to the Costa Blanca, I recall being told by one consular official that, "The Brits come here to die". I quickly discovered that nothing could be further from the truth. In my newly appointed role as a newspaper reporter, I quickly realised that far from going to the Costa Blanca to die, the Brits and other expats had moved to the Costa Blanca to live - and a very good job they were making of it too!

Many people that I met had finally been released from the crippling pain of arthritis and other conditions linked to a cold, damp Northern European climate and had quickly realised that a whole new world of mobility was waiting for them. Others had realised their dream of a home in the sun, inspired by the many "You can do it too" TV programmes, earlier in life - thanks to rising house prices and the newly found equity that they had discovered in their homes. All had one thing in common, fulfilling the dream of a new life and adventure in the sun.

I quickly discovered tap dancing groups, where it was not unusual to discover ninety-year-olds treading the boards, orchestral groups and brass bands, salsa classes, walking groups and drama groups. The area was buzzing with activity and it always amazed and delighted me to see so many British, Scandinavian, German, Irish and Spanish, as well as many other nationalities, enjoying being together. One thing that united many expats was the desire to see a rapid improvement in animal welfare, and I am convinced that the present level of animal welfare in the Costas, although still not ideal, is due to the efforts of the many expat groups, working alongside their Spanish counterparts.

Now that I am living in the Canary Islands there is, of course, a much smaller expat population. The climate is such that much of the expat social life revolves around the bar culture. There are few activities that expats are involved in, although there are plenty of Canarian music, drama and cultural groups to be found, but the enthusiasm for joining these is less obvious than in the Costas. There is also a much younger expat population living on the islands, whose main focus is earning a living and paying the rent or the mortgage. This does not leave a great deal of time for other activities in an area where wages are low and unemployment is high.

Sadly, some expats do not succeed in their attempts to create a new life in the sun. For many, 'living the dream' rapidly becomes 'living the nightmare'. Illness, relationship problems, bereavement or unemployment drives many to return 'home' disillusioned, but wiser. In time, I hope that these would-be expats realise that no experience in life is ever wasted, and that the broader experiences that they will have gained, will stand them in good stead for the future, whatever they choose to do.

Some time ago, I met someone who was well versed in spiritual matters, and commented that ancient ley lines intersect these islands. As a result, these islands draw in a certain kind of person and let go of those it does not want. I remember him commenting that these islands have a force that cannot be avoided. I was sceptical at first, but I have noticed over the years that I have lived here, that of the many would-be expats who have arrived and returned disillusioned, a significant number of these have returned to the islands again a few years later and settled successfully. Many will say that this is due to a positive change in personal circumstances, and a desire to seek the sun and warmth once again. However, maybe, just maybe, the islands have drawn them back again?

Airports and Travel

A Bit of a Wrench

Airports give me problems. Whether it is excess luggage or simply that the wretched security alarms will just not stop bleeping when I enter their territory; it is always an annoying and often embarrassing experience. My recent visit to the UK was a case in point.

Some time ago I was tempted to purchase a new kind of adjustable spanner. It was marketed heavily on television and in the national press and after a sorry incident with our downstairs loo - I won't go into detail here - and many hours of grappling with all manner of antiquated tools, I decided that if I had one of these new 'super spanners' the job would have been done in a flash. Although I dropped many hints to my partner, sadly one did not appear in my Christmas stocking.

After Christmas none were to be seen in the shops and it was my brother who came to the rescue. He would order one from Amazon and give it to me when I returned to the UK. Why he could not have had it sent direct to me I did not like to ask and so I looked forward to collecting the magic tool during my next visit to see the family.

"Now then sir, is this your bag?" came an officious sounding voice at Gatwick Airport security. I had just been frisked once again by a security officer and had thought that my ordeal was over for the time being. I nodded.

"Would you mind coming over to this table whilst I empty your bag? We have just x-rayed your bag and you have two suspicious items inside. I would like to examine these items more closely and in your presence." I was beckoned to a nearby table whilst the security officer donned rubber gloves and began removing all the items from my bag. Oh dear, here we go again!

"My, sir certainly likes his toys, doesn't he?" frowned the security officer as he removed a laptop computer, three mobile phones, various adapters, Tom Tom navigation unit and accessories as well as a number of cables, dongles and plug ins. He frowned again as he retrieved a number of small Christmas presents carefully packed by an elderly relative. He waved one of the small items in the air. "This is one of them. Do you know what's inside?"

I had no idea, but suddenly realising that this was not the correct answer, I replied, "A potato peeler. I cannot get a good one at home and Auntie Gertie thought we would like it."

The security officer smiled. "Hmm, yes, it feels like it. It would be a pity to open it, wouldn't it? Would spoil Auntie Gertie's surprise. I'll x-ray it again and see." This time he was being remarkably helpful and I thanked him. After a moment or two he returned to the table with a spring in his step.

"Yes, that's it. A potato peeler it is, but don't tell Auntie Gertie I told you." He laughed heartily. "Now what about this other item?"

The security officer proceeded to remove the last items from my large and heavy bag. "Hmm, now if I am not mistaken, I think you will find that this is the problem." He triumphantly held my brother's gift - my new adjustable spanner in the air. "You cannot take this on board, sir. This wrench is potentially a dangerous weapon."

"You cannot be serious," I responded angrily. "It is not a wrench, it is an adjustable spanner," I protested, but sensibly recognising that a dialogue about the Oxford Dictionary definition of both spanner and a wrench would not be entirely appropriate at this point. "Look it is still in its plastic packaging. You would need a strong pair of scissors, if not a sharp knife, to open it. We all know that any self respecting terrorist would only consider carrying out his dastardly deed with a pair of nail scissors or a nail file, but I cannot see any terrorist wanting to use my spanner without first removing it from its plastic packaging. To do that they would need scissors or a sharp knife which, as we both know, are banned," I added triumphantly.

This was the wrong response and for a moment I thought that I was about to be arrested. The security officer frowned. "This item, sir, is a dangerous wrench and in the wrong hands it could be a lethal weapon just as it is, plastic packaging and all. I have no alternative, but to confiscate it. You will just have to tell your Auntie Gertie that we are sorry, but she really must not send you back on flights with dangerous items in your hand luggage."

Dear Auntie Gertie, who died long ago I might add, would be spinning in her grave if she knew that an innocent potato peeler and an adjustable spanner, attributed to her generosity in the spur of the moment, were considered even possible threats for an act of terrorism. Now her heavy handbag and sharp stiletto heels were an entirely different matter... Sorry, Auntie!

A Pair of Shorts and a Toothbrush

As much as I love visiting friends and family in the UK and Ireland, the necessary air flight fills me with dread, which is why I avoid this tortuous ordeal as much as possible. No, it is not the actual flying part, nor the possibility of catching pig flu from all that recycled air, nor being crammed into airport buses and queues and not even the major airports' policy of processing passengers like sardines. No, my horrors begin when packing my suitcase, or several in my case, a week or so before the trip. Recent luggage restrictions are ridiculous, after all, my wash-bag alone is almost the entire weight allowance. Add to that, two shirts a day for 14 days, all the necessary vests and thermal underwear, gloves, scarves and hot water bottles - all so essential for a trip away from home, as well as a more than generous inclusion of essential gadgets and their necessary chargers and adapters and you will understand the pain, suffering and soul searching that I have to endure. Yes, I know, I am not alone in my whinging and I do fully understand all about global warming - as if an extra shirt or two would make any difference...!

A very good friend of mine recently took me in hand after I had explained the distress of my forthcoming situation. I listened carefully as he, in whispered tones, revealed some of his travel tips. He laughed, rather cruelly I thought, when he heard of the number of shirts and socks that I had planned to take. "You will be wearing vests, so take just three shirts. Make each one last for two days and then go to the launderette," he laughed. He passed on other gems too - all equally drastic measures.

Hmm, and a good dose of deodorant, I thought to myself, but not wishing to appear ungrateful I continued to listen to his pearls of wisdom. After all, my friend was an ex-marine who had travelled throughout Laos, Thailand and Vietnam for several months with little more than a pair of shorts and a toothbrush. He taught me how to roll and not to fold my clothes. Did I really need to take an electric shaver, electric toothbrush, hairdryer and iron? He thought not and I, after several stiff brandies, eventually agreed, albeit reluctantly.

The big day arrived and I tentatively balanced my suitcase in my partner's hands as he balanced on the scales. After the deduction of his weight and a few adjustments I smugly realised that the overall weight of the proposed luggage was now just 16 kilograms! That was indeed a record for me and I set off to the airport with a new air of confidence, knowing that I had four kilograms available for newly purchased goodies!

Two weeks later I was standing at the dreaded Gatwick airport, queuing to have my bags checked. I had suffered two weeks of just three shirts, visited the launderette twice, had plenty of showers and used lots of deodorant. No one had commented about my wearing the same items of clothing for two weeks and I stood with confidence in the queue waiting my turn. Certainly I had bought a few things, collected the usual batch of Christmas presents from generous relatives. I had bought two large bottles of Vitamin C tablets as well - have you noticed the acute shortage on the islands?

"Had a good trip, sir," came a friendly voice from a spotty youth wearing a smart uniform. This chirpiness took me back a little as both age and experience has taught me that such chirpiness from anyone official in airports throughout the world usually means trouble.

"You're a little overweight, sir," continued The Spotty Charmer, grinning broadly. I thought he could have chosen his phrasing a little more carefully. After all I have been wasting away on a diet for three months or so.

"How much overweight?" I snapped coldly, not about to indulge in pleasantries.

"Ten kilograms, sir. You must have bought a lot of stuff in the UK. I hope it's worth it because that little lot will cost you £100." The Spotty Charmer had suddenly become officious and demanding in his voice, but he continued to smile broadly, although the breadth of the smile was thankfully restricted by the brace on his teeth.

"That's impossible," I replied. "Anyway, ten kilograms at £5 per kilogram is only £50. You are trying to overcharge me, young man."

39

"Not so, sir. If you pre-book your excess luggage before your flight then you can have it for £5 per kilo. If not, it is £10, sir." I no longer liked the way he referred to me as "sir". It had an evil resonance about it.

"What rubbish," I spluttered. "How can I possibly foresee what the overall weight of my luggage will be until I have completed my trip. How can I judge that beforehand?"

"Well, that is your problem sir. Will sir be taking anything out of his case or will sir be paying by credit card?"

"This is preposterous," I exploded. "Sir will certainly not be taking anything out of his case," I retorted proffering my well-used credit card.

"That'll do nicely," beamed The Spotty Charmer, whisking the card out of my hand and into his evil machine.

I sighed, knowing when I was beaten. How my friend had travelled the length and breadth of Asia with a pair of shorts and a toothbrush I shall never know!

Holiday souvenirs

For those of us who live in the Canary Islands, we already know how fortunate we are as these islands have a great deal to offer residents and tourists alike. However, sometimes visitors may get a little more than they bargained for.

At the end of our holidays many of us often like to take home a souvenir of the places that we have visited, either for relatives and friends or as a happy holiday reminder for ourselves. As for which gift to take home from the Canary Islands, I find that locally produced rum generally goes down well or maybe some of the many items produced from the local weed - the medicinal aloe vera plant. Personally, I have learned to steer clear from the dreaded turrón (a strange tasting nougat) commonly disguised as a Christmas 'treat'. Yes, I know that Canarians and Spanish are said to love the stuff, but has anyone actually ever seen a local buy a bar, let alone eat it? I think it is a sinister plot to offload as much of the foul tasting stuff as we can onto unsuspecting tourists. Now what about taking home a nice plant instead?

The first thing to say about this one is that plants are not allowed into the UK without an approved licence. Do please check the rules carefully on this one otherwise you may get rather more than you bargained for. Even so, I do know that many holidaymakers purchase cactus and other plants to take back home. After all, what could be better than a really sharp, vicious looking cactus as a treat for your least-favourite aunt? Maybe give her a packet of turrón as well for good measure. I know from experience that it works wonders with false teeth and should keep her quiet for an hour or two!

So what about the odd termite or two as pets? The UK press recently carried a report from scientists saying that Britain's only colony of termites has survived 12 years of attempts to wipe it out using chemicals. These determined little beasts, which can destroy a house by eating it, were thought to have been destroyed after an expensive eradication programme.

So what has this to do with your holiday in the Canary Islands I hear you asking? Sadly, these wood-devouring mini-beasts were discovered in 1998 in two adjoining homes at Saunton in North Devon. Scientists now believe they had been brought to the UK from the Canary Islands in a plant pot.

Since their discovery, a £190,000 eradication programme, funded by the UK Government, has tried to wipe out the colony of these determined little visitors using a variety of chemical weapons. Under the programme, the area within a 500 metre radius of the two houses was monitored, and an "insect growth regulator" called hexaflumuron was supposed to prevent the insects maturing so they would be unable to reproduce.

They were thought to have been destroyed, but the latest survey of the site has found evidence of new infestation. The scientists and exterminators have gone back to the drawing board to discover a new way of finally eradicating these unwelcome foreign visitors, although rumour has it that they are now claiming political asylum and wish to live in peace in the UK.

So if your holiday is drawing to an end, may I suggest that you hurry along to the shops and purchase some of our wonderful locally produced rum and please don't forget to take home as many packets of turrón as you can carry! We need to get rid of this foul concoction one way or another!

Airport Security

One of the many additional hassles of returning to the UK, even for a fleeting visit, are the security checks. Yes, I know that these checks are essential to thwart the potential terrorist who intends to attack a plane armed with little more than nail scissors and baby teething gel. However, I do wonder why it is me that is nearly always frisked. I can see the security officers 'eyeing me up' as I enter the 'control zone' and I have yet to discover whether it is because I look shifty or whether they just find me irresistible in some way and cannot wait to get their hands on me! Anyway, whatever the reason, I do find it mildly annoying, although often entertaining, and I just hope that they warm their hands first and get it over with as quickly as possible.

This time I approached the Gatwick security zone with supreme confidence. Yes, I had remembered to remove my watch, removed loose change and keys from my pocket, removed my belt (is this really necessary?) and checked for surprise eye piercings, nose studs or anything else that I might have overlooked and that just might set off their sensitive security system.

It was all to no avail because as I walked through the magic electronic archway a piecing alarm sounded and I was duly stopped in my tracks, firmly yet politely, by a burly, but not unattractive, security officer.

"Now what are you hiding in there?" he began pleasantly, whilst I resisted the temptation to refer to a Kalashnikov hidden in my Marks and Spencer's underwear. Yes, I know that such comments are unnecessary and potentially dangerous, but nevertheless I suddenly had an urge similar to that experienced by many - that of pulling the communication cord on the Orient Express or maybe the 16.45 from King's Cross. I smiled benignly and said nothing.

"Well, we'll just give you a quick once over, sir," he grinned, prodding me with a large instrument and waving it around my body like a magic wand. The alarm bleeped again. The security officer looked puzzled. He then discovered my mobile phone in a side pocket, which I duly removed both humbly and apologetically.

"Never mind, sir. It happens," he said pleasantly, waving his magic wand around me once more. "I see you have an iPhone, they are great gadgets, aren't they?" The alarm bleeped once again.

"Now then, sir. You having games with me? Keys? Cash, any hidden piercings that I should know about?" I didn't like the way that he said "hidden", with a smirk, and I shook my head wincing at the very thought of a Prince Albert, although I did wonder how one would get through security if one actually did have this rather painful addition to the natural order. The security officer once again waved

45

his weapon around my body furiously, but sadly I still bleeped. This was it; I was about to be strip-searched.

"Hmm," he looked puzzled. "Maybe it is your trousers." He rubbed his hands up and down my trousers once again. "Yes, I can see a couple of small studs on the pockets, maybe that is the problem." He prodded me firmly rather like a farmer does to a bullock before sending the poor creature off to the butcher. "Yes, I am sure that is it. I think I can let you go."

I heaved a sigh of relief and thanked the security officer profusely after, not for the first time, imagining that I would be taken off to some nearby room and inspected closely with the aid of rubber gloves. I shuddered at the thought although no doubt it depends upon exactly who is officiating.

"Next time, I'll have all your clothes off," he grinned. Once again I was speechless, but made up my mind that the next time I was in Gatwick Airport I would ensure that I was wearing a new pair of Calvin Kleins and not Marks and Spencer's thermal underwear!

What Does a Scotsman Wear Beneath His Kilt?

It was another windy day at the airport. Nothing, particularly unusual in that, Canarian residents might say. After all, it is the continuous gentle breezes that make Gran Canaria such an idyllic place to live. Without these breezes, the island would be far too hot a place to live, let alone to work, during the summer months.

If you are an expat, you will possibly recognise that much of our lives tends to focus around the airport. Collecting friends and family from the airport is always a great delight, although returning them is often a very different matter. At other times, for me, regular visits to the airport are necessary to collect letters and parcels, as well as to have coffee in one of the rather good coffee shops in the airport.

I am often entertained by the antics of visitors arriving and leaving the island, and a few minutes watching returning holiday-makers in those endless queues at the Thomas Cook or Thomson check-in desks often brings its own rich rewards! I am continually amazed by the way in which those calm tour representatives mostly manage to keep their tempers under control! Recently however, my attention was drawn to the check-in desk for the flight to Morocco. It was, as usual, full of chattering men and women many of whom were dressed in elegant robes. Again, as usual, they were surrounded by massive boxes containing television sets, refrigerators, microwave ovens and washing machines. Certainly it is clear that they have a more generous baggage allowance than most of us are given for flights to the UK.

My eyes fell upon an elegant middle aged man dressed in a brilliant white robe edged with gold braiding (a jellaba). It looked splendid and, in many ways, reminded me of a bride-to-be - apart from the greying hair and beard, that is! This gentleman was clearly bored and being accompanied by several other men, who looked as if they were servants or aides, strode away from his collection of boxes and headed towards the door of the airport. He rummaged inside his splendid robe, no doubt in order to locate a packet of cigarettes or his mobile phone, and lo and behold an enormous gust of wind swept around him and lifted this gentleman's robes high above him!

Initially the gentleman looked a little embarrassed, but regaining his usual regal serenity managed to pull the offending garment once more fully around him and immediately headed for the safety of the inside of the airport - the need for a smoke now forgotten for the time being. I can now reveal the answer to the question that I am sure you have been wondering. What was he wearing beneath his glamorous robe?

Pantaloons! The gentleman was wearing baggy, flowing, purple pantaloons that looked remarkably similar to those worn by Aladdin in the pantomime, cartoon and story books. They also looked very much like a pair of curtains that I remember my Aunt Gertie having in her dining room...

So, what of the Scotsman and the kilt? Sorry, actually it was just a ruse to get you to read beneath the title! After all, 'What does a Moroccan wear beneath his jellaba?' sounds nowhere near as interesting as 'What Does a Scotsman wear beneath his kilt' does it?

Post, Phone and Email

A Drag Queen at the Correos

Like so many ex-pats living in the Canary Islands and Spain, I love receiving post from home. Be it a letter or postcard from friends or family, or maybe the occasional magazine; it is good to know that we have not been forgotten. Although there is no shortage of quality shopping opportunities in the Canary Islands, I am a strong supporter of the delights of Amazon and the QVC Shopping Channel and I am often tempted to order the occasional book, DVD or latest gadget on-line.

The world's market place really opened up when I discovered the wonders of eBay some years ago. Now, I can find almost anything on the pages of this wonderful creation. Items ranging from long obsolete batteries for my minidisc (yes, I adore iPods but somehow they never seem to meet the genius of minidisc), replacement parts for an ancient, but much loved Russell Hobbs coffee percolator to very cheap yet effective mosquito netting all find themselves winging their way to one of these tiny islands in the Atlantic.

I have to say that, in the main, the Correos postal service has been very good and I am pleased to report that everything that I have ordered has safely arrived either at our home in the Costa Blanca or the Canary Islands - eventually. However, there was very nearly one rather nasty exception.

Several weeks ago I ordered a rather splendid electronic item from Amazon - I won't bore you with all the details now, but enough to say that it was sufficiently exciting to have me waiting expectantly for the postman each day for nearly five weeks! Amazon told me confidently that delivery would take somewhere between three and seven days. Yes, that did seem a little optimistic, but we often receive post from home that has taken only three days to get to Gran Canaria. Anyway, this item was travelling by courtesy of Deutsche Post and if I know anything about our German friends, it is that an efficient postal service is one of the major assets of their country. I waited with hope and expectation...

Three weeks later the parcel had still not arrived and by the end of the fourth week I was becoming anxious and contacted Amazon. Their advice was to give it "another week" and so, once again, the anguish of waiting for the postman each morning was to be repeated.

Just as we were entering the fifth week and I had all but given up any hope of receiving it, there was a buzz on the door bell and a new, very cheery, postman was holding out a box for me! Yes, it was the long expected parcel from Amazon.

"Are you new to the job?" I asked the young postman, accusingly.

Yes, it turned out that our new postman had just been appointed. I asked what had happened to our previous postman - a very nice man who was also a part-time drag queen by night. Maybe he had deserted his postal deliveries permanently in favour of the bright lights and a wardrobe of new frocks, wigs and feather boas?

The young postman shook his head. No, it turned out that some three weeks earlier our normally reliable postman, and part time drag queen, had chopped off his middle finger during a rather nasty incident with a set of ancient curling tongs, a jar of cocktail cherries and a machete - no, please don't ask me for the gory details! As a result he could no longer continue with his postal round and it had subsequently taken Correos three weeks to appoint his replacement. Ah, so that was the reason why my parcel from Amazon was delayed. How very inconsiderate!

Keeping in Touch

Are you good at keeping in touch with the folks back home? I mean to, but somehow other things just seem to get in the way and time goes so quickly over here. Thank goodness for electronic communication. A quick call or message now and again says it all, or does it?

How do you keep in touch with the folks back home? Email, text messages, telephone, Twitter, Facebook and Skype maybe? I wonder how many of us actually write letters to our loved ones and friends nowadays?

Old habits die hard and, as an ex-teacher, I find it hard to resist reading the results of current educational research. One recent survey of 1200 seven- to fourteen-year-olds conducted for the children's charity, World Vision, surprised me. The survey discovered that one in five children had never received a handwritten letter. A quarter of children surveyed had not written a letter in the last year and 43% had not received one.

With all of us increasingly relying on email and social networking sites to communicate, the research found that a tenth of children had never written a letter themselves. Teachers and experts said that they feared young people were missing out on the pleasures and developmental benefits of letter writing. Maybe they are just over-reacting and creating a news story?

However, if we think about it, handwritten letters do seem much more personal than electronic communication. Maybe it is because by going to the trouble of physically committing words to paper, going to the post office to buy a stamp and posting a letter. Yes, I do know that queuing for a stamp at the Correos in Spain can push us towards breaking point! However, when we write a letter to someone we care about we show our investment of time and effort in a relationship. I guess that is why we tend to hang on to personal letters as keepsakes. I still have some letters written to me as a child by my grandfather and my favourite aunt.

The child gains too. The very effort of writing is a real one. Painstakingly manoeuvring the pencil or pen across the page, thinking of the best words to convey a message, and struggling with spelling and punctuation. Maybe it is an effort worth making, because it is only through practice that we become truly literate – and the experts tell us that literacy is the hallmark of human civilisation. Now, there's a really big thought for us to ponder over our gin and tonics!

So what has happened to all those letters from grandparents that I certainly remember? A letter at Christmas or birthday would often include the added bonus of a postal order too. Do you remember the excitement of opening those? Perhaps the letter even had one of the new definitive stamps stuck on if we were really lucky. Such simple pleasures!

The experts say that if we care about real relationships, we should invest in real communication, not just the quick fix of a greetings card, text or email. Hmm, maybe just for today I'm going to put away my beloved Mac laptop and write real letters to my nephews and nieces. Ah, would that mean a morning queuing at the Correos? Well, maybe not today.

"Lots of Love" or "Laugh Out Loud"?

Forget learning to speak Spanish! It is Textonyms or Textese, also known as SMS language, chatspeak, texting language or txt talk, that we should really be learning as the new language in our newly adopted country.

It all used to be so beautifully simple. In the old days it was rather easy. As a schoolboy, if one was feeling particularly lovesick, passionate or saucy we would blush deeply and include something like SWALK ("Sealed With A Loving Kiss) on the back of the envelope containing our illicit message and wicked intentions. Indeed if one was feeling especially naughty, or totally outrageous, we would write 'BURMA' on the back of the envelope. ("Be Undressed and Ready My Angel"). Straightforward and to the point, wasn't it? We all knew where we were and there would be no misunderstandings, right?

Goodness knows what the jargon of today really means. I love to receive text messages, and particularly those from one of my friends in the UK, but I have to confess that I rarely understand them. Although a perfectly competent speller in real life, the dear boy suddenly seems to enter a world of total linguistic incompetence, nay insanity, when sending text messages to me. It is not only that they read as total nonsense, but also they don't seem to save on many words or letters. In any case, do mobile phone companies really charge for the number of letters that are sent nowadays or is it that we all need an excuse to reduce the English language to the barest of bare bones in order to communicate effectively on these modern devices?

I have, in the past, been very pleasantly surprised to receive messages from texters and emailers ending with LOL, which I had assumed was a term of endearment, if not affection, meaning lots of love - endless affection that, if you think about it, is rather nice. These are very pleasant to receive and make one realise that the world isn't such a bad place after all. However, my naive bubble has at last burst and I can confess that I have been saddened to discover that these promises of endless, unending affection are not what they seem. Actually, it means "laugh out loud" or "loads of laughs", which I don't find at all amusing. It is highly disappointing to at last face the reality that all my friendly texters didn't actually love me after all.

Yes, I know that anyone over the age of 40 is now regarded as a boring old fart with one foot in the grave, but my plea is that I do try. I do understand 'gr8' means "great", 'ru' means "are you?" and that 'cryn' means "crying", but why not crayon? See my problem? In my youth we often used to use the expression 'TTFN' - maybe following the expressions of some comedian of the day, I cannot remember whom, which meant, quite simply, "Ta, ta for now", simple eh? Nowadays, modern texters even use a combination of jumbled letters in their text messages which are little more than secret code that would have made the secret agents very proud. So if they say 'ttyl, lol' they probably mean "talk to you later, lots of love" not "talk to you later, laugh out loud"; and if someone says "omg, lol" they probably mean "oh my god, laugh out loud" not "oh my god, lots of love". Are you confused as well?

It seems that for words that have no common abbreviation, texters simply remove the vowels from a word, and the reader is forced to interpret a string of consonants by adding the vowels when they receive the message. So "dictionary" becomes "dctnry", or "keyboard" becomes "kybrd". It is up to the frustrated reader to interpret the abbreviated words within the context in which it is used.

Yes, I know that language develops and grows and that it is natural for children and young people to play with and adapt language for their own use. We all did it, except that we didn't send text messages, just verbal abuse, which was so much pleasanter. Context is the clue to all this business of trying to read and interpret txtese, and is probably the reason why I shall do my best never to use it. Just imagine the problems that we could get ourselves into! BBFN (bye, bye for now)!

Postal Express?

I know from my previous work as a reporter that many expats quickly become frustrated by the antics of some of the state monopolies in Spain. Dealings with the Town Halls, water and electricity companies, Correos and Telefonica - to name a few, can become incredibly frustrating experiences and can be the stuff of nightmares. With most of these companies, I still get the feeling that they think that we are here for their benefit and not the other way around. The situation is very similar to that in the UK 15 to 20 years ago, when the then UK monopolies maintained a similar arrogance towards their customers.

My problem began several weeks ago when a Spanish friend in Alicante decided that he would like my old laptop computer. I thought I would give Correos another try, particularly as they offered a two-day Postal Express service to Peninsular Spain. It cost 24 euros - not bad in view of the size and weight of the package, and with a guaranteed two-day delivery from Las Palmas to Alicante...

Three days later I received an anxious call from my friend. No, the package had not arrived. My friend was particularly concerned because he had just called Correos in Alicante and they had told him that the package was still in Madrid.

Several days later, I received another call from my friend. He had just received a letter from the Aduana (Customs) to say that they were holding the package in Madrid. There was tax to pay and he had to complete a form and return it to them. My friend challenged this assertion, pointing out that the package was being sent from one part of Spain to another, but this logic does not enter the world of the Aduana.

The laptop was worth only about 100 euros at best because it was several years old. Apparently, because I had purchased the laptop in the Canary Islands (and had only paid 5% IGIC tax on it when it was new), if it was sent to the Peninsular the taxman would want to claim additional tax because the Canary Islands are seen as being outside the EU and Spain for tax purposes. At this point my friend and I wondered whether it really was worth paying tax on the item. We agreed that when it was delivered, and if the tax was too high, he would reject the package and it would eventually be returned to me.

One week later, the Postal Express package had still not arrived. My friend was due to go away on holiday two days later and there would be no one at his home to receive the package. He complained to Correos in Alicante and they agreed that the package would be dispatched that same day and would arrive the following day. Needless to say, it did not arrive as promised.

Two days later, just my friend was preparing to leave for the airport, the package arrived, together with a demand for 25 euros tax. He paid up and went on holiday. The time that the package had taken to get from the Canary Islands to my friend's home in Alicante was just over two weeks - not exactly within two days as promised in the Correos advertising and, indeed, guaranteed in their terms of service.

Yet again, I decided to challenge the lumbering dinosaur and filed a claim against them for breaking the terms and conditions of their service contract. Although my Spanish is not good, I followed this up with a letter outlining the problem and sent it to Correos, convinced that I would hear no more.

A few days later I received a very apologetic letter from Correos, accepting full liability for the problem, and assuring me that I would receive a full refund of all postal charges. True to their word, the postman called today to give me a cash refund! Victories against these lumbering dinosaurs are few, but when they do come, the taste of victory is sweet!

Tomorrow, Tomorrow...!

I guess that many of us have a love/hate relationship with our utility companies. Somehow the electricity, water and telephone companies have little of the charisma of some of our favourite shops and suppliers that we can actually choose. In the UK, even the rigours of enforced de-nationalisation and expensive publicity and marketing campaigns seems to have done little to improve the perception of these lumbering beasts in the eyes of the general public. The same is true in Spain and the Canary Islands, where we are currently going though the same tedious processes of being offered 'alternative suppliers' for our electricity, water and telephones calls - even though we all know that it comes from exactly the same source! I was really touched to receive a letter a few days ago from the old nationalised company assuring me that they would give me a two per cent discount off our electricity bill - if we stayed with them. They omitted to mention that prices were going up far in excess of this anyway! However, I digress.

Last week, I called the electricity company to advise them of a change of postal address. Not that I am actually moving house, I am not, but a post office box tends to be a more reliable way of receiving mail rather than having it lobbed over the gate, as is the favoured method of delivery by our usual postman, the part time drag queen I mentioned in an earlier Twitter, and who clearly has his mind on other things!

As usual the telephone lines were very busy. Earlier dealings with the electricity company had always been less than successful. I was certainly prepared for a long wait with a large glass of wine and a packed lunch at the ready. The telephone rang and rang although, surprisingly, it was eventually answered by a real person, it sounded like a young woman. Over the sound of canned music, I was given a pleasant greeting and she enquired how she could help me. So far, so good. The young woman had some difficulty in making herself heard, as she shouted over the incessant loud chattering and laughter, as well as loud canned music in the background.

I made my request for a change of address and was not that surprised to hear the response, "No, it is not possible over the telephone. You must come into the office with your passport, national identity number, birth certificate," inside leg measurements and all the other requirements for pieces of paper that our bureaucratic Spanish friends seem to love so much! "Ah, so it is not possible to do this over the telephone?" I enquired. I was then told that this was not possible, but that I could send a fax to the company and this would be quite sufficient! Although I was puzzled as to how this would actually prove my identity, I had learned long ago that, apart from their love affair with paper, Spanish officials also adore fax machines - they are far more popular here than in the UK.

I was then put on hold whilst the young woman took some of the details. What was that music playing in my ear? It sounded familiar. Well, it was certainly appropriate for the electricity company, none other than a shrill song from that, in my personal opinion, ghastly, cringe-making musical, Annie (my ears are still recovering from the shock!), "Tomorrow, Tomorrow, I'll love you tomorrow, You're only a day away...!" Someone at the electricity company certainly has a sense of humour, although I doubt they are aware of the irony!

Food and Drink

A Recession Busting Breakfast

In our Canarian village we are blessed with three small grocery stores. They are not very large and it can be a bit of a squash if there are more than a handful of customers in the shop at a time. Despite being surrounded by spacious, modern supermarkets in nearby large towns as well as in Las Palmas city, we have discovered, as have many villagers, that the prices in our local shops are very competitive with the larger supermarkets and usually we prefer to shop locally. There are also other benefits; for example, one shop happily delivers anything to our home, which is a boon for such items as large bottles of water and anything that is particularly heavy. They are also very reliable - items purchased are always delivered to our home later the same day and nothing seems to be too much trouble. I guess our village shops are reminiscent of village shops and post offices in the UK that have since given way to the out-of-town hypermarkets.

On one weekly shopping expedition in the village store, I patiently waited at the cheese and processed meats counter for my turn. There was an elderly Canarian woman in front of me and she seemed to be having some trouble in deciding which cheese she should buy. Eventually she stabbed her finger on the glass counter and pointed to one of large slabs, asking if she could try it. As in all the best UK delicatessens, the shop assistant nodded and cut off a generous slice and passed it over the counter on a cardboard plate for the old woman to try. Ancient, well-worn fingers slowly crumbled the cheese into small pieces and I watched as she savoured each tiny piece of the creamy white cheese. The shop assistant, anxious to return to the girl on the till to continue the morning gossip, watched in silent anticipation.

Eventually, the old woman put the cardboard plate back on the counter with some satisfaction, looked inside the glass cabinet for a second time and pointed to another large slab of cheese of a different variety. Again, she asked for a sample. The shop assistant nodded and cut off another slice, this time not quite as large as the first, and handed it to the elderly woman. Again, she broke it into tiny pieces, savouring each delicious mouthful with relish before nodding and placing her plate on the counter. To my increasing disbelief, once again the old woman repeated the process of pointing to yet another slab of different cheese and, without a word, the shop assistant cut of a small piece and handed it over for the old woman to sample.

By now, there was a small queue of people patiently waiting their turn. Most Canarians are very tolerant by nature (this tends to distinguish them from their Peninsular Spanish counterparts) and we all stood watching with some amusement as the old woman then pointed to some slices of ham. Again, a sample of ham was handed to the old woman to try. This same process was then repeated for two different varieties of olives - each time the old woman savouring each delicious mouthful with considerable enjoyment.

Eventually the old woman appeared to be satisfied. At last she smiled and pointed once again through the glass display cabinet to the first slab of cheese that she had sampled. We all heaved a sigh of considerable relief as a small chunk was cut off, weighed, and carefully wrapped in both plastic as well as tin foil and was finally handed to the old woman, who popped it into the jacket of her cardigan and wandered over to the till to pay for her purchase.

Walking home from the shop I wondered if the old woman repeated this process regularly in all three of our village shops? Certainly, the shop assistant seemed to know the routine well and I admired her uncomplaining attempts to satisfy her customer. I wonder just how accommodating the Saturday girl would be to this old woman in a Tesco's delicatessen in the UK? "There's no such thing as a free lunch," they say, but maybe there is such a thing as a free breakfast!

Marmite soldier, anyone?

There is no doubt that many readers are in uproar after hearing about a most worrying series of thefts in the UK. If you are not already aware, a current wave of thefts from garages and small shops in Northamptonshire is terrorising the UK for fear that this moral decline spreads beyond the confines of this county.

So what is the object of this desire? Well, no other than a much-loved (and often hated) addition to a decent slice of toast - Marmite! Many reports of this heinous crime have been noted in recent weeks, but the current spate of incidents has taken the police by surprise and is particularly alarming with 18 jars of Marmite, with a 'black market' value of around £50, being taken from a single garage shop. The thefts have become so serious that shop owners are now being forced to keep this unique product under the counter for their more discerning customers, or not stocking it at all for the time being. We live in fear of an imminent Marmite shortage.

Marmite can, in my opinion, be equated with Blackpool or Benidorm - you either love it or hate it. There simply is no halfway point. Personally, I like nothing better than a slice of hot toast and butter with a thin spread of Marmite with my morning coffee. Our dog, Barney, who sadly died recently, loved it too and he would sit beside me adoringly, salivating until it was his turn for a Marmite soldier, which he gobbled down with great glee. Bella, our Spanish fruit bat-type dog, on the other hand, obviously detests the stuff and although she knows better then to decline the offer, takes the offending morsel grudgingly between her teeth, so as not to touch her mouth with the foul sticky stuff and swallows as quickly as she can before gulping down a bowlful of water. You see, you either love it or hate it.

Despite promises from the various British supermarkets that have come and gone over the years, occasional appearances in Spar or Carrefour, a regular supply does seem to be missing. European Governments would do well to remember that the temporary shortage of Marmite's main competitor in Australia - Vegemite, very nearly toppled a government!

Marmite, along with the elusive 'J' cloth, pump action Sensodyne toothpaste, Linda McCartney sausages and vegetarian gravy granules are just a few of the products that I always ask friends to bring back to the island for me whenever they visit the UK, or maybe if visiting family and friends wish to bring us something special.

Having just returned to the island from the UK, and being an avid Marmite lover, I can already imagine some unkind comments from a few people who know of my love of this product. I can assure my family, friends and readers that I have nothing to do with this incident. Besides I already have a dozen or so jars safely stored at home - just in case!

Tortillas are not always what they seem

I cannot pretend that it has always been easy being a lifelong vegetarian. From my early childhood days in my home village in fenland Lincolnshire, where my parents thought that I would expire from lack of protein, to my current life in the Canary Islands, I have had to ask, demand, compromise, challenge and examine the contents of my plate very closely. The early days in Spain were very difficult at times, and often still are in some of the more remote villages in the Canary Islands. Many locals thought vegetarians very odd, although would usually attempt to understand and provide an excellent salad or maybe a Spanish Omelette. This is often where the problems began.

Working on the principle that I will not eat anything that has had a face or a mother (and please don't get me on to the subject of eggs!) you first need to understand that many Spanish and Canarians still think of tuna as a plant. Of course tuna is not living and breathing and it is perfectly acceptable to include it as an item in a salad... Fortunately, there are now many cafe bars and restaurants in the Spain, as well as in the Canary Islands, who now know that tuna is most definitely not a plant, but a fish. Yes, but, how about some ham...

There is a small, traditional, yet very friendly bar, just outside Torrevieja, where I would often call in for a glass of wine and maybe some tortilla. It was family owned and I quickly realised that the tortillas were not of the wet and slimy pre-packaged variety that you can easily buy in the supermarket, but a delicious, genuine homemade Spanish tortilla - made by grandma herself. The barman very quickly introduced me to grandma and she beamed with toothless delight when I complimented her upon the quality of her tortillas. From that day on, whenever I called in, there would always be slices of freshly cooked tortilla available. Often the flavours would change and sometimes the old lady would add cabbage, maybe peas and sometimes carrots to the traditional mix of potato and onion, and they were always delicious.

As time went on, the experience began to remind me a little of Letitia, the weird, well meaning old lady in the TV comedy, the Vicar of Dibley, because there were amazing similarities between grandma's experiments and Letitia who, if you recall, would make amazing, yet disgusting, concoctions with fish paste, jam, anchovies and chocolate sauce - all at the same time. I could never be too sure as to what would be the ingredients of the day. I felt trouble brewing, but was never quite sure when it would strike.

Fortunately, on one memorable day, just as I was about to tuck into a slice of the latest experiment that, I was told, contained chopped red peppers, I had the uneasy feeling that all was not quite what it seemed. I removed the mouthful that I was currently chewing into a napkin and examined the contents closely. No, it was not red pepper; it was finely chopped ham. I walked over to the bar and the old lady appeared from behind the plastic strip curtain. She beamed her toothy smile and looked at my enquiring face expecting her usual compliment. This time I shook my head and she looked bitterly disappointed. In faltering Spanish I explained that the tortilla contained ham and that vegetarians do not eat meat. She looked angry, her hand swept up in horror and a babble of unintelligible Spanish flooded in my direction. Her son shook his head sadly and explained in faltering English that grandma was bitterly disappointed with me as she thought vegetarians ate ham. She could not understand why I had declined her latest tasty offering and took it as a personal insult. It was clear that I would no longer be welcome and I fled.

From that day to this I will only eat genuine Spanish Omelette - tortilla de patatas or maybe one with onion - tortilla de cebolla, containing the traditional mix of potatoes and/or onion! Whatever I am told about the innocence of the ingredients of the tortilla on offer I decline gratefully. Sorry grandma, but real vegetarians most certainly do not eat ham!

A Drop of the Hard Stuff

A couple of years ago I bought a rather good camera on eBay. It was only slightly used and I reasoned that it would serve my interest in photography for a few years to come. It was one of those, to some, unnecessarily large single lens reflex digital cameras with all the bells and whistles and megapixels that anyone could wish for.

For the last two years the camera has served me well, taking high quality photographs in readiness for my next book. As and when I could afford it, I bought an additional lens, better flash and so on.

Imagine my horror when, towards the end of August, I retrieved the camera from its resting place in a cupboard and discovered that it had partly melted. Maybe 'melted' is a bit of an exaggeration, but the rubber/plastic handgrip and side panel were now oozing a sticky black gunge - very similar to melting tarmac that we see in the UK after a particularly hot day. The black stickiness was so unpleasant that I could not hold the camera without it leaving a thick black residue on my hand. It covered my shirt in a black oily stain when it brushed against the rubber handgrip and side of the camera. Obviously, it was almost impossible to compose a decent photograph!

I know we have had a very hot August with temperatures approaching 40°C on our terrace, but I am quite sure that cameras are meant to withstand extremes of heat and cold, otherwise there would be no jungle or arctic photos to be seen anywhere!

My first port of call was, of course, the Internet, as this is the modern way to solve most problems. There are few things in life that have not happened to someone else, somewhere before. My search proved fruitless and so I posted a message on one of the camera web-forums asking for help. I received one reply suggesting that I may wish to apply Johnson's Baby Powder regularly to the offending parts of the camera. Now, I know that this stuff is great for babies' bottoms, but I also know enough about cameras to realise that applying a fine dust, however gentle on the skin, anywhere near an expensive camera is just asking for trouble.

I visited several camera shops whose sales staff looked at the camera with disgust. One suggested that I may like to buy a new one, and the other two sales assistants made that sharp sucking-in-of-breath-between-the-teeth sound that I hate so much. It always means expensive trouble. I was right, and fled on both occasions.

I sent emails to two camera repair specialists in the UK. One resisted the temptation to reply and the other suggested it might be my sweaty hands - I think not! Eventually, I received a reply from the camera manufacturer suggesting that I may like to send the camera to their service division and that the cost would be about £200 to replace the handgrip and side panel! This, I suspect, is rather more than the camera is worth.

I sat and reflected over the day's problems with my favourite tipple - a neat Scotch. I came to the conclusion that I was yet again the victim of planned obsolescence that affects so many appliances and gadgets nowadays. Suddenly, I had an idea! I grabbed the nearest piece of clean cloth to hand - my unused handkerchief - and dipped it into my glass of the wonderful golden liquid. I then rubbed the cloth gently over the rubber handgrip and, to my immense surprise and pleasure the black sticky residue began to disappear. I poured more Scotch onto the cloth and rubbed the offending pieces of rubber.

I am now pleased to report that my camera once again looks like new. The black rubber handgrip and side panels now gleam, and they are no longer sticky or leave a residue on my shirt. All it took was a very small quantity of whisky and a clean handkerchief!

Not only does my favourite tipple taste good and help me to unwind, and is a wonderful cure for colds and flu, but is now highly recommended to clean black, sticky gunge off expensive cameras. Cheers!

Environmental

Saving the Planet with a Plastic Bag

I am thoroughly confused about climate change. Like many people I am confused by what seems the overriding evidence that it is man who is responsible for climate change and that unless we act quickly and with determination our planet is doomed. On the other hand, we have the so-called sceptics who maintain that these dire predictions are the result of political and economic reasons and have nothing at all to do with man-made climate change. I guess I am now an agnostic on this issue, but surely if there is any doubt at all, it is best to be on the safe side. Best not to play Russian Roulette with our planet - we may not live to regret it!

This brings me to the thorny subject of a certain French supermarket chain of which I am not too fond. It is one of those annoying stores where I have had a number of arguments about things that annoy me, and which have met with a totally disinterested response. Witnessing and commenting about an elderly woman who tripped over a box of bananas left in one of the aisles due lack of lighting - you actually need a torch to read some of the labels on a cloudy day - met with the defensive comment, "Ah, you see, we switch lights off because we are trying to save electricity and the planet." Never mind the poor old soul being carted out of the store on a shopping trolley like a sack of potatoes and into a waiting ambulance...

On another occasion, whilst buying fruit and vegetables, something I try to avoid in this particular store as they are far cheaper and fresher in my village, I complained that several items on the shelf were already rotting and it was clear what was left would not last long once it had been taken home. It was during a calima when we all know that the island becomes unbearably hot for a few days and that, if possible, it is best to stay indoors with a cooling fan or air conditioning. On these rare occasions most food stores make the most of their air conditioning whereas this supermarket had it switched off. It was clear from watching the staff, who I noticed were already very pink at the gills and sweating uncomfortably whilst the sensible ones had their heads stuck inside freezing cabinets for relief. The lack of customers in the store should have given management a clue that maybe it was too hot to be comfortable or safe. I mentioned this point to one of their 'customer service team' who gave me the reassurance. "Ah, that is because we have the air conditioning switched off. We are trying to save electricity and the planet."

A few days ago I arrived at the checkout with a small quantity of shopping. I usually prefer to shop locally, but my needs were urgent and time was short. I paid the cashier and noticed that there were no plastic bags and asked if I could have some. The cashier shook his head with a smirk. "No, we no longer give them out. You can buy one if you like, but it will cost you 10 cents."

I shook my head and demanded to know why this sudden change of policy was introduced, whilst tempted to tell him exactly where he could place my shopping - back on the shelves where it came from, but thought better of it.

"Ah that is because we are trying to save plastic and the planet," was the immediate, and predictable, reply.

Now, I am fully aware of the evils of plastic bags and particularly the problems that they cause landfill sites and, yes, it would have been better if I had arrived at the checkout with my own bags, but I had not. What particularly annoys me is that it is not that plastic bags are no longer to be used, but that we now have to pay for them. I wonder if anyone has noticed a reduction in prices in return?

I also like consistency and I cannot see why, if the store is trying to save plastic as well as the planet, they are now giving out plastic bags freely at the entrance to the store in order to security seal purchases made at other stores in the shopping centre. At least I used to recycle the old plastic bags for dog poo!

Scotch and Oestrogen, Sir?

A few days ago I made a return visit to Firgas, a delightful small town to the north of Gran Canaria, and a municipality in its own right. This is the home of Firgas bottled water - sparkling mineral water, which originates from a plentiful spring some three miles from the town. It is said that the bottling plant produces around 200,000 bottles a day - no wonder it is popular throughout the islands.

Before moving to Spain, I was totally opposed to the idea of drinking bottled water. I felt strongly that the making and discarding of plastic bottles was not environmentally friendly and, in any case, I had read somewhere that the plastics that the bottles were made from contained many harmful substances that polluted the liquids they contained. Apparently, the environmentalists told us, we are unwittingly absorbing cancer causing chemicals from the plastic into our bodies. No doubt the same can be said for many food and drink products and not just water in plastic bottles. Anyway, I reasoned, I certainly wouldn't be paying for bottled water. After all, I had been drinking the stuff right out of the tap for all my life and it hadn't done me any harm, or had it?

One of the first things that we were told when we arrived in the Costa Blanca was "not to drink the tap water". I knew this, of course, from the many holidays that we had already spent in the country, and it was reassuring to be told by an experienced 'expat' that "tap water is quite safe to drink, but you might get a stomach upset from the minerals if you do... Drink bottled water instead". With this advice from one who knew, I cast my inhibitions aside and decided to drink bottled water instead. After all, when one moves to another country it is important to show some flexibility...! We also invested in a rather clever water filtration and chiller system. These units are supposed to purify and remove any harmful substances that may have found their way into tap water, as well as removing most of those nasty tasting chemical additives and it would mean no more plastic bottles.

Bar room gossip and chat can be a wonderful source of, mostly inaccurate, information for the newly arrived 'expat'! The influence of cheap booze and the fact that few expats take the trouble to learn Spanish before they arrive in the country can result in outrageous claims and notoriously unreliable information freely given to anyone who will listen. However, on one occasion, I had the good fortunate to meet with a, still sober, engineer who worked for one of the water companies in the UK. He confirmed that most substances in ordinary tap water could be rendered harmless by filtration, adding chemicals and the rest, with the exception of oestrogen. I pricked up my ears upon hearing this piece of information and quickly learned that too much oestrogen is certainly not too good for you. Indeed, in men, too much of the stuff can lead to the development of breasts. Now, gentlemen, unless you really crave for a nice pair of breasts, or are seriously considering a career change to become a drag queen possibly, it is best to avoid too much of the stuff. Sadly, my engineer friend gave me little more information than I have repeated here. He had already downed more than his fair share of lager before announcing that this was why he always stuck to drinking lager and rarely touched a glass of water. "But surely...?" I began, and then thought better than to discuss the subject with him any further.

If you 'Google' oestrogen (or estrogen) you will quickly discover the definition that "Oestrogen is the main sex hormone in women and is essential to the menstrual cycle." This is lovely for the ladies, I am sure, but I am not sure that we should be drinking the stuff in our 'Café con Leché'. Indeed, can you imagine placing an order at the bar for a "Double Scotch and Oestrogen"? Ah, you already have.

Returning to Firgas bottled sparkling water. It is a lovely refreshing drink and I am reassured that it is sold in glass bottles. Cheers!

The Canarian Calima

Newly arrived residents and visitors to the Canary Islands often mistake the Calima as haze or overcast weather. Actually, it is a fine layer of very oppressive dust and sand laden wind that covers the islands occasionally during the winter months, but more often during the summer. Right, now for the geography and science lesson.

The Calima, like it's 'big brother', the Sirocco, blows from an area of high pressure usually over Northern Africa and the Sahara and is driven by South Easterly winds out into the Atlantic and over the Canary Islands. Such storms and the rising warm and humid air can lift dust 5,000 metres or so above the Atlantic blanketing hundreds of thousands of square miles of the eastern Atlantic Ocean with a dense cloud of Saharan sand, often reaching as far as the Caribbean.

The Calima originates in the Saharan desert, where a unique microclimate exists, known as the Saharan Air Layer. This consists of a dry, dust-laden pocket of air that forms over the desert, normally between spring and summer. This pocket then hangs over the desert up to a height of a couple of kilometres into the atmosphere. However, if the wind swings round to blow across the Canary Islands from the south east, it can bring a Calima at any time of year. It picks up the Saharan Air Layer and drives a proportion of it across the water to the islands, whilst the rest is dispersed across the Atlantic or via rainfall.

The effects of this dust storm can be felt in a variety of ways. Most notable is the sudden rise in temperatures that a Calima brings – even in the winter months. The dust which lies in the atmosphere creates a barrier for rising hot air, trapping it closer to the earth's surface. Combine this with the fact that it is often a hot wind that brings the Calima here in the first place and it is easy to see why they result in a mini heat wave.

As can be expected when a substantial quantity of fine dust particles is suspended in the air, the Calima often causes a range of side effects for local residents' and holidaymakers' health alike. Particularly for those suffering from asthma and other related breathing difficulties. It can also irritate the sinuses, eyes, ears, throat and stomach as a result of exposure.

Canarian Calimas can last anything from a few hours to about a week. However, the Calima generally lasts for two to three days on Gran Canaria and during the summer months is accompanied by a significant rise in air temperature. The air turns a reddish-brown shade. This fine film of dust and sand can creep through doors and windows and creates havoc with outside patios, outdoor furniture and cars, which all need a good wash and scrub when it ends.

Sometimes locusts are also blown over from the Sahara region of North Africa, but they usually don't live long after their journey, which is probably just as well for the farmers and gardeners of the islands. The dust from calimas that originate in the Sahara can be carried across the Atlantic Ocean much further than the Canary Islands and can reach as far as Florida and Puerto Rico (and not the town in Gran Canaria).

Conditions can deteriorate to such an extent that it sometimes forces public life and transport to a standstill. In January 2002, the airport at Santa Cruz in Tenerife had to be closed because of poor visibility - pilots could see for less than 50 metres in front of their planes.

Locals tell me that the best thing to do is, and my apologies for this very sexist statement, if you are a man, to stay indoors with a few mates and a ready supply of cans of beer and watch football on the television, whilst the women usually head for the local commercial centres!

The Magic Blue Ball

It was just one of those regular shopping trips to the local hypermarket. Not only do I like the store but, as a lover of all gadgets, the self service checkout machines do intrigue me, despite the fact that I invariably have to seek assistance from the patient lady supervising the operation. After all, when is a tomato not a tomato? When it is Canarian and on special offer is the answer. How about multiple items? Hmm, well practice does make perfect they say.

"Have you tried one of those new Magic Wash Balls?" asked our friend, who was lingering by the checkouts. "They're wonderful. They're hard to get, you know, but they have just got some in today. George swears by them."

I was intrigued. Anything that George swore by was well worth checking out. However, intrigue was replaced by cynicism when I heard that this magic blue ball, now apparently all the rage in Portugal and Spain, did away with the need to use washing powders, liquids or indeed any of the less than environmentally attractive yet expensive additives that we have all been conditioned to use over the years. It seemed that one Magic Ball lasted for at least 1000 washes (around 3 years), did not need topping up with any expensive refills and, as well as being environmentally friendly, meant that a low temperature wash could be used.

"It can't be. How does it work?" I asked.

"We don't really know, but we are hoping to pick up a couple now. As I said, George swears by them."

As I handed over 15 euros to the cashier for this very doubtful piece of plastic I could hear my mother extolling the virtues of Persil, Omo and Daz in my ears. All these distant memories from childhood were now to be replaced by one rather uninspiring blue ball.

Two months on I am pleased to announce to the world that it does work! I have since bought a second Magic Blue Ball, as advised by the manufacturers for use with a very large wash. I calculate that we have already saved a small fortune in washing liquids and powders, not to mention reduced electricity and water bills. No longer is the nasty powder clogging up the pipes and drains, or polluting seas and rivers that, I have to confess, does make me feel a little smug.

"What about the perfume?" asked one cynic, her eyes flashing dangerously at the mere suggestion that she should abandon her Persil whiteness (and it shows! You see, how the advertising jingles have got to me?). I gently reminded her that we wash to make clothes clean and not just for the nice smell. In any case, I suggested, she could always use fabric conditioner for the perfume. My reasoning fell on deaf ears.

Yes, I am now an unashamed apostle for the Magic Ball. I tell everyone how wonderful it is, but I have learned not to mention it to those who, shall we say, are a little set in their ways. After all, not everyone wants to save money and are happy to clog their machines and pollute the environment.

The Week The Planes Stopped Flying

The day has been silent. We live quite close to the airport and are used to seeing the many flights arriving each day with their cargos of white, pallid, passengers, released from the tight grip of a Northern European winter, looking forward to the comforting warmth of the Canarian sun. Often, we see the same passengers a week later at the airport, this time in the departures queues, looking browner and healthier, if not sadder, as they prepare for their weary flights home.

Today was different. There were no queues of frustrated travellers and irritating tour representatives herding their reluctant passengers into long queues to await their turns at the check-in desks. The waiting area was empty. The glaring departures board screamed the one word that no one wanted to read, 'CANCELLED'.

The volcanic ash from Iceland has done its worst for our islands, already teetering from the effects of recession. Hoteliers, bar and restaurant owners and shopkeepers, all looking forward to the heady days of a springtime tourist revival, shook their heads as they shared and commiserated together the events of one of the worst weeks in the tourist business on the islands. The planes had stopped coming and in their hand-to-mouth business, so too had the hard earned currency that would help them to keep their businesses open for another season.

Back in the airport, I spotted activity around the customer service desk of one of the low cost airlines.

"I need to get home before then, my son's medication has run out," cried the grey haired mother with her disabled son standing silently at her side.

"We'll give you a flight back next week, but other than that you are on your own," came the harsh reply to one desperate family, surrounded by pushchairs, a crying baby and a screaming toddler.

"You pay nothing and you get f**k all," came the words of an angry young man clutching a rucksack. "I should have known. I will never fly with this bunch of cowboys again."

The customers of another low cost airline - the one with the smart orange tracksuits - fared rather better. This airline appeared to be treating their customers with the respect that they deserved. Not only were they booking passengers into alternative flights, but they were also putting them up in hotels. They may not have been where they wanted to be, but at least their clients would not have to spend a night on the beach.

The local television crew arrived to film the antics and the anger outside the office of the low cost airline. The passengers instinctively turned their backs against their cameras - after all, why should their misery be the stuff of the evening's television entertainment?

I left the airport, disturbed and saddened and began to muse upon a world without the precious, noisy, fuel-guzzling machines that dominate our planet. Our reliance upon these monsters of the sky, carrying their bellyfuls of passengers to exotic destinations is something that we all take for granted. Once they stop flying, even for a few days, holidays and finances are ruined, perishable goods such as fresh fruit, vegetables, food items and flowers lay rotting in warehouses in Las Palmas, London and Nairobi and national economies begin to crumble.

Maybe one day in the future the planes really will stop flying. Children will gather to hear tales of giant flying metal birds carrying people to destinations in the sun. Will we also be telling them of tales of complaining passengers, sitting in silence watching noisy cartoons on large screens, who have only paid the price of the latest best seller for a ticket to a far away destination? Will we tell them about the food and drink in plastic trays and beakers and the complaints that it is not as good as they could get in their local takeaways? What about the planes themselves? Will we visit them in museums and both admire and loathe them for the way in which they changed our planet forever?

In a week of chaos and inconvenience, maybe we should be grateful for the silence, and the opportunity that the volcanic ash from Iceland has given us to reflect upon a world without these whales of the sky, and begin to imagine a flight-free world in their place?

Water from Wind

Turning water into wine is a great idea, but how about turning wind into water? I have always loved windmills. Their graceful form and natural motion have always fascinated me. However, I know that many people also hate the sight of them as yet another of man's intrusion upon a beautiful landscape. However, now that a new era of limited fuel supplies is upon us, harnessing the wind to provide a cheap and sustainable source of fuel to feed our unending desire for electricity seems much more attractive.

A drive to a Canarian village near my home, Pozo Izquierdo, near Vecindario, will provide a physics lesson that is not easily forgotten. Not only is it a great place for a good walk with the dog and some fresh air, but you will be in the centre of a wind farm that not only produces electricity from the wind, but also any excess electricity produced is used to desalinate water from the seawater that surrounds this island paradise.

Saving water, one of the island's scarcest resources due to the lack of rain, has led to extensive research in the desalination of seawater and using wind power to operate small desalination plants. The islands are not short of wind power – the Trade Winds, with their moderate speed and direction, are constant throughout the year. This technology and ideas have since been exported to many other parts of the world.

One of the main objections to wind farms has always been that they produce a varying amount of electricity. This variability of supply in the electricity grid means that there must be other power generators, such as gas fired units, that can come 'on line' at short notice – in order to avoid wide fluctuations of power and your television or washing machine blowing up. Keeping these generators 'at the ready' is an expensive use of resources and is often the quoted reason for not using wind powered generators.

Now this is the clever part. The desalination of water is an expensive process and requires a lot of electricity. However, scientists found that the wind generation of electricity and the process of desalination of water can work together successfully for the simple reason that electricity cannot be cheaply stored, but water can. Using surplus electricity from wind farms such as the one in Pozo Izquierdo to desalinate seawater is the ideal solution. When there is a falling amount of surplus electricity, the number of desalination units operating is reduced. The water produced when the wind farms are in full production can then be stored relatively cheaply until required. Clever stuff, eh?

Cars from Bananas

I like eating bananas and, since coming to live in Gran Canaria, I am now a passionate advocate for this humble fruit, which, incidentally, is also called "the fruit of the wise". From a health point of view, it really is a wonderful addition to the weekly shopping list, as it contains vitamins and minerals essential for the human body. Bananas contain Vitamin C, potassium and dietary fibre, but do not contain sodium, fat or cholesterol. Bananas also contain three natural sugars, sucrose, fructose and glucose and gives an instant and substantial boost of energy. They also contain Vitamin B6, which helps protect the immune system and the functioning of the central nervous system. Pretty good stuff, eh?

Yes, I like bananas. Not those perfectly shaped and tasteless Caribbean Eurobanana varieties that grace the shelves of the UK supermarkets, but that gem of all bananas - the Canarian banana. Small and sometimes misshapen they may be, but the creamy yellow flesh and sweet taste make them very special.

Maybe I am just a little biased, because after all, I am surrounded by them. However, 18% of all the bananas eaten in Europe are produced in the Canary Islands, and very important to the islands' economy they are too. Amazingly, around 10 million banana plants are grown in Gran Canaria each year - that is a lot of bananas for one small island, and this produces an awful lot of waste.

In the past, banana plant waste was used as a support for growing the equally popular tomato plants, and in crafts such as basket making and artificial flowers. The plant waste was also used as fodder for cattle and goats, but factory farming has replaced this with concentrated feeds. Today, this vegetable waste is deposited in ravines on the islands where they naturally decompose. An estimated 25,000 tonnes each year of natural fibre is found in this waste. Indeed, what a waste!

Not any more, it seems. The European Union is currently funding something called the 'Badana Project'. This imaginative scheme is focused upon developing a process that will convert this natural organic waste into plastics that will be suitable for making cars, washing machines and kayaks, to name just a few of the intended uses.

It appears that there is money in banana waste too. Judging from the list of organisations sponsoring the project with the European Union, along with universities in the Canary Islands, Spain and Belfast, and companies from the Canary Islands, Spain, the Netherlands, Hungary, Bulgaria and the UK. The old truism, "Where there's muck there's money", springs to mind. Maybe it should now read, "Where there's bananas there's plastic."

Just a few more facts about the humble banana. The word banana is derived from the Arab word "banan," which means finger and, unlike most other fruits that grow on trees, bananas grow on plants.

Incidentally, the word 'badana' from the 'Badana Project' really is the fibre obtained from layers of the banana stem and not just 'banana' spluttered by a European Union official with a bad head cold!

Seaside Burps

"Oh, I do like to be beside the seaside!" goes the familiar music hall song and maybe most of us agree with the sentiment. It is also a pretty safe bet that if you are reading this 'Twitter' you are either living by the sea or thinking about doing it!

We Brits love our traditional seaside holiday resorts. Strolling along the promenade wearing a thick pullover, gloves and scarf on a cold, wet day, breathing in the fresh sea air just makes us feel so glad to be alive, doesn't it? Alright, we also look forward to going back home to a cosy fire and a hot cup of coffee to thaw out. We Brits are mostly a hardy lot and somehow, at the time, the cold and damp didn't seem to matter too much because we were breathing in all that fresh ozone. It is just so good for us, or is it?

As a child growing up in rural Lincolnshire, it became a family tradition that if we were recovering from a cold or flu, my father would take us to Skegness for the day. "This'll blow away those germs, lad," he would say, although privately I suspected that when I got home, I would end up with pneumonia anyway. Yes, Skegness was just so bracing and that sea air, well...!

So, Skegness it was to be for much of my early life, later to be superseded by the delights of seaside resorts that I still know and love. Blackpool, Weymouth, Bournemouth, Brighton, Benidorm ...!

Benidorm, now where did that come from? Like many of us, I quickly learned that to enjoy more of the delights of the seaside that didn't require the protection of a raincoat, scarf and gloves would mean a move overseas.

As I grew older, the longing for the seaside was never far away. Those bracing walks with the dogs were quickly followed by a leisurely look through the holiday brochures to plan our next holiday in the sun. One thing was for certain, even though I didn't like the cold, wet, grey Bank Holidays by the sea in the UK, I did feel a longing to be beside a sea that was blue, clean and sparkling. Like so many before me, I dreamt of sunbathing on golden beaches, and not the muddy flats of coastal Lincolnshire.

Maybe it would be the Costa Blanca, the Costa del Sol, the Canary Islands, Portugal or further afield if funds permitted? Very quickly the dream of living by a seaside that I could visit anytime that I wished became too much, and this is why I am now living only a very short distance from the sea in the Canary Islands; a move that I am very thankful for.

So what is it that gives the seaside its distinctive flavour? The sand? The endless rolling waves or the distinctive smell maybe? Maybe it really was the "bracing ozone" that my father was convinced would do us the power of good during our period of recuperation? It took me some years to discover the truth.

So what is it that gives the sea its distinctive smell; the unmistakable whiff that we associate with summer holidays? Without wishing to ruin the romantic view of the sea that many of us share, that wonderful smell of the sea is actually due to nothing more exotic than flatulence; wind, burps and farts to you and I! Cows do it. Horses do it. People do it after drinking lager, or while eating a spicy curry. We all pass gas and lots of it too.

The seaside's familiar "bracing" smell is caused by a chemical produced by coastal bacteria, which is present in very low concentrations. Basically it is micro organisms in the sea, tucking into tasty morsels of plankton that they like best, and relieving themselves with a little burp afterwards.

So, the next time that you are enjoying a spot of sea air, just remember and be thankful for the countless millions of microscopic organisms enjoying their lunch in the sea, and relieving themselves of excess wind afterwards. Breathe deeply now!

Language and Culture

Fax Machines and Bureaucrats

Expats living in Spain will quickly become aware of how much Spanish officials adore reams of paper and boxes of rubber stamps. Well, closely, allied to this obsession is the heady adoration of that once wonderful, but now antiquated technology of the past - the fax machine. Yes, I have to admit that I used to be fascinated by the thought that a piece of paper could be put into one of these machines in London and yet, almost in real time, it would pop out from another very similar machine in New York. If you think about it, it really is a very clever process.

However, times have moved on and we now have the Internet, emails and text messages, and somehow the humble fax machine looks like something rapidly destined for a museum of 1970's technology - or is it?

Since moving to Spain I have come to realise that it is essential to have a fax machine at home or at least to have ready access to one. Its use is still demanded by the many faceless officials oiling the wheels of the Spanish bureaucratic machine. Without it, the newly arrived expat will undoubtedly face a life of complete misery and degradation. "What, you don't have a fax machine?" I can hear the bureaucrats spluttering, as they tuck into their mid-morning breakfast at their desks, a ham filled bocadillo in one hand and mobile phone in the other.

A few days ago I decided to change the bank that I use to pay one of my direct debits. My initial thoughts of a quick phone call to the company concerned to change the bank details proved not to be the case. Several hours later I am still trying to achieve what would be, in the UK, a very simple procedure. My initial telephone call earlier this morning was greeted with astonishment that I should even want to consider the process of changing a bank, followed by a request that I make another request, this time by fax, confirming what I wanted to do and giving the necessary account details. Surely I could send an email? No, it had to be a fax, Maria, the lady at the end of the phone insisted politely.

My hastily typed and faxed letter was then followed up by a return phone call from Maria. Did I really want to change the bank details? Yes, I confirmed. Well, in that case, would I send a send a letter or a document from the new bank confirming my account details? This, of course, had to be sent to Maria by fax.

Once again, I plugged in the fax machine, and this time sent another letter, together with a letter from the new bank confirming the account details. This was followed by another phone call from Maria, who was now sounding a little more aggressive, complaining that although she had received my letter and the letter from the bank - the faxed letter had omitted to include my full name and fiscal number. Would I send them another letter, preferably the front page of my cheque book, which would include both my name and account details - once again, by fax. Oh, and by the way, could I fax them a copy of my passport and residencia certificate at the same time?

Three hours later, and as I type this, a simple process that should have been dealt with in a few minutes, is still grinding on. Once again, Spanish bureaucracy is beginning to wear me down and Maria will be spending all her day changing my one direct debit and I won't get any writing done. Maybe I won't change banks after all!

Love thy neighbour - Canaries style!

There is an old saying that we get the neighbours that we deserve. I have had some lovely neighbours over the years, but there have been a few strange ones, which have left me wondering what I have done to deserve them!

Do we ever really know our neighbours? From a quick glance at the rotary clothes dryer, we know that the lady of the house next door has a liking for daring red underwear, and that the gentleman of the house likes to use his power drill early on a Sunday morning. Goodness only knows what he is doing, but surely there are only so many holes that can be drilled in a lifetime with a Black and Decker? We also know from the ghastly smell that wafts over from the adjoining wall, that barbecued fish is a speciality and a delight to look forward to each Saturday evening, whilst Wednesday afternoons is the time when mother-in-law arrives to give the house a good clean.

If we are truly honest with ourselves many of us may admit that most of us rely on our neighbours for entertainment, as well as friendship and the occasional 'cup of sugar'. Over the years, I have witnessed plots and scenarios that would put Eastenders and Coronation Street to shame. I vividly remember the dear old couple next door when we were living in the UK. Mary was a charming woman, a member of the local Women's Institute and pillar of the community and a keen ballroom dancer, who would regularly make us delicious cakes and biscuits, and occasionally walk the dogs. Little did we know at the time that she was planning to do away with her husband and run away with a bookmaker boyfriend, also a keen ballroom dancer, to Corfu on the proceeds. As she was escorted from the house into a waiting police car, we realised then that Mary's famous chocolate cake would no longer be appearing on our doorstep. It was a supremely sad day for us all. Ballroom dancing has a lot to answer for.

Even though those "very nice people next door" or "the charming couple across the street" seem respectable enough people who happily water our pot plants for us or look after the cat when we are away, or do some shopping for us if we are sick, do we really know what goes on behind those shutters? It seems not.

A recent local news item caught my eye the other day. Apparently two men living in a neighbouring town owned very similar cars - both white Ford Fiestas. One was slightly smarter and more importantly, a newer model, than the other and so one neighbour decided to switch the number plates from his own Fiesta for those from his neighbour's car. The renegade neighbour then duly parked the car as his own in the same street.

Not surprisingly, the owner of the older vehicle noticed that something was wrong and alerted the local police and told them that there was a car, identical to his own, parked in his own street. The police investigated further and noticed some cosmetic changes made to the vehicle, including new painting on the wing mirrors, a set of new hubcaps, and a new tinted rear window. The true identity of the vehicle was confirmed once the police had checked the chassis number. The police are now searching for the errant neighbour, which shouldn't take too long as these islands are quite small.

I doubt the two men will be good neighbours for some time to come, which only goes to prove that to remain good neighbours, "Thou shalt not covet thy neighbour's Fiesta"!

The Sunday Slowdown

As a child and teenager growing up in rural Lincolnshire, I always hated Sundays. For me it meant a day when nothing ever happened. I was forbidden from playing with my friends, riding my bike, playing loud music and doing the normal stuff of everyday life. Usually, I was told to "sit quietly and read a book" with maybe the highlight of being sent to Sunday school in the afternoon.

Maybe it was my grandfather's influence upon the family. He didn't believe in modern day technology. The telephone, radio and certainly not the television were considered to be loathsome instruments that were the work of the devil and steadfastly refused to have anything to do with any of them. He was a firm advocate of "The Sabbath is the Lord's Day and to hell with the rest of the world" syndrome and even shaved late on Saturday evenings so that he didn't have to lift a finger and offend the Lord on Sunday morning. I could never work out the logic of this one because surely hair grew at the same pace, even on the Sabbath?

Sunday School was another disturbing influence in my life. There are only so many of those wretched sticker stamps of religious figures that a growing lad can stick in an album without having a breakdown, assisted by the monotonous drone of a half-witted, rapidly balding Sunday School teacher. Even then I knew it was a con, because Jesus always appeared as a white-skinned tall figure with long flowing blonde hair. I knew a little geography, thanks to all those books I had to look at on Sundays, and reasoned that he couldn't have that colour skin given where he came from. Fortunately, Scott, one of my best friends, alerted me to the fact that the local sweetshop was open on Sunday afternoons and for many months after this glorious discovery we would meet there, spend the Sunday School collection money on gobstoppers, liquorice, sherbet dips and all manner of sweet junk, stuff ourselves silly and then go home claiming to have been at Sunday School all afternoon.

Later, when I went to college, the freedom of doing what I wanted, when I wanted without feeling guilty on this dreaded day was bliss and it took some getting used to. However, for me, there was still one problem. All the shops and anywhere of interest were closed on a day when I had the time to look and enjoy all that was on offer. Why did the government insist that everything was closed on Sundays? It just didn't make any sense.

Later, of course, politicians of all persuasions came to their senses and grudgingly allowed Sunday shopping, albeit within a number artificial constraints. This period of relative freedom was, initially, bliss. I could visit Tesco, B&Q and all manner of stores when I wanted. I had my own home by then and it was perfect for buying the bits and pieces needed to renovate the cottage that we were living in at the time. No, my parents, and certainly my grandfather, would not have approved of my use of a Black and Decker drill late on Sunday mornings.

Moving to Spain and the Canary Islands was a shock to the system in many ways, and certainly the Spanish attitude to Sundays. All the shops, other than those designated for tourists, are closed. The large department stores and commercial centres are closed too. There are few flights to and from the usually busy airport. There are few cars and very few people around until at least midday. It is only at about 2.00pm that I catch a sniff of the gut-wrenching, foul smelling odour of fish being barbecued by the neighbours as the family arrive for Sunday lunch.

Even the usually vociferous dogs seem to know it is a day of rest and cease their barking until at least midday. There are no children to be seen, or heard. Strangely enough, I seem to have come full circle. Maybe it is best if I settle down quietly and read my book after all.

'The Big Sleep'

Have you noticed that often when we go into a shop in the UK, and the item that we need is out of stock, we are told that it will be "in on Tuesday"? Similarly, in Spain, the response is usually the predictable, "mañana". However, this is not the case in the Canary Islands. Here we have the more elaborate response, given with a shrug of the shoulders, of "It will be about six weeks, as it has to come by boat from Barcelona". It is something, that after the initial frustrations, we learn to accept. After all, we do have the most wonderful climate and the worry about getting a certain design of wall tile quickly fades into insignificance.

Does 15 August mean anything to you? Well, it is the Feast of the Assumption, Independence Day for India, Liberation Day for South Korea and Madonna's birthday for starters. Yes, the 15 August is an important day for many people around the world and, most importantly for the good people of these small islands, it is the official beginning of 'The Big Sleep'.

I say it is the official beginning of 'The Big Sleep' because, in reality, it has really been going on since the beginning of July and will, no doubt, continue to the end of September. The 15 August is more like the 'official climax' to a summer of doing very little or maybe doing nothing at all, which is even more poignant during this period of recession and major unemployment on the islands.

As much as I enjoy living and working in Spain in general, and the Canary Islands in particular, I have to confess that I do find 15 August irritating. Of course, it is the traditional beginning of the two-week summer break taken by many people of the Mediterranean countries. After all, the days are hot and sticky and the temperature is not conducive to any form of excessive physical activity. It makes a great deal of economic, health and common sense to close down building operations and any form of manufacturing during these heady summer days, and I have no problem with this at all.

What I do have a problem with are post offices, banks and council offices. Why is it that post offices, banks and government offices also decide to reduce their opening hours at a time when the holiday season and the numbers of visitors are at their peak? Why, in the comfort of their air-conditioned palaces, do post office, bank and government staff suddenly decide to operate a go-slow for most of July, August and September?

Postal deliveries are all but suspended, customers wishing to post a postcard home or pay their water bills join an endless queue - little realising that it will be at least two hours before they escape their torment. Good natured, but wily Canarians know all about such trials of life. After all, they usually have the good sense to bring a packed lunch with them and camp inside the Post Office or bank for much of the morning and treat it is a social occasion. After all, they have been through it all so many times before!

There seems to be no concept of staggering holidays for workers in these offices, let alone providing relief staff to cover holiday absences. These services tend to grind to a near standstill, yet it only seems to be the British, Germans and Scandinavians who show any form of irritation. Most Canarians simply shrug off the inconvenience with a smile and return in September.

So, on the basis of, "If you can't beat 'em, join 'em," maybe it is time for us all to shift into another gear. Well, I'm off for a swim, a lounge on the sun-bed with a good book and another gin and tonic. Have a wonderful 15 August and enjoy 'The Big Sleep'!

The End of The Siesta?

A recent report by a Spanish Government backed commission urging the country to switch its clocks to Greenwich Mean Time will, no doubt, strike at the very heart of Spanish culture and tradition, if not the Spanish psyche. The proposal is aimed at shaking up the typical Spanish daily existence – with its lengthy coffee breaks, two-hour lunches and late evening meals and is the result of a survey conducted at Spanish embassies in other European countries into host nations' daily timekeeping.

It has taken me several years to adjust to the idea of the siesta and, I have to confess, it has been one of the most difficult adjustments that I, as a Brit, have had to make in Spain. However, the initial irritation of finding that shops, offices and the like have all closed at the time when I need them most has all but disappeared, as I too have adjusted and now take part in the siesta tradition.

The siesta is a very sensible idea in a hot climate when the temperature is at its fiercest. What better than a snooze after a leisurely lunch? The siesta was born not just out of the necessity of slowing down in the afternoon heat, but the fact that, traditionally, many Spanish men and women have two, relatively low paid part-time jobs, with the second job beginning after the siesta. Typically, the Spanish working day begins at about 8.00am, with a 30-minute break at 11.00am, then lunch usually starts at 2.00pm or 3.00pm, with people returning to work about two hours later, then often working on to 8.00pm, dinner as late as 10.00pm or 11.00pm. It is a long day and the siesta has become an essential way of life for many Spanish working in towns and villages, although much less so now in the cities than in the past. However, returning to the recent report, Spain has been identified as one of the least-productive countries in Europe despite the fact that, in theory, it is the European country where most hours are spent at work.

In the Canary Islands we already have Greenwich Mean Time and the pattern of life is very similar to that on the Peninsular, so I doubt that a change to GMT would make much difference to the local way of life there either. I well recall visiting our newly built property in Gran Canaria early one afternoon to take some measurements before completion. Although the property was unlocked I could see no one working there. Initially alarmed by the lack of security, I entered the property and went upstairs only to find four workmen fast asleep on flattened cardboard boxes in the main bedroom. It was siesta time and I didn't have the heart to disturb them.

Reports such as this latest one from the strangely named, 'National Commission for the Rationalisation of Timetables' come and go and, if I am not greatly mistaken, it will take much more than a report to wrench the beloved siesta from the hearts of our newly adopted countrymen. Forgive me, I must go now, it is time for my siesta.

The Spanish Mistress and The Gym Master

I am often asked what I consider to be the essentials when planning a new life in another country. My answer is always the same, to learn the language.

I won't pretend that learning Spanish has been easy for me. It hasn't. Indeed, you could say that I am not a natural at learning languages. As an eleven-year-old I was forced to learn French, a language that I did not like. Maybe it was the teacher, the quality of teaching or simply the sound of the language that I disliked, but I quickly learned, in the style of Del Boy, that 'un petit pois' was not for me.

Latin hit me in a slightly different way. Dead and dusty it may have been, but the subject was taught in a more effective fashion and with a degree of humour by my old headmaster. He was a strict disciplinarian whom I liked and respected, and I made adequate progress. However, I could see little point in the endless conjugation and chanting of those wretched verbs: "amo, amas, amant..." that will forever ring in my ears.

Eventually, crunch time. I had already dropped Latin and was doing my best to avoid French, using a variety of avoidance tactics of which I was a master. As I completed my fifth year at the school, I was told in no uncertain terms that I had either to take on another language or it was an additional two lessons a week on the playing field. To me this possibility of yet more 'hell on earth' really was sufficient motivation to find another language very quickly.

German was an option and eagerly followed by many of my peers as we entered the sixth form. However, for me the language is far too guttural and makes sounds that I wouldn't wish to make in polite company. Now, what about Italian? Yes, a musical language that is one of beauty, sincerity and where, I was assured, my Latin would come in useful, and they really are such attractive people, aren't they? The only problem was that my school didn't offer it.

The truth finally dawned. I reasoned that I would need just three languages to do anything anywhere in the world - English, Chinese and Spanish. My request for Chinese lessons was greeted with a stony faced, disinterested stare from my housemaster before I was bawled out of his study for wasting his time. Undaunted, I decided to have a chat with one of the school secretaries, a charming young women who rather liked me. A hurried whisper when her colleague disappeared into the stock room revealed that "Spanish lessons are off for the time being". This, I learned, followed an unfortunate incident between the newly appointed young Spanish mistress and the middle-aged gym master in the sports equipment cupboard the previous week. In those days, I was far too naive and polite to ask for further details, but I had a vivid imagination. So Russian it had to be.

Sadly, that was to be a disaster too. Mr Edwards had recently returned from studying a crash course in Russian at Leningrad University and was only a few pages ahead of his students in the textbook. However, I did learn sufficient to ask about the weather in Moscow and to say "I love you" in Russian, which was a bonus.

Many years later, as a school inspector in Wales, I was amazed at the ease with which four- and five-year-old English-speaking children could learn a second language - Welsh. My exposure to these children in the playground during break times, experiencing the ease with which they switched from their mother tongue to another, admittedly very difficult language to learn, both humbled and amazed me.

Learning Spanish later in life is not easy. However, I am pleased to say that I can now understand far more of what is said and written and I have growing confidence in being able to speak the language. That young Spanish teacher and the gym master in the sports cupboard at my old school have a lot to answer for, don't you think?

Not exactly cool...!

Who remembers the Reliant Robin? If you are of a certain age, you will remember the Reliant three-wheeler - the much loved (and tolerated) ageing, battered transport of Del Boy and Rodney of TV's 'Only Fools and Horses' fame. Apart from having only three wheels to worry about, this remnant of British motoring history's main claim to notoriety was that it could be driven on just a provisional or motorcycle licence; it did not require the full driving test.

I remember only too well the fleeting temptation of getting such a vehicle shortly after obtaining my first provisional licence, but as a student I could afford neither motorcycle nor three-wheeler at the time anyway, and so the idea was quickly forgotten.

This brief recollection of the past brings me to the situation regarding the little Aixim cars that are so often seen tootling along the roads between Las Palmas and Maspalomas in Gran Canaria (and, I guess, much of Spain, France, Italy and Portugal). These irritating little cars are usually very easy to spot, as they rarely move faster than 30 mph and are often trailing behind on the verges of many roads, leading a parade of angry drivers with faster vehicles frantically tooting their horns.

These vehicles can be described as 'micro-cars' and the main reason for buying them appears to be that they can be driven without any licence at all over here. This seems to be an anomaly in the motoring laws and I understand that the police are anxious to review the qualifications for driving them - for obvious reasons! I don't think I have ever seen one in the UK, probably because they are classified as a quad bike, in view of their weight and power output. This, very sensibly requires either a full driving licence or a full, unlimited capacity motorcycle licence to legally drive them in the UK. However, this may change in the future, as these little cars are very economical to run with a relatively spacious body made from a strong alloy frame, covered with non-rust plastic panels. Their low-emission engines (which sound a little like motor mowers 'on heat') make them exceptionally 'green' vehicles; and it is now possible to get various versions that run on electricity. No doubt we shall be seeing many more of these 'kerb crawlers' in the future!

Historical

Greenwich Mean Time and the Canary Islands

Maybe the real reason why time traveller, Doctor Who, has a continuing pre-occupation with sorting out problems with aliens in the City of London is not really to do with ever shrinking location budgets at the BBC, but more to do with the fact that Greenwich is the centre of time. A recent news item celebrating the 125th anniversary of the decision to make the Greenwich Meridian the centre of time, reminded me of a history lesson that I still remember from my school days. Co-incidentally, it also has an interesting link with the Canary Islands. Maybe this was the true beginning of my journey to these wonderful islands.

The Greenwich Meridian is an imaginary and arbitrary line that cuts through Spain, UK, France, Algeria and Ghana. It divides the Earth into east and west in much the same way as the Equator divides it into north and south. It enables us to navigate the globe, as well as synchronising the world's clocks. However, this has not always been the case.

Before the all-important decision 125 years ago to make Greenwich the centre of world time, many countries and, indeed, large towns kept their own local time. This was based upon the hours of daylight and there were no international rules as to when the day would start or finish. With the growth of railways crossing international borders and marine activity, it became essential to set a global time. Before an important meeting in Washington took place in 1884 there were, in Europe alone, some 20 different meridians - you can imagine the confusion!

The Washington meeting, naturally, brought with it many different views, no doubt based upon national self-interest. The final conclusion was to make Greenwich the standard for setting time with a vote of 22 to one, with only San Domingo voting against and Brazil and, predictably, France, abstaining. France suggested that the new agreed meridian should run through the Canary Islands, and this suggestion was not just French awkwardness - it had some foundation.

Back in AD 127, the Greek astronomer, Ptolemy, made astronomical observations from Alexandria in Egypt. Ptolemy selected the Fortunate Islands (the Canaries) as the physical location of the prime meridian when he created an accurate grid system upon which the location of individual cities from the farthest known land west to the farthest known land east could be accurately placed. From that time onwards, early Mediterranean navigators used the meridian through the Canaries, as their first, or prime, meridian as they were then thought to be the most western part of the habitable globe. During the 15th and 16th centuries, when the peoples of Western Europe emerged as sea traders, almost every maritime nation used as a prime meridian, a meridian passing through its own territory. The French, for example, used the meridian of Paris; the Dutch, that through Amsterdam; and the English the meridian through London. You can only imagine the chaos and confusion and inconvenience caused to mariners by the existence of a multitude of prime meridians!

So you see the Canary Islands have a strong place in history in setting the centre of world time. Imagine the prestige (and confusion) if the world's clocks were set to Canaries Mañana Time and not Greenwich Mean Time!

World War Heroes

One of the many things that I love about our island in the sun is the 'live and let live' approach of its people. No, I don't mean the thousands of tourists, but the true Canarian people, those who were born and have stayed in this little corner of Paradise. As long as it is broadly legal and does not interfere with anyone else, in the main, anything goes. For many of its present day expat population, with its heady mix of faith, culture, colour and sexuality, it takes time to get used to not being judged. Maybe this stems from the time, it is said, when Spain's General Franco, intolerant of gay men in the military, would ship them off to Gran Canaria, which became a kind of penal colony for homosexuals. Whether there is real historical substance to this claim or whether it is an urban myth, I do not know for sure, but it sounds reasonable enough to me!

For me, one of the real unsung heroes of the Second World War was the code-breaker, Alan Turing. It was thanks to this mathematical genius that the war against Nazi Germany ended when it did. He managed to intercept and crack ingenious coded messages that gave detailed information to the Allies about the activities of German U-boats. However, there was only one problem with Alan Turing - he was gay.

Alan's reward for his pivotal role in cracking intercepted messages was quickly forgotten when, in 1952, he was prosecuted for 'indecency' after admitting a sexual relationship with a man. As an 'alternative' to imprisonment, this unsung war hero was given 'chemical castration' - a newly devised treatment for such 'disorders' at the time. In 1954, at the age of 41, he killed himself by eating a poisoned apple. I rather like this part of the tragedy - the ending is just so dramatic!

Or was this the end of Alan Turing? This amazing man is also credited with creating the beginnings of computer technology and artificial intelligence, which led to the development of one of the first recognisable modern computers. Alan Turing's brilliance and personal life came to the attention of present day computer programmer, Dr. John Graham-Cumming, who began a petition asking for a posthumous apology from the government. Many thousands of people signed it and the previous UK Prime Minister, Gordon Brown, finally apologised for how Alan Turing was treated in the 1950s. Whether it was through political motivation or genuine compassion for this brilliant man, and I like to think it is the latter, he said that "on behalf of the British government, and all those who live freely thanks to Alan's work, I am very proud to say: we're sorry, you deserved so much better."

My thoughts also go out to the many thousands of gay men and woman who have been persecuted over the years - just for being themselves.

All this serious stuff brings me back home to Gran Canaria. Spain's General Franco certainly had his faults, but I cannot help thinking that being shipped off to a life in the sun in the penal colony of Gran Canaria, just for being gay, was a far preferable alternative to 'chemical castration'!

The Virgin and the Pines

Tuesday 8 September is a very important day in Gran Canaria and one that is ignored at your peril! Not only is it yet another essential public holiday, complete with a very convenient bridging day on the day before and, no doubt, the day after - if not the rest of the week, but it is also a fiesta day when homage is paid to the Virgin of the Pines - the Patron Saint of Gran Canaria. Whatever your religious affiliation or beliefs, it can only mean one thing on this island - party, party, party!

The town of Teror is one of the most attractive towns in Gran Canaria, and is the site for this most important of religious festivals. Visiting Teror during the week of the festival is highly recommended, with one important caveat that I will mention later, as this pretty town is decked out in all its splendour and ready to receive thousands of visitors for this annual festival and pilgrimage.

Legend has it that in 1481 a vision of the Virgin Mary appeared to some shepherds on the top of a pine tree, and since then the Virgin of the Pines has played an important role in the history and the everyday life of the people of Gran Canaria. Pope Pius XII proclaimed her patron saint of the island in 1914 and Teror, with its beautiful church, became the religious capital of the island. Since that time, every year, on the 8th of September, the Fiesta of the Virgin of the Pines is celebrated and numerous pilgrims from all over the island come to Teror to pay reverence to the saint.

The beautiful Basilica de la Virgin del Pino, the church in the centre of the town, contains the 15th century carving of the Virgin and is suitably adorned. The day itself is a day of pilgrimage and many islanders, as well as visitors, walk to the town from all over the island as many believe that the Virgin has healing powers. This fiesta is not only the biggest event in the region – it is also the most important religious festival on the island's calendar and the celebrations usually go on for one week, as do the parties!

Just a few words of advice, if you do decide to visit the town it is best not to take a car with you if you wish to retain complete windscreens! When we first arrived on the island, we tried to visit the town during the week of this fiesta only to be met by groups of town vigilantes insisting that we park our car in their field, rear garden, patio or whatever at hugely inflated prices. As these hooligans were brandishing sticks and clubs at anyone who tried to park without their blessing we hastily drove away. Indeed, it was less than a warm and spiritual welcome to the town of the Virgin and the Pines!

Health

The Boob Job

Ladies, have you ever thought about breast enlargement? Gentlemen, have you ever considered having your 'man boobs' removed or maybe 'levelled off' a little? How about a 'nip and tuck' or maybe teeth implants or eye surgery? Well, you will be pleased to know that in the Canary Islands we can offer all such delights and at a much lower price than in the UK and many parts of Europe. In short, if it is hanging off, bulging, or not working as well as it did then we have specialists on hand here to help you!

It was only recently when I met Karen in one of the busy tourist bars in the south of the island a few days ago that I realised that the medical tourism business in the Canary Islands is growing so fast. Karen, a bride to be, with a six-year-old daughter, Shelly, from her previous marriage had always felt self conscious about her figure and she felt that she had reached the 'now or never' time of her life. When the new love of her like, Mike, finally popped the question, and they decided to get married, Karen decided that as a special treat to herself, as well as for Mike, she would have breast enlargement surgery.

After considerable research and recommendation, Karen came on holiday with Mike and Shelly to Gran Canaria to have her operation in one of the private hospitals. As part of the package, she was accommodated in one of the five star hotels close to the hospital. Karen told me that she received wonderful treatment and excellent post-operative care, as well as the ideal conditions for recovery. Mike and Shelly flew back to the UK the week after Karen's operation, allowing Karen a further week on the island for recuperation.

A new pair of breasts seems a strange souvenir to take back from holiday, but Karen assured me that she would do it again if she needed any other kind of cosmetic surgery. Hospital superbugs are virtually non-existent in the Canary Islands, and the cost of treatment is up to 40% less than other UK and European medical tourism destinations, even with the current exchange rate. These benefits, combined with the fact there are no waiting lists, appear to make the Canary Islands an ideal destination to meet medical needs safely and in a superb location for recovery.

As I bought Karen another drink, I asked her if it was really Mike that had persuaded her to have the operation. Karen dismissed the suggestion and assured me that it was all her own idea and that Mike was now considering having his man boobs reduced. "It's either that or a honeymoon cruise," sighed Karen.

Personally, I am quite happy to resist the temptation of assessing the various qualities of ladies' breasts, because there are greater experts than I. However, I thought Karen looked confident, fabulous and indeed beautifully proportioned. Indeed, I am happy to reassure readers that there would be absolutely no question of Karen drowning should she fall overboard during her honeymoon cruise!

A Playground for the Wrinklies

I have always liked the small Canarian coastal town of Arinaga, situated on the eastern side of the island of Gran Canaria. Unlike the sun-drenched tourist beaches of the south, Arinaga tends to attract a hardier type of holiday-maker and resident who shun the expense and crowded beaches of the south in favour of a calmer, more genuine Canarian seaside environment. True, despite the magnificent bay, the beach itself boasts grey sand rather than the white or golden variety, but at least it is natural and hasn't been imported from the Caribbean! However, the promenade more than makes up for any deficiency with its rich variety of restaurants and bars - just right for enjoying a bracing walk. I say bracing, because this must be one of the windiest parts of the island. However, for those of us who have tolerated a miserable few hours in the heat of the summer in the baking heat of Puerto Rico - this breath of fresh sea air comes as considerable relief.

The only thing I don't like about Arinaga, and the main reason why I could never stay there for long, are the lamp-posts that follow the length of the promenade and bend dramatically towards the sea! Even the lifeguard lookout station leans at a frightening angle! I have no doubt some renowned architect or town planner thought it a good wheeze, but as someone who likes tidy, straight lines I personally find it highly disturbing and wish they hadn't bothered! Homage to the sea can be demonstrated in so many other less-challenging ways!

Maybe it is the same reason why the Leaning Tower of Pisa does absolutely nothing for me and, in my opinion, would be better knocked down and rebuilt - and this time vertically!

Since arriving in Gran Canaria, I have been fascinated and impressed by the politics of the small municipality of Aguimes, of which Arinaga is part. Locals tell me that, in the time of General Franco, Aguimes was one of the few municipalities in the islands to put two fingers up to the fascist dictatorship in Madrid, and continued with their fiestas and other celebrations as normal. These flamboyant events had been generally banned by the General and his regime at the time - but this was totally contrary to the Canarian spirit. By all accounts, this local opposition was mostly ignored and the locals were able to get on with their fiestas as normal. The group in power in the Town Hall at the time were mostly young idealists of communist/left wing socialist persuasion and it is these young "firebrands" of yesterday who continue to advise and mentor the new generation of politicians in the municipality.

Aguimes continues to take its social responsibilities very seriously. It is one of the municipalities that takes its concern for single parents, women alone at home, elderly people, the disadvantaged and the education of the young very seriously. One example of this concern can be seen during a walk along the impressive promenade at Arinaga. Here you will find an assortment of machines that would not look out of place in a well-equipped gymnasium. After initially thinking that these were modern equivalents of playground equipment for children, I noticed a sign that indicated that the equipment was not to be used by anyone under the age 15. Further investigation revealed that this equipment was intended for use by adults. Stepping machines, machines to strengthen legs, arms and all parts of the body were there for anyone to use - and completely free of charge.

I noticed two elderly woman taking advantage of these facilities. One had great difficulty walking, yet was using one of the machines to gently exercise. Another was tugging at the machine that would help to strengthen arm muscles. Both women seemed quite content exercising and chatting whilst enjoying the sea view. Where else would we find facilities of this kind so freely available and in such a wonderful setting? Well done, Aguimes and Arinaga! I hope your very local brand of politics, with people and their needs at the very heart of what you are trying to achieve, continues successfully for many years to come.

A Question of Convenience

One of my favourite stores in Spain and the Canary Islands is El Corte Ingles. This chain of stores is a combination of the UK's House of Fraser and John Lewis department stores, with a Spanish flavour thrown in for good measure. Prices may be a little on the high side, but customer service is generally very good and, a real plus point, they have toilets that are free to use! This is a real bonus in a country where public conveniences are not the norm. Indeed, although bars are obliged by law to make their facilities available to non-customers, I find that I cannot use them without ordering a drink and so the whole process starts once again. Yes, El Corte Ingles breaks this vicious cycle of events and provides considerable relief to many!

A few days ago, it was heart warming to hear a conversation between a father and his small son in the washrooms of El Corte Ingles. Father was insistent that his small son washed his hands with soap and water and after inspecting them he reprimanded the small boy for not doing so thoroughly and made him repeat the process. This, the small boy did, although he failed to put his paper towel in the bin. Again, the father made the small boy pick up the paper towel and place it correctly in the rubbish bin. This made a pleasant change from the increasing trend for men not to wash their hands after using urinals and, horror upon horrors, not even washing their hands after using the cubicles. No doubt they then go on to have a coffee and croissant in the bar! This reminds me of recent research relating to the analysis of bowls of peanuts left on the bar for customers to dip into, but I won't go into this horror story here!

Most of us have some regrets in life, and this incident in El Corte Ingles reminded me of one that still haunts me from when I was the head teacher of a large primary school. It was in the days when we were all given our own school budgets to manage. After one particularly irritating school governor made the comment at a meeting that, in his view, we were using an excessive amount of paper towels and toilet rolls. We had a drive to reduce budget expenditure on cleaning materials. Questions were asked and after much analysing of computer print-outs and soul searching we discovered that, yes, it was true, we were spending far too much upon these disposable items. So much so, as the school governor pointed out to me with great glee, we could afford to appoint one 40th of a class teacher if we reduced this spending. I pointed out that, appointing one 40th of a teacher or not, hands still needed to be washed and bottoms wiped, but to no avail...

The result was the installation of hot air hand-driers. Now, in those days, this really was high tech stuff and I looked proudly on as the gleaming white boxes were carefully installed on the walls of the toilets, at appropriate child height, with great satisfaction. Yes, it was true that for the next few days, infant pupils kept disappearing to the toilets to "wash their hands", but, I reasoned incorrectly, this novelty attraction would soon wear off. Sadly, this was not to be the case and it was during one of my patrols that I discovered a small boy alone in the toilets during lesson time, standing on an upturned plastic milk crate with his bare bottom placed strategically a few centimetres away from the hot air blower! The poor boy had wet himself in class and, full marks for initiative, thought that this would be the best way to overcome his embarrassment.

I soon discovered that hot air hand driers never really work - not for small children anyway. They are in far too much of a hurry to get on with life. After the initial novelty, it was clear that children either did not bother to wash their hands at all, or left the toilets with hands dripping wet, resulting in chapped hands during the bitterly cold weather of winter time. It was a great mistake and if I ever see that particular school governor again, I shall have great pleasure in telling him so. Oh, and the small boy's name? I kid you not, it was Jeremy Rowbottom!

"We love the NHS!"

Last year loud voices were raised on each side of the Atlantic concerning the best way of providing a health service that is based upon need and not the ability to pay. The raucous screeches of the Republican far right were unusually successful in creating an unholy alliance between the UK political parties, mostly stoutly defending the UK Health Service and the principles of its founders. Surprisingly, the issue appears to have, for once, united the views of the previous UK Prime Minister, Gordon Brown and the previous Leader of the Opposition, David Cameron, with each posting their comments on the "We Love the NHS" Twitter site.

There were a number of frightening statistics quoted in the press during that period. Yes, I know that statistics can be manipulated to say almost anything, but the claims that around 27 million people in the USA have insufficient medical cover and that a further 48 million people have no medical cover at all are, if true, very worrying. How can this be in one of the richest economies on the planet?

It is easy to forget in this debate that the National Health Service is no longer unique to the UK. Similar, broadly based services are in operation throughout Europe - as the many tourists to these destinations each year will testify. I know many expats living in the Canary Islands who have benefited from the excellent Spanish health service successfully treating serious conditions such as heart attacks, brain surgery and strokes - services freely given, based upon medical need and not the ability to pay.

I remember when living in the Costa Blanca talking to Robert, one of our neighbours and a good friend. Like us, he moved to Spain to start a new life in the sun. However, Robert's dreams were to be cut cruelly short just as he and his wife were purchasing their new dream villa. Robert was diagnosed with terminal cancer and his doctors in the UK gave Robert just a few months to live - and with a much reduced quality of life. Robert and his wife still moved to Spain and set about living their dream, albeit with this devastating nightmare hovering around them, knowing full well that their time together in their dream home was shortly to come to an end.

Robert went to see doctors in the Costa Blanca, where he was given a number of tests. Eventually, the Spanish specialists came to broadly the same conclusions as their counterparts in the UK. However, instead of giving Robert only a few more weeks to live, Robert's Spanish consultants prescribed drugs and care that would not only enhance his quality of life, but also to extend it. This was treatment that was not made available to Robert in the UK. Robert lived for a further two years, relatively discomfort free and gave him a quality of life that he thought had been denied him. Until the day he died, Robert was continually full of praise for the Spanish health service - a service that he had received totally free of charge, under the reciprocal agreements with the UK.

Surely, it is the cornerstone of any caring, compassionate and civilised society that the poor, elderly and needy are cared for and that the sick are treated, not according to their ability to pay, but based upon their medical needs. I applaud President Obama for honouring his election promise to bring affordable health care to all sections of the American public, and not just those with fat bank balances and expensive insurance policies.

Legal and Financial

Whack a Banker!

The human race has always enjoyed finding a minority to persecute. Whether it is the colour of skin, sexuality or religion, we always manage to find a convenient scapegoat for grievances, and particularly during the bad times. A recent UK survey of 'people's worth to society' concluded that bankers are a drain on the country, because of the damage they caused to the global economy. It certainly appears that bankers are the new persecuted people...

Have you heard of the new, very popular, and delightfully named, arcade game called 'Whack a Banker'. Apparently, it is all the rage in the UK and involves whacking bankers on the head with a wooden mallet. These are not real bankers, I hasten to add, but plastic, bald, faceless 'lookalikes that pop on a board ready for the player to bash them on the head with a wooden mallet. Punters pay 40p a time to hit as many bankers as they can in 30 seconds. When a customer wins, a voice says: "You win. We retire. Thank you very much to the taxpayer for paying our pensions." Hmm, now there's an idea…

So, will this delightful game take off in Spain? I suspect it might if a suitably modified language version becomes available. Just as with banks in the UK, Spanish banks vary in their approach, flexibility and quality of service to their customers. However, one thing that they do have in common is their general lack of customer service.

When I arrived in Spain, I quickly learned that in most, but not all banks, customers should be prepared for a long wait, taking a flask of coffee and sandwiches if necessary, in order to stand in a queue awaiting their turn for a good half morning. In most banks the one and only cashier struggles to carry out the simplest, as well as the most complex, of transactions, answering endless queries, as well as ever intrusive telephone calls - both mobile and fixed (bank as well as personal).

I can never understand this because invariably the branch appears to be full of non-engaged staff either chatting to each other, engaged in non-essential tasks or having a cigarette break outside the front door. Maybe a little flexibility is in order here; for example, if a non-engaged member of staff sees a lengthy queue, maybe they could help out? Simple stuff, eh?

I can never understand why the telephone has priority over the customer, patiently waiting for their turn. Surely if we have been waiting in the bank for an hour or so, we should be the priority over the customer who calls on a whim, asking for an account balance and whose query is answered immediately?

In general, I have found that the savings and local banks, similar in their mutual constitution status to the UK building societies, have a much greater understanding of their customers' needs than the large countrywide institutions that appear to hold the nation's financial cards. They have no shareholders and the good ones actually put money back into charitable causes, as well as the local community. Now there's a good idea for UK bankers. Maybe, if they did more of this instead of looking to their bonuses, they wouldn't be disliked (and whacked) quite so much.

Until death do us part (or until someone better comes along)

Recent divorce statistics from Spain's National Statistics Office are, at first glance, alarming. The figures show that in the Canary Islands the rate of 3 divorces per thousand of the population is the highest in Spain, where the divorce rate has fallen by 10 per cent since the time of the last survey in 2008.

Given that, for many, these islands appear to be an island paradise that draws many Northern Europeans to the islands, begs the question "What has gone wrong for these couples?" I can only guess that most of these breakdowns will be in the younger age group and are linked to the stresses caused by a lack of jobs, homes and a bleak future.

It is traditional for Canarians to marry when they are young. Many are still not out of their teenage years when the pressures of many overbearing families, and a mostly symbolic Church, forces them to take their wedding vows. It is not unusual to see, what appears at first, to be a brother and sister taking a baby out in the pram or playing with a toddler on the beach. It is only when chatting to these 'brothers and sisters' that we discover that they are in fact husband and wife and that the child is their own.

Needless to say, many of these young couples do not have the financial resources to rent a flat or to start a mortgage and, as a consequence, they are forced to live with their in-laws. This brings its own pressures on any couple. In the past, this has meant that grandmother has taken on the burden of raising the child and later providing after-school care, whilst the young parents are able to finish their education or start a career, but times have changed. The pressures of living within an extended family for far longer than in the past, and the inability of obtaining a home of their own, places unbearable pressures upon many families.

The problems have become more acute in recent years with the influx of expats moving to these islands. The best and most affordable properties have been snapped up by expats, forcing house prices, goods and services to increase as a consequence. It is an anomaly that despite the popularity of these islands as a holiday destination, they remain the bastions of unemployment, low pay, long hours and a reliance on 'black money' rather than secure contracts offering a living wage to local people.

The islands' government has attempted in recent years to provide affordable housing for young families, but the supply and availability of such properties has been slow and requires a steady income, which many young couples do not have. As many of us will remember from the UK, affordable housing, starter homes and other such well-meaning schemes do not remain affordable housing for very long.

We are often told that Spain is a very family-orientated society, and so it is - far more than many would consider realistic or desirable in the UK. In Spain, it is customary for all members of the family to take responsibility for, and to look after, the young, elderly and sick members of their family. In the Costas and the Canary Islands, residential homes for the elderly are few, with the exception of several run by nuns for the elderly with no families.

Island living, although idyllic in many ways, also brings other pressures that are often not realised. Island living often creates, by definition, an insular view of life. Despite attempts by schools to widen their pupils' experiences, many have never left these islands. Whereas school leavers in Peninsular Spain and other parts of Europe attend universities far from home, gaining rich experiences and meeting a wide variety of other people, as they complete their formal education, many Canarians study locally and have never left the islands.

I recall putting the question of travel to Peninsular Spain and further afield to one young Canarian in his thirties. His reply was, "Why should we? We have everything that we need here." However, it is this insularity of knowing maybe only the people that we went to school with, or those from the same town or village that creates its own problems.

Hopefully, these recent statistics will provide opportunities for some soul-searching amongst clerics, local and national politicians. The statistics will also provide useful fodder for university researchers and the like. Hopefully, society too will look seriously at the pressures that young Canarian families currently face and take action. However, in these days of recession and financial cutbacks, I somehow doubt that anything positive will happen to address an obvious problem.

The Telemarketing Plague

Do you receive endless email spam messages advertising all kinds of competitions, pills and potions and, in particular, Viagra? The Viagra ones are particularly sinister, I find. After all, do they know something that I don't? They are, of course, easily dealt with by using the delete button, and some email providers also provide very sophisticated software that will weed out some of the most annoying and offensive messages and blast them into the ether. Sadly, it is a fact of modern day living that most of us are bombarded with all kinds of advertising, junk mail and unwanted phone calls.

The Spanish love their mobile telephones and it is customary for all businesses, Government offices, banks and services to ask for a mobile telephone number. I realised long ago that this was mainly a ploy to sell future services and, as a result, I usually give an old mobile number that I never answer anyway. However, it is the endless and uninvited calls to my new mobile phone, when I have only given that number to family and friends that I find most annoying.

This morning we received a total of four uninvited calls to our two mobile phones, as well as the home line, and that was before coffee! Be it the beast Telefonica, Movistar, Vodafone or Orange, the result is always the same. After a few weeks with a new mobile or landline number, the calls begin. These calls used to be mainly to tempt us away from one phone operator to another by offering an additional service or a special offer, some of which were quite useful. Now, I find that these numbers are sold on, and most calls are now advertising lotteries, asking me to take part in a 'survey' of some kind, offering a range of financial and insurance services, as well as some offers of a very doubtful nature. Not only are these calls annoying, but also they can be very distracting when working or driving. These calls must be a particular problem for the elderly or sick, particularly when received very late in the evening.

I always used to answer my mobile phone in Spanish. This, I thought, was the very least I should do when living in Spain. However, I would find myself drawn into an endless and confusing conversation about various products and services that I had no intention of buying or had the time to listen to. I am also well aware of the number of sales people who are desperate to make a living and earn a very tiny income from such calls. Somehow, it also seemed impolite to cut off the caller and I have, in the past, tried to be patient and courteous with them.

My attitude has now changed. Whenever I receive a mobile phone call, I now always answer in English. There is usually a brief pause and as soon as the caller realises that I am not Spanish, or unwilling to speak in Spanish, they cut off. Problem sorted!

Sadly, my new approach has still has not solved the problem of the phones ringing late into the night and, short of switching them off, there must be another way. I have tried calling the mobile operators requesting that my numbers be removed from their calling lists and their unbelievable response was that "it is not possible to do this in Spain". Unlike the 'Mailing Preference Service' for post and the ease with which such telephone calls can be blocked in the UK, this seems to be a real omission in consumer rights in Spain. If anyone does know how to block these endless calls, do please let me know!

The Parking Ticket

Last week I received a denuncia. Yes, the very word, 'denuncia' tends to strike fear in the very soul of the newly arrived expat living in Spain, but I have been around long enough to know that it only means 'police report' and, in my case, 'a parking ticket'. Even so, it was not pleasant to receive; such a nasty shade of yellow - cheap quality paper too, rather like the tortuous Izal toilet paper of my childhood, and stuck to the windscreen of my beloved Suzuki. My crime? Well, I had committed that most heinous of crimes - parking Suzy in an area where I was not supposed to park - despite there being no signs or lines telling me not to do so. What was even more annoying was that there were many other cars parked in the same road as well - but only Suzy had a ticket. Maybe she just exudes 'Brit Abroad'!

Trying to be a good citizen, I felt it my duty, two days later, to make the trip to the Town Hall to be absolved of my sins. Being well aware of the Spanish love of documents, I had the foresight to take with me my passport and residencia - originals not copies. You see, like so many, I have been caught out on that one before! I also took the documentation for the Suzuki, insurance documents, local tax documents and even my inside leg measurements, just to be on the safe side! You just never know what local officials will insist upon - many like to send you home, having to return with that elusive piece of paper another day.

Eventually, I managed to find the ticket machine for the queue and realised that something to do with 'multa' seemed to fit the bill. I joined the lengthy queue of criminals ready to plead for penance and hand over their fines. There were forty or so other miscreants in front of me and I began to wonder if the warning from a hardened expat when I first arrived in Spain was true. "Watch out for parking tickets and fines just before Christmas. They try to get extra money in for their Christmas party..." Certainly, the length of the queue indicated that this year's Christmas party was going to be a very good one indeed.

Eventually, two hours later, with my blood pressure far higher than when I had arrived, I sat at a grey table opposite an equally grey, wizened and thoroughly depressing official. Without a word, he took my shabby yellow piece of paper, peered intently into a computer for several minutes, grabbed my residencia document and then disappeared. A few minutes later he returned, clipping a copy to his newly printed documents, applied the obligatory 'bonk' of the rubber stamp and sat back in his chair. I asked how much it would be. With a smirk, he told be it would be one hundred and eighty euros, but that as I had been a good person in applying for forgiveness early it would be discounted to 90 euros. That was double what I had expected. I offered him my credit card in payment, but I was merely waved over to another equally long queue in another room.

This was another depressing and thoroughly irritating experience. The queue snaked around the room and out of the door. At the side of the cashiers' office was a branch of a well-known bank, together with a cash machine - all obviously essential if the fine means that you need a personal loan or mortgage to pay it. An hour or so later, I eventually presented the sheet of my now disintegrating 'toilet paper' to yet another unsmiling, equally wizened, clerk. After demanding my residencia and passport, she grabbed the credit card and ran it through her machine. She paused and glared at me.

"British?" she asked. I nodded.

"That'll do nicely", she replied, with the first smile of the morning.

Be warned, if the size of the fine doesn't hurt you, then your patience and possibly your pride after a morning at the Town Hall certainly will. I came to the conclusion that the misery inflicted at the Town Hall is part of the punishment process and that, if there is a next time, I will be better prepared. If you are ever unfortunate enough to have to follow in my footsteps, I advise you to take a flask of coffee, some sandwiches and a picnic chair!

Police Crackdown on Speeding Infants

I never cease to be amazed by the total lack of road sense shown by some drivers in Spain. No, I am not just talking about Spanish and other European drivers because, I understand from reliable sources, that it is more often than not the Brits who are responsible for many of the road accidents over here. After all, it is still not unusual to see British drivers driving the wrong way around a roundabout or speeding down a one-way street in the wrong direction. It's all very well complaining that, "These Europeans drive on the wrong side of the road," but I doubt that argument is a sound defence in court.

In our village it is not unusual to see a toddler sitting on his father's lap driving the family car around the village. At first I used to think it was very tiny men driving the cars, but once I had my new glasses I could see exactly who was really driving; my discovery was very worrying! I regularly see many a confident two-year-old confidently grasping the steering wheel of the car, whilst peering over the dashboard, whilst father proudly operates the clutch and, I hope, the brake.

The Christmas and Kings' Day festivities bring with them a new tranche of expensive gifts for many over-indulged children. For the last two years there have been an ever-increasing number of micro motorbikes and tiny four-wheeled vehicles, especially designed for the seven-year-old who intends to have everything, available in shops and large superstores.

Advertised as "a snip at five hundred euros" these 'toys' are indeed generous gifts, and which many children are more than happy to receive!

Christmas Day and Kings' Day is when these lucky infants, and their proud fathers, are anxious to try out their new roadsters for the first time. Although these micro bikes and mini four-wheel drive vehicles are tiny, they are packed with a considerable amount of punch, with many having a petrol engine capacity that would make a Black and Decker hedge trimmer feel envious! However, instead of taking them to the park, a disused airfield or scrub land, these micro infants bomb around the local village streets as if there is no tomorrow and some, according to many irritated neighbours, may well find that they have their early days of motorised transport suddenly sabotaged by randomly strewn packets of tin tacks! These irritating little vehicles, with engines that sound very much like swarms of constipated wasps, buzz, wail and whine from mid-morning until late evening. Thankfully, these tiny vehicles eventually run out of petrol or the battery runs down and both the vehicle and the infant are at last hauled home by their now despondent fathers.

The increasing trend for these tiny vehicles and their infant drivers to use public roads and pathways is worrying, and the consequences potentially lethal. Many local drivers are not careful and considerate road users. These tiny vehicles are not intended for road use and as such give poor protection against injury. It is very rare to see helmets worn and the issues concerning insurance and the protection of pedestrians is a minefield.

However, all is not lost. I am pleased to report that whilst driving out of the village yesterday I saw two police officers apprehend an unaware infant speeding in their direction on his brand new micro four-wheel drive (with father clinging on the back for good measure). The speeding infant was stopped just as he approached the main roundabout outside our village. The small boy, whom I doubt was much older than seven years, and his embarrassed father were in the process of being given a good talking to by one of the less than amused gentleman in green; the infamous yellow documents were already in the process of being filled in.

Be warned, motorised infants! I doubt that many seven-year-olds will have a denuncia for a Kings' Day present from the police!

Attitudes

Build 'Em Up and Knock 'Em Down!

A conversation with some friends visiting the Canary Islands from the States a few evenings ago made me think. "Why is it that you Brits build folk up and knock 'em down again so quickly?" was the question.

The comment was made in the aftermath of Cleggmania that swept Britain for a couple of weeks during the recent General Election campaign. Nick Clegg, an essentially unheard of leader of a relatively minor political party in the UK was suddenly swept into the public gaze during the televised debates of the three political leaders and the public liked what they saw, or so it seemed. Interviews, chat shows and the full glare of media attention was poured into questions such as the best sex that Nick had ever had, his shoe size and what he liked eating for breakfast. The fact that he has a Spanish wife and was rather fond of Europe didn't go down too well with the Eurosceptics, but it did propel Nick Clegg into the Hall of Fame - as far as the tabloids were concerned anyway.

As the dust is settling, Cleggmania has evaporated and the poor man is now being vilified in the tabloids. The question from my friends from the States has once again entered my mind and, yes, they do seem to have a point about the Brits.

As much as I love my fellow countrymen and women and a county of which I am still very proud to have as my heritage, it is an unfortunate trait of the Brits, in general, to build people up and then to take great delight in knocking them down. You have only to think of Fergie, Princess Diana, David Beckham, Tony Blair, Jonny Wilkinson, Katie Price, Susan Boyle ...the list is endless, to see what my American friends meant. For a time these people are treated like heroes, they become almost God-like in the public eye, only to have scorn poured upon them and be vilified by the tabloids shortly afterwards.

My contact with Spanish, German and, indeed, people from many nationalities on the island, leads me to believe that this is an unfortunate trait in the British as a race. Maybe it is a gene thing or maybe, as an island people, the days of Empire still have a considerable bearing upon our collective national psyche. Maybe we resent change, have become too cynical and resent the success of others.

Taking the argument once step further, I remember many of my friends and acquaintances over the years who have had the inspiration and courage to start their own businesses. No easy task for anyone in this day and age, I know. I remember initial comments ranging from "I doubt it will succeed," or maybe "Good idea, but it won't work" or if the business is successful, I hear grudging comments such as "He's just been lucky..." Believe me, experience tells me that there is no such thing as luck - you make your own 'luck' in this world.

Even more depressing are the comments that I hear if the business has failed. "I knew it wouldn't work" or

"John just hasn't got what it takes..." I could go on and yet I am quite sure that most of us have heard very similar comments.

Contrast this to the attitudes across the Atlantic. Would-be entrepreneurs, people with ideas and the spirit of 'get up and go' to get something done are applauded and, in the main, encouraged. True, businesses and enterprises also fail there, but would-be entrepreneurs are applauded in the States for having tried even though they may have failed and not, as in the UK, despised and made fun of for having tried and failed. That is the great difference between our two cultures.

The British have rightly gained an enviable reputation throughout the world, developed and honed over many generations, for their sense of fair play, justice, fairness and empathy with others. Why is it then that this is such a major deficiency in the nation's character? Why is it that we love to build 'em up and knock 'em down? Maybe it just makes us feel that much better about ourselves.

The UK Election and the Euro Brit

As a confused teenager growing up in rural Lincolnshire, my mother always insisted that I refrain from talking about politics, religion, vegetarianism or sex at the dinner table. Three of these "no, no's" I was quite happy to avoid, but there was one that I never quite managed to avoid, and I will leave you to guess which one. In later life, I applied the same principles to many conversations - in polite company. Anyway, during the pre-election period in the UK, I will break this now self-imposed taboo and raise the question of Britain's place within a united Europe.

Why is it that the British, a tolerant, decent and principled people when at their best, are some of the worst when it comes to xenophobia, building people up and then taking great delight in knocking them down, and so cynical when it comes to the question of national and European politics? It continually amuses and amazes me that when speaking to expats living and working in Spain, and often the British seem to be the worst offenders, that many have little time for Europe. Indeed, they have little time for the country of their birth either, which is presumably one of the reasons why they are now living in Spain. Unequalled by any other nation, just gather a group of British expats together, mention Gordon Brown, and the tirade of abuse that floods from the lips of those who have not lived or worked in the UK for the last 20 years or so hits one's ears with a vengeance. Even David Cameron seems to take his own fair share of stick, particularly those who remember the divisive policies of Thatcher's 80s, and I doubt that the Lib Dems will be safe from voter abuse for very long either.

Since moving to Spain, I gave up my right to vote in UK elections long ago. During this election period, we are reminded that we can vote in the UK elections for up to 15 years after we leave the UK. Even after two years away from the UK, I felt that I no longer had the moral right to vote, but would become an amused and interested observer of UK 'goings on' within a European context. What interests me now is the political situation and social progress made in Spain where we now live and work. Surely this is more relevant to the expat living in Spain?

I recall speaking to a colleague in Spain some time ago. He had not lived or worked in the UK for nearly 30 years, having lived in South Africa for many years and left 'in a huff' when black South Africans took the responsibility for running their own country. He moved to Spain, but spent most of his time criticising the UK, which I could never understand because he left the UK when he was very young. Be it education, family values, motoring or immigration issues, he always had a negative, cynical view of what was happening in the UK. He also had very strong views against the South African government of which he was, and still is, vehemently opposed. However, not once have I heard him comment about Spanish politics, laws, government and political progress in the country that he has adopted as his own for the last fifteen years or so, and which has been very good to him. He is, in the true British tradition, quite happy to whinge, moan and criticise anything that he can - from a safe distance on his terrace in the sun. I wonder if this is a healthy pre-occupation?

I hope that no readers of this book come into this category, but if you do, I really would urge you to try to forget the vicious, neo-fascist ramblings of some of the UK tabloids and try to understand the politics, traditions, culture and language of the country that you now live in. It is not only about taking; it is about giving something back to our adopted country as well. Most of us living here have benefitted from the European dream by the very fact that we are freely living and working in Spain, so maybe a little understanding of the European Union ideal that made it possible would be a good idea as well.

Sorry Mum, but it had to be said. Yes, I will leave the table now and go to my room...

The Beautiful Game?

I have always hated sport. Yes, I've said it aloud at last and I feel much better for it! It stems from the days when I attended my grammar school in Lincolnshire. I still have nightmares about those cold, wet and interminably long Thursday afternoons on the rugby field wishing, begging and pleading for the game to be over for another week, and I could return inside to the warmth. There were just so many things that I did not understand. Why was the ball that stupid shape anyway? I could see the point of football, but we were neither allowed to mention, let alone play soccer from the moment that we arrived at that ghastly institution at the tender age of eleven until we managed to escape its clutches forever.

Maybe it had something to do with having to wear my brother's elderly rugby boots. I really do believe that Noah had this particular pair in a cupboard in the Ark - just waiting for one of the tribe to play rugby! By the time they were handed down to me they were real antiques and, my goodness, didn't the other boys let me know it! They were made from painfully strong, inflexible leather and how my feet hurt afterwards. What I would have given for a pair of modern Nikes! Most of all it was the weather. It was always cold, wet and foggy and how I wished I didn't have to be the hooker yet again!

However, I quickly learned escape tactics. Although I couldn't physically escape from the game, match or whatever it was called, unless I had yet another sick note from my mother, I did retreat into my own very special world. Daydream, make-believe or fantasy, whatever you like to call it, but it was a far better place to be and I spent much of my time there. This probably explains why I was always the last boy to be chosen for the team. Mind you, this world of my own special creation is still a wonderful place to be, and, now that I am a writer, it has proved to be invaluable resource. Maybe I did learn something from that place after all.

I now realise that the main reason that I hated sport so much was that I couldn't actually see the ball! Not very well anyway, and so maybe things would have been very different if that little problem had been corrected many years ago. Nevertheless, I suspect that I would always have daydreamed and my own special world was never very far away. Athletics, and javelin throwing in particular, were yet another issue of considerable concern. Readers may be relieved to know that teachers quickly realised that letting me loose with a javelin was not a good idea and forced me to 'put the shot' or 'shot the put' (I can never remember which it is) instead.

Over the last few weeks, my attitudes and opinions have gradually changed because of the World Cup. I have seen the pleasure, involvement and excitement of local Spanish and Canarian people, as well as people of all nationalities visiting the islands on holiday. It has brought welcome relief at a time when we all need a break from the recession, financial and work problems, politicians, corruption and all the usual things that plague our daily lives. I love to hear the cheers and groans from the bars as yet another goal or penalty followed by the crazy tooting of car horns, cheering, fireworks and tremendous camaraderie following the recent Spanish victories on the playing field.

Possibly, I am a reformed sports person and maybe I have finally changed my mind about football after watching the World Cup finals. I now realise that perhaps I should have given it a far better shot than I have so far. Maybe in a different time and place, I would have done. Even so, it doesn't change my mind about that sport of the Devil - cricket, but that's a story for another time!

Fancy a change of career?

"French Air Traffic Controllers on strike!" screamed the headlines of one UK newspaper that I picked up recently. So, hand on heart, do any of us really remember when these lovely people were not on strike and were actually working? I think maybe not.

For as long as I can remember, French air traffic controllers have always gone on strike. It is one of the things that the French do best. After all, the concept is as much an intrinsic part of the French way of life, as eating fine food and farm subsidies. Sadly though, it happens at the most inconvenient of times, namely the summer months. It seems much like the 'British Disease' of the 70's and '80's when everyone seemed to be going on strike and hang the consequences for everyone else. Anyway, the fact that the French air traffic controllers are going on strike yet again seems to make little real difference to passengers this time, as recent arrivals to the Canary Islands confirmed, that they simply flew a different path instead. "The old expression, "Crying Wolf" springs to mind."

For tourists heading to Spain's Costas and the Canary Islands this summer a far more serious dispute is looming. Passengers could face travel misery because of a row over Spanish air traffic controllers' pay. The Spanish government wants to slash salaries after it was revealed that some controllers are taking home an astronomical £800,000 a year. Yes, you did read this correctly and it is not a typing error! This dispute could spark a "summer of discontent", with strikes and delays ruining holiday plans.

Although maybe not as noticeable as the French strikes, Spanish air traffic controllers have held many strikes over the past few years, causing travel problems for holidaymakers. Now, understandably, the Spanish Government wants to stop high wages and plans to slash more than £11 million off air traffic control costs. Recent statistics have shown that out of 2300 air traffic controllers employed by Spain's state operators AENA, 10 were paid between £725,000 and £800,000 last year - 10 times the salary of the Spanish Prime Minister. In Britain, the average wage of a controller is around £60,000, which may seem rather good to the rest of us.

Only a short time ago, passengers were hit by long delays because of staff shortages among controllers in the Canary Islands. Two runways were closed at Madrid Barajas airport recently for the same reason.

It is worth remembering that Spanish air traffic controllers caused heavy delays in 2002 and 2003 by striking. In 2003, they proposed 10 days of summer strikes because of a proposed change in the law they claimed would limit their rights. Regular travellers to Spain may well remember that in June 2002, hundreds of flights were cancelled after they ordered strikes to protest against unemployment benefit reforms. Maybe at a time of recession and the anger over bankers' bonuses they would do well to remember that no one is indispensable.

Boot-camps, (Arch)Bishops and Blogs

An item about a Chinese teenager who is now in a serious condition with chest and kidney problems after being beaten at a boot-camp caught my eye this week. This follows another incident where a fifteen-year-old was beaten to death in a similar 'treatment centre'. Their 'crimes', along with thousands of other teenagers across China, was 'being addicted to the Internet' and who are sent to 'boot style' camps across China to cure them of their addiction. Reports indicate that parents are willing to pay around £450 to have their teenagers 'cured' from playing too many on-line games, as well as the unforgivable sin of peering at the world outside China. A chilling quote from one of the 'therapists' responsible for setting up such camps is reported as saying, "Physical punishment is an effective way to educate children - as long as it can be controlled." With around 300 million Internet users, these boot camps are going to be kept busy controlling, punishing and torturing young Internet users for many years to come.

This article contrasted with, or maybe I should say was supplemented by, a recent article from Vincent Nicholas, the recently appointed Roman Catholic Archbishop of England and Wales, who took it upon himself to criticise social networking sites such as Facebook, MySpace and Twitter, as well as text messaging and emails as "undermining community life."

The Archbishop then went on to say that skills such as "reading a person's mood and body language were in decline", and that exclusive use of electronic information had a "dehumanising" effect upon community life. Apparently, social networking sites such as Facebook and MySpace are encouraging a form of communication that is not "rounded".

Well, there you have it. I thought, along with many other thousands of expats living in the Canary Islands and Spain, that using new technology in such a way that we can easily call and video-conference family and friends in the UK, send and receive text messages and renew friendships on social networking sites was actually enhancing family and community life. Obviously, I am completely wrong, and as it is such a heinous crime it is best stopped forthwith, if we are to avoid being sent to 'boot camps' in our thousands.

Oh, and to answer the Archbishop's comments, I cannot help thinking that if Jesus were around today he would be blogging, texting and 'Twittering' along with the rest of us!

People, Pets and Places

'From Teacher to Drag Queen'

My first novel, 'Journeys & Jigsaws Book 1: From Teacher to Drag Queen' finally hit the shelves of bookshops, and the warehouses of all the on-line bookstores. This novel had rather a long gestation period - it was about three years before that I first put pen to paper, or rather first hit the keys of my laptop in a hotel room in Fuerteventura. Pressure of work from the newspaper that I was editing at the time prevented me from writing much more for nearly two years. The novel was about many issues that had troubled me, and people like me, greatly during those often dark, sinister days of the 1980s.

Now it is finished, as is the sequel, and like all authors I enjoy responses from readers, but sometimes with some trepidation. One of the main questions that I have been asked by folk from the media or friends that I have not seen for some time, after the initial pleasantries, is "Barrie, are you a drag queen?" Let me try and answer this first question!

A drag queen is a unique performer and storyteller. Someone who can capture an audience and make them laugh, and maybe even cause them to be frightened or worried. A drag queen is someone who wears a very visible mask. Everyone knows there is a mask, yet everyone accepts that this is normal for the performance. Let me explain further, if you ever visit Las Palmas in Gran Canaria during Carnival you will find very few men, actually dressed as men - because most of the men are dressed as women! Everyone wears a costume and a mask and it just seems almost normal during that festival period. Indeed, you are very much out of place if you don't join in!

So as a writer, I hope that readers will be entertained. Many will laugh, be sad, frightened or may be worried when they read 'Journeys and Jigsaws', and certainly I hope that I will have challenged readers' preconceptions and views. So, if I have captured my audience in this way, perhaps I am a little like a drag queen! Maybe the short answer to this question is, no I am not a drag queen, but I am a great believer in career changes!

A Canarian Garden

Some of the few things that I miss from the UK are luscious green gardens, grass, flowers and trees. As the UK springtime approaches, I begin to crave for Cornish gardens with their snowdrops, bluebells, daffodils, camellias and all the wonderful plants and flowers that announce that springtime has finally arrived. All this is in such stark contrast to our small island off the Atlantic that basically has two seasons in the south, hot and very hot, whilst the more temperate north has a little more rain and cooler, cloudier days, which is more conducive to the growing of plants. In the south of the island, we have to content ourselves with a variety of palms, cactus and succulents that require very little moisture and can cope with soaring high temperatures and little rainfall.

In any case, I am not convinced that our Canarian neighbours would choose to garden, even if the temperature and rainfall were conducive to this very British of activities. Most appear content to lay patio tiles on any available patch of ground, with maybe the odd container plant that is rarely watered, shrivels up and dies within a few days of buying it from the small garden centres here - no tea rooms and greetings cards for sale in these garden centres, I'm afraid! There is a wonderful Botanical Garden in the north of the island, but I am not too sure how popular it is with local people, the few visitors that I usually see there are visitors to the island and not locals.

One of the first things that we did when we moved to our Canarian home was to install a watering system that switches on and off twice each day for just five minutes. This is similar to a wonderful system that one of our good friends and neighbours in the Costa Blanca insisted we install when we moved into our new home in Torrevieja. You would be surprised at the variety of plants that will grow even with this very small quantity of water. Even so, as I said earlier, this passion for gardening is not usual here - the outside living space being seen as an area for having family barbecues, as well as sitting and chatting with friends over a bottle of wine until the early hours of the morning. After all, gardening is such a waste of time and energy!

However, all is not lost. In the village where I live, there is a new housing estate. On one side there are the mountains and on the other there is the sea. In between and surrounding the estate is open, wasteland used for little more than exercising dogs and where some of the local teenagers choose to race their motorcycles. Ideally, this area should be planted with grass and trees, but this is not a viable option on these dry islands and so it remains an empty, unloved space.

Last year, whilst walking with my dog, Bella, I noticed that someone had marked out a piece of this wasteland near the footpath with large stones. Over the next few weeks more and more plants began to appear. Cactus, succulents and a whole manner of different plant life was planted and, what's more, were being watered. It was good to see, as I had suspected that this would be a short-lived wonder that would quickly be forgotten and the plants would be left to shrivel and die. Not so. Over the following months the plants flourished, and it was clear that someone was painstakingly watering them by hand with a bucket or watering can - and with no water supply nearby this is no mean achievement. Later, a small, home made, wooden garden seat appeared together with an old log and part of a wooden beer barrel.

Today, I walked past this garden again with Bella to find a small boy sitting on the garden seat. "He loves it here," remarked the young woman with the pushchair. "He likes looking at the plants." I asked if the young woman had created the garden and she shook her head. "No, I don't know who did it or who looks after it. It just appeared. What a pity there aren't more on this patch of land."

I agreed, and we both marvelled that the garden lay untouched by vandalism or litter for so long - created by someone who wanted to make something ordinary just a little bit better for all to enjoy. The wonderful thing is that further on my walk I noticed another row of stones marking out another new garden on the wasteland. Someone else is going to join in the fun!

Walking the Dog

Each day I take my dog, Bella, for a walk. We love her dearly, and inside our home she is a well-behaved, loveable and playful friend - in fact, a delightful and valued member of the family. As a puppy, she looked just like a tiny fruit bat and these distinctive features still remain. She is loyal, inquisitive and likes to be at the centre of all that is going on. During our holidays, when she goes off to kennels, she plays happily with other dogs and, we are told, that she is no trouble at all. However, it is a very different matter whenever we are out for a walk together, because she will growl and bark at any dog, cat or moving object that she sees. Dog experts tell us that this is because she is trying to protect us and, given her background as an abandoned puppy in the Costa Blanca, I tend to take their word for it.

I also still remember the trauma when Bella slipped her collar and went missing for several hours in Cartagena. As a result, she now wears a harness and I swore that I would never let her off her lead outside her home again. As a result if this deficiency in her all but perfect nature, Bella remains firmly at the end of a short lead on short walks, but we use a long extending lead on open spaces. She seems to be quite happy with the arrangement. At least we are well aware of the flaws in Bella's nature and take steps to ensure that she is safe, as well as ensuring that she does not annoy or inconvenience others.

One of the things that annoys and distresses me, both in the Costa Blanca as well as the Canaries, is the tendency for many Spanish families to let their dogs roam freely by day and then return home at night to eat and sleep. This used to be the traditional way, but with increased traffic, the rural idyll has all but disappeared in most neighbourhoods and many dogs and cats are the cause of road accidents.

I had little sympathy with a neighbour whose dog was killed by a speeding car a few months ago. We have since noticed that the dead dog has now been replaced by another, who also roams the streets. The lesson has not been learned.

It is true to say that the dogs seem happy enough with the arrangement - roaming, playing and generally having a fabulous time with their mates. The downside is that many a playful encounter with the 'bitch across the road' leads to the distress of yet more unwanted and abandoned puppies and this is something that is taking time for the locals to fully grasp.

Although neutering dogs and cats is promoted on the island, this is not always too successful, particularly during a recession when the costs are seen by many owners as being too high.

You can imagine the annoying scenario when walking Bella on a lead. Many an uncontrolled dog suddenly leaps forward to play with Bella. There is often no owner in sight resulting in a tussle between dogs wanting to play and Bella who does not. On several occasions I have had words of abuse, fortunately shouted in my direction in Spanish so I could not really understand the finer content of what was being said, telling me that I should let Bella run off a lead and then there would be no trouble. Hmm, that's what they think, but I tend to think that a few vital organs would go missing if I did!

A Cat and Dog Story

I have always been of the opinion that we are born as either golfers or dog walkers. Sorry, I can already hear some of you complaining, "But I play golf and I have a dog!" Well, maybe, but perhaps one takes clear precedence over the other? Personally, I am a dog walker and not a golfer. Maybe this is in much the same way that most people tend to prefer cats to dogs or dogs to cats. It's all about personal preference and, more often than not, whether we were brought up to love and respect animals during childhood, and whether we come from cat or dog families or maybe neither.

It was another hot, sunny day on the island and it was time for Bella's midday walk. Yes, I know all about "Mad Dogs and Englishmen and the Noonday Sun", but if Bella doesn't get her walk at lunchtime, then all hell breaks loose. So a very short walk it had to be. We walked over to the dry and dusty wasteland, after all it hadn't rained on the island since February, and Bella pulled with determination towards some old dry shrubs. In the UK it would have been called a hedge, but maybe that would be stretching the imagination too far over here. I tugged at her lead, assuming that she was on the hunt for yet another lizard, but she firmly refused to leave and stood her ground barking at whatever she had found beneath the dried out shrub. I knelt down and peered beneath and discovered what she had been barking at. It was a tiny bundle of matted, dirty white and grey fluff - a tiny kitten.

The tiny scrap of life hissed, growled and tried to scratch and bite, as I put my hand towards it and carefully lifted it out. Surprisingly, Bella, who usually hates cats, did nothing, but watched as I gathered up the poor little creature, wrapped it in my handkerchief and made our way home. The little kitten was only a few weeks old and not in a good state. It was very weak and clearly dehydrated from the baking heat, and I doubted that it would last the night. Still, I reasoned, at least we could make it comfortable during its last few hours.

We managed to buy a tin of cat food from the local shop and began to tempt the kitten with a teaspoon or so of the foul smelling contents of the tin. The kitten began to lick and then eat a little from the spoon and after a while hungrily devoured a tablespoon of so of the meat. He then lapsed into a deep sleep. We repeated the process again an hour or so later, and continued throughout the evening until the kitten could eat no more. Even so, by the time I went to bed, I doubted that the little thing would see morning.

Early the following morning, I peered anxiously into the old cage where we kept the kitten to see him standing and looking at me with enormous eyes. He hissed and growled, and tried to scratch as I picked him up. He ate several more large helpings of cat food during the day and was clearly recovering from his ordeal! Phone calls, Facebook, Twitters and emails to cat-loving friends brought us essential help and advice at a time when it was most needed. Thank you! We went out and bought the correct kitten food, cat litter, travel bag, scratch post and all the other necessities of life for the modern kitten. Adopting the kitten certainly gave the credit card a hammering!

As I write this Twitter, one week later, I am delighted to say that the vet has declared that Mac is a three-month-old boy. She thinks he is basically fit and well, although he has another examination next week, and has treated him for fleas, worms and diarrhoea! Even in this short space of time he is growing into a happy, contented, if nervous kitten that will happily spend his time on my knee purring and having his tummy and chin tickled. Thankfully, he no longer scratches, hisses or spits - at us anyway!

Mac will stay with us and has already become a much-loved member of the family. That is with the exception of Bella who, I fear, will regard the finding of Mac as the worst day's work that she has ever done in her life. Mac spends much of the day staring at her with big, threatening eyes and growls and hisses whenever she gets too close. I also suspect that it will be cat and not dog who will be in charge!

The Uniqueness of Gran Canaria

I often receive emails from readers asking why I moved from the UK to the Canary Islands, and to Gran Canaria in particular. In this 'Twitter' I will attempt to answer the question, but my apologies if it sounds as if I work for the Tourist Board. I don't, but I just happen to love the island!

Gran Canaria is often called a "continent in miniature". It is a fitting title because of the island's uniqueness of having several climatic zones within the one relatively small island. There can be snow on the mountains, whilst you are swimming in the sea or sweltering in the heat of the desert. In Gran Canaria, there are craters, volcanoes, waterfalls, mountains, pine woods, palm groves and beautiful sandy beaches making it a naturally stunning and interesting place to visit or to live. With its seemingly endless sandy beaches, dramatic mountains, deep ravines, sweeping sand dunes and lush green vegetation many have come to regard Gran Canaria as the jewel of the Canary Islands.

Whilst the north of the island frequently experiences dense, low cloud, often blocking out the sun for hours at a time; the southern coast of the island is perpetually cloud free and guaranteed rain free during eight months of the year, making it a popular destination for sun-seeking tourists. Average temperatures on the island are 24°C in summer and 19°C in winter. Unlike some of its neighbours, Gran Canaria has extremely varied landscapes with

European, African and even American vegetation. There is hardly anywhere else in the world where you can find such differing landscapes and climate zones in such close proximity to each other.

What is the reason for this uniqueness of the island's climate? One of the reasons is the unusual shape of the island, which leads to a great variety of microclimates. While the climate is dry and sunny almost all year round in the coastal regions, particularly in the south, as you move up to higher altitudes, the influence of the sea is reduced and the clouds are retained by the mountains. This produces great variations in temperature from the temperate zones of the lower regions or valleys and subtropical forests to the highest zones where the temperature can fall to 0 °C. It's not too unusual for people to go sunbathing and swimming on the beach and then to find themselves playing around in the snow on the mountain tops just one hour's drive later.

The sea is equally as warm with temperatures fluctuating between 18 °C in the winter months and 22 °C during the rest of the year. This, together with the estimated annual rate of 2,700 hours of sunlight in Gran Canaria allow you to make the most of the day, whether you are on the beach, playing a sport, on a day trip or enjoying an outdoor activity.

People often mistakenly think that if the winter is so warm on the islands then the summer heat must be overwhelming, but this couldn't be further from the truth. The summer in the Canary Islands is softened by the trade winds that refresh the islands and give it mild summers. Indeed, one small village on the on the island's east coast, Pozo Izquierdo, is often said to be the "windiest place on earth" and there is rarely a shortage of a refreshing breeze. However, in the last couple of years there have been one or two weeks in August where the temperature has climbed higher than usual. As a bonus, research from the international scientific community claims that the island's capital, Las Palmas, is one of the cities with the healthiest climate in the world.

I could go on, but I am fast running out of space. All I can say is, come over and see for yourselves. You will be made most welcome!

EXPAT SURVIVAL

Celebration

Canary Islands' Day (Día de las Canarias)

30 May is a day for all Canarians, as well as for all those who love the Canary Islands, to be proud! Proud of our beautiful islands, our rich heritage, the way of life and the enjoyment that they give to so many people. This is the day when the Canary Islands, a Spanish Autonomous Community, became integrated into the European Union as a peripheral territory deserving of preferential treatment. It marks the anniversary of the autonomous Canary Islands' Parliament's first session, which took place on May 30, 1983.

The Canary Islands are a long way away from the Spanish Peninsular, yet are very much part of Spain and also part of Europe. It is easy to forget that Gran Canaria is at the southernmost tip of Europe and our closest neighbours are those parts of Africa with a more European outlook. The islands are a bridge between Africa and Europe with a strong link to parts of America. It is worth remembering that America opened its doors wide for the thousands of Canary Islanders who crossed the Atlantic in times of hardship looking for a better future. Many have since returned with their children and grandchildren. Europeans, Africans, Asians and Americans meet in the Canary Islands, a true intercultural link and an open, welcoming land for the millions of tourists who come to discover the beauty of these islands.

Many cultural activities and celebrations are arranged for Canary Islands' Day each year. Schools make a special point of teaching children about the rich history and culture of the Canary Islands and organise parties and events for children in the days before the special day. Many people hold private parties at home or in restaurants on the evening of May 29. It is a time for great celebration and joy.

Now for the history and geography lessons. The Canary Islands consist of seven inhabited islands off the coast of Africa, which are: Gran Canaria, Fuerteventura, Lanzarote, Tenerife, El Hierro, La Palma and La Gomera.

There is also the Chinijo Archipelago, which includes the tiny islands of La Graciosa, Alegranza, Montaña Clara, Roque del Este and Roque del Oeste. Although these islands form an autonomous community within Spain, they are closer to Morocco and the Western Sahara. The Romans too were aware of the Canary Islands, but they remained independent until the Spanish invasion of the islands in 1402, when the islands became part of the Kingdom of Castile in 1495.

This is a day when we celebrate with pride and wish to share just a taste of these wonderful islands with our visitors, as well as those who live and work here. If you have never visited us, maybe one day you should.

"Your hat looks wonderful, my dear!"

Nothing says "Royal Wedding" quite like an ostrich's bottom joined to your left temple. No, I had told myself, I would not be spending the day watching the wedding celebrations and associated hats of a couple I did not know, would never meet and who were representing a country many miles away. It was a country that I had left many years ago and would be unlikely to return to. Participating in such an event from a small island in the Atlantic did seem a ridiculous way to spend a day, when I had far better things to do. Although I respect and admire the Queen, I suspect that is more to do with the fact that she represents continuity in my life, rather than a wish to celebrate the wedding of her grandson. I had another chapter of my book to write, and that was the way that I fully intended to spend the Royal Wedding Day.

How wrong I was. After being initially drawn by the excitement that was building on the radio, curiosity led me to switch on the television. The atmosphere was infectious, and by 10.00am, I found myself watching and sharing the events on television with around 2 billion other people in at least 150 countries around the world.

The enthusiasm and excitement of the crowds waiting and watching brushed away all the usual cares and sorrows of the world. Gone, for the day anyway, were thoughts of war, rebellion, recession, bankers' bonuses and students' tuition fees. In its place came a kind of raw innocence, one of belief and hope for the future, and a sense that history was being made without the intervention and manipulations of politicians and big business. It was a simple hope and belief in the future that the union of two people always brings, and an infectious joy that is so hard to put into words.

How we marvelled at the hats - as ridiculous as some of them were. After all, wearing a dead parrot, or the entire contents of a florist's catalogue on your head does not look particularly 'cool', or stylish come to that. "Please do not turn your head whilst in the pew, Madam, otherwise you will flatten the gentleman to your left." Did these ladies actually look at themselves in the mirror before they left home? Were their partners too frightened to make a negative comment, or were they just too subdued after being crammed into a morning suit and trussed up like chickens for the day? I suspect that one of the young princesses, who was wearing part of a tree on her head, learned the hard way when the cameras caught her leaning forward at an angle of 90° in order for the limousine to accommodate both her and her generously proportioned hat on the way to the palace for the obligatory canapés!

Spirits were lifted whilst listening to the music of some of the great British composers in the spectacular and familiar surroundings of Westminster Abbey, now decked with beautiful, fresh green trees. Innocent looking and freshly scrubbed choirboys singing their new M & S socks off, fusty Archbishops, Cardinals and Deans, with far too much white facial hair, all brought back memories of earlier times of national celebrations long ago.

Along with most other people watching, I was drawn into the spirit of an event that I could not explain. Watching the beautiful bride and her handsome prince is, I guess, the stuff of fairy tales and early childhood memories. Yes, I too felt a lump rising in my throat and found that I had moist eyes at several times during the service. This was surreal and quite ridiculous to be feeling and behaving like this, I told myself.

Mums, dads, children, grannies and granddads swarmed down the Mall to watch the newly wedded couple appear on the balcony. A sea of different coloured skins, ages and nationalities greeted the cameras. Awkward and surly looking teenagers admitting that they too were having a great time and were waiting to see 'that kiss' made me feel that I had somehow slipped into an alternative universe for the day, but maybe that was the effect of Victoria Beckham's spiky alien creation. People were just so happy!

Later I found myself attending a 'Royal' barbecue and joining in with a toast to the happy couple. It was a sincere toast, not only to the Royal couple, but to the love of all couples everywhere, gay or straight, and with the sincere hope that they will have found their soul-mates and can live in happiness together for many years to come.

The Twelve Grapes

Tradition has it that on New Year's Eve in Spain and the Canary Islands, twelve 'lucky grapes' known as 'Uvas de la Suerte' have to be eaten around the stroke of midnight. It is important to eat one grape at a time with each stroke of the clock and, of course, washed down with liquid refreshment, and usually a lively Spanish bubbly wine called Cava. It is believed that this tradition came from ancient wine growers; well, after all it does fuel the sale of grapes on New Year's Eve doesn't it?

This fine tradition, as with a number of so-called traditions, has a number of flaws. Without appearing too cynical about the whole business of grape swallowing, I have witnessed several unfortunate incidents concerning the hasty swallowing of grapes since I have lived in Spain, and I repeat these as a warning for this and future New Year's celebrations.

Most importantly, grapes grown in the Canary Islands are of the seeded variety. The process of hastily swallowing twelve grapes in twelve seconds may be perfectly acceptable with the unseeded variety, but what exactly do you do with the pips in the seeded type when you are in polite company and do not wish to swallow them?

My Mum used to warn me about swallowing grape seeds with the threat that I may get an immediate attack of appendicitis and would have to be whisked to the casualty department of the nearest hospital for an immediate operation. It is strange how memories from childhood are triggered by small events in later life. According to Mum, this pip swallowing may lead to an acute case of peritonitis and if you were really unlucky you would be dead before the end of New Year's Day. Yes, Mum was a little inclined to exaggeration when it came to matters medical. All that inconvenience for a grape pip. Is it really worth all the trouble?

I recall one unfortunate occasion at a New Year's party that I attended in the Costa Blanca, when an elderly lady swallowed a pip that 'went down the wrong way'. It started as a cough, gentle at first and then becoming increasing violent. She was given a glass of wine and later a glass of water to ease the problem. Her coughing became increasing troublesome and I really did not like the shade of pink that she was turning, as a few helpful people thumped her vigorously on the back to dislodge the offending item. Sadly it was to no avail until one helpful gentleman, who claimed to be a first aider, wrapped his arms around her chest from behind and gave her a sudden squeeze. The old lady moaned, and not with pleasure, as her false teeth shot across the room. The offending pip had been dislodged and the party continued with the old lady later leading the Hokey Cokey.

So have a wonderful New Year and remember the old adage, 'It is always safer to spit than swallow.'

The South American Factor

The Canary Islands have a richness, colour and diversity that are probably unequalled in most parts of Europe. No, I am not talking about the flora and fauna of these islands, but its people. Here you will find people of all colour, faith and no faith, straight, gay and transgendered. In the main, all rub along happily with each other and this is one of the many reasons why I adore these islands so much. The islands offer a culture of 'live and let live' with tremendous energy, vitality and enthusiasm - feelings and impressions that are quickly sensed by our many thousands of tourists to the islands and why they return year after year.

One of my favourite events in Gran Canaria is Carnival in Las Palmas and I would urge anyone who has not experienced this colourful and amazing spectacular to choose (or make) a costume, pack a bag and stay in Las Palmas for a couple of nights during the height of the festival. Be prepared to stay up all night and be hoarse by the end of it all! If you hate late nights, loud noise, crowds of people and thoroughly enjoying yourself then please don't go! So why is it that Carnival is larger and livelier than most events that you will find anywhere in Europe? I put it down to the South American factor.

My dentist, accountant, lawyer and eye surgeon are all from Argentina, and very good they are too. As most residents will already have discovered, there are many people from South America living and working in these islands and this is one of the reasons why Carnival in Las Palmas is sometimes described as "Second only to Rio". It certainly puts Peninsular Spain to shame when it comes to this spectacular annual event. Indeed, many professional people, as well as bar and restaurant staff from South America, now live and work in the Canary Islands. It is interesting to talk to some of these people and to discover the reasons why they are attracted to these small islands in the Atlantic.

Since the 18th century there has been an outflow of Canary Islanders to parts of South America and to parts of what is now the USA. At one time this was part of Spain's strategy to colonise and populate the newly discovered Americas, and the Spanish Government looked to the Canary Islands for recruits to increase the size of the army in Louisiana, with the dual role of defending the territory, as well as populating it.

In more recent times, there was an outflow of migrants from Spain and the Canary Islands and particularly during the periods of economic troubles, avoidance of the obligatory military service, the 1936 - 1939 Civil War, as well as during the period of General Franco's dictatorship between 1939 and 1975. During this time, many Spanish citizens fled from Spain as a result of the Civil War, as well as sending their children to South America for protection. These refugees from Spain eventually settled in Argentina, Cuba and Mexico, as well as other countries in Latin America.

Cuba was a particularly welcoming destination for many Canarians and there are still strong links between the Canary Islands and Cuba, at both the Islands' Government and personal levels. There remains a strong feeling of gratitude towards this island in the Caribbean that became home to so many Canarians fleeing from repression and poverty.

Many of these migrants are now of an age when they wish to return to their country of birth and Spain, to its credit, is doing its best to help these Spanish emigrants and particularly by supporting the elderly.

Pensions, as well as return visits to Spain for these 'children of the Civil War' and who have not visited their country of origin for many years are now provided by the Spanish Government in an attempt to redress some of the injustices that forced them into exile during the Franco dictatorship. Temporary changes to Spanish law under the 'Law of Historical Memory' has allowed many children and grandchildren of Spanish emigrants living in Latin American to obtain Spanish citizenship.

At times of financial crisis, history teaches us that the weakest and most vulnerable members of society are often singled out for criticism and often worse. We heard a great deal about the perceived problems of immigration into the UK during the last General Election. However, in the Canary Islands, we can reflect upon this as a more positive story and one that has contributed greatly to island life.

It makes me feel alive!

Expats tend to spend a great deal of time at airports. My regular visits to the airport often give me the opportunity to indulge in one of my favourite past times - people watching. Although I tend to avoid the misery of 'Departures' like the plague, watching the 'Arrivals' is always an entertaining business. 'Spot where they are from' - is quite an easy game for me to play nowadays, and one that I rather enjoy.

I can easily spot an Irishman, a German or a Spanish national with just a quick glance, although defining which Scandinavian country the tourist is from does require a much more detailed observation. It is amazing how comedy stereotypes of the individual characteristics of different nationalities are often so true. As for spotting an Englishman, well that is just so easy, although I sometimes do get them confused with Germans – yes, the two nationalities really are alike in so many ways!

My eye was drawn to a young man in a wheelchair being pushed by an elderly woman from the arrivals lounge and into the main airport corridor. He looked painfully thin, with a pallid unhealthy looking skin, and his frail body was strapped into his wheelchair. An elderly man followed the wheelchair, pushing several suitcases on one of the airport trolleys.

It was clear that these passengers did not travel light. I immediately recognised the Welsh accent as being from the valleys when the elderly woman began speaking to the young man. However, I could not decide whether the elderly couple accompanying the young man were his elderly parents or grandparents.

The young man beamed as soon as he was pushed into the corridor. "Look Ma! Look!" he shouted, "The sun! The sun's shining on our island again!" The old lady nodded, "Yes, Colin, it is. You like it here don't you?" She took a tissue out of her pocket and wiped the young man's mouth gently.

Colin caught my eye. I smiled. He beamed at me, displaying a broad, toothy smile. It was a genuine smile, full of happiness and joy.

"Hello," I said. "You look really pleased to be here. I hope you had a good flight?"

Colin nodded, and beamed again. "I love it here. I always love it here. It makes me feel alive".

I smiled and nodded, and wished the young man a happy holiday and moved on to my next errand.

Later, whilst waiting at the Post Office, I began to think about Colin and his elderly parents. His words, "It makes me feel alive" played on my mind. Colin was clearly disabled physically, as well as mentally. He looked so poorly, yet I have rarely seen a smile so broad and genuine, a smile of pure elation and joy, as I did on this young man.

As I was leaving the airport, I spotted Colin's father waiting for a taxi. I suspected that they were waiting for one especially designed for disabled visitors. "Colin's going to have a really good time," I said. "I can see it in his face."

The old man nodded. "Yes, we try to come here as much as we can. He loves the island and is so much better when he is here. We don't know how much longer Colin will be with us, but we want to make sure that each day is special for him. He gives us so much joy".

I left the airport with a lump in my throat, reflecting about this very special young man and his caring, loving parents. I hope the family has a truly wonderful holiday and that Colin can store many happy memories for the future.

Happiness and joy is contained within us and is a state of mind. It need not be connected to our health, mental and physical abilities, the amount of money that we have or the amount of booze that we consume. I think I am beginning to understand what Colin meant when he said, "It makes me feel alive."

"It's Hot Up My Barranco!"

"Phew, it's hot up my barranco today, darling," gasped Miranda as she staggered down the street carrying two large and heavy bags of clattering bottles from the local supermarket. Before you get too carried away by imagining a doctor about to don a pair of surgical gloves for some emergency female probing, I should explain that Miranda is one of the village's more colourful characters. She is a school assistant in one of the less classy private schools by day and a tattooist by night. I once asked if there was any conflict of interest between her two jobs. She screeched loudly in my ear, before resting her mug of gin on top of my car.

"No, not at all, darling. It's a great way to help the kids with their reading."

I must have looked puzzled, as I thought I knew a thing or two about teaching children to read, and she seemed to read my thoughts.

"You see, I have all the letters of the alphabet tattooed all over my body somewhere, so I use those to help children to read. If it's Tina the Tiresome Transvestite we are reading, I just point out this letter "T" on my arm and then we find the picture of the Tina on my back. Easy, the kids love it."

"So you have all the letters and associated pictures somewhere on your body?"

"Oh, yes, darling, but I should say that some are more difficult to find than others. We tend to keep off the "Y" and "Z" words otherwise I would get the sack, darling. If you know what I mean!" She guffawed loudly, as she nudged me in the ribs and winked knowingly.

By now, I think you are probably getting the idea of what Miranda is like. A lovely lady, but back in the UK I would be surprised if she had a job at all. However, over here, we are all much more open-minded.

As Miranda dropped her bags by my front gate and she propped herself on my parked car, she watched what I was doing with some amusement. I stopped washing the hedge (actually it is one of those plastic ones, but I do like to freshen it up a bit from time to time) and it is always a good opportunity to remove the crisp packets and condoms from its branches.

"You are home early today. Is everything alright?"

"Darling, it's the heat. It is just so hot. I tell you, darling, it was 41°C up my barranco at lunchtime. It was just too much darling. We sent the little dears home early, because they were just fading away."

I tried to imagine Miranda's boisterous pupils fading away and thought it highly unlikely. We have a number of calimas, although some people call them siroccos, on the islands each year, and the islanders are generally conditioned to withstand them, and it is the expats who suffer. They can be a little unpleasant for a few days, bringing with them very high temperatures from Africa and the Sahara. In my own village, when the wind disappears, it is a case of staying inside as much as possible with air-conditioning on and plenty of cool drinks. These heat waves can occur at any time during the year, but they are less common during the cooler months.

Miranda's school is situated in a barranco, a Spanish word for ravine. Some would say that was a foolish place to build anything, because of potential sudden rainstorms, but I guess the land was cheap. Anyway, I suspect it was built to withstand the heat and would have air conditioning installed as essential.

"I was pleased to get home early, darling. I needed to get ready for the bonfire this evening."

"Bonfire? In this heat!" I exclaimed.

"Darling, tomorrow is the Festival of St John the Baptist. A most important religious festival! You mustn't miss that. We are having a bonfire party tonight to celebrate. Not here you understand, but outside Telde. It's traditional you know, darling. You really must come. You don't have to be a Catholic, just bring a bottle!"

So there we have it. We are in the middle of a calima where daytime temperatures are around 40°C, in the shade, and the good people of Telde are planning a bonfire party to celebrate St John the Baptist. The activities on this island never cease to surprise me.

Culture and Heritage

Agatha Christie and the Canary Islands

Many residents and holidaymakers are well aware of the recuperative properties of the Canary Islands, yet few know of the strong links between the popular novelist, Agatha Christie, and these islands.

Agatha Christie visited the Canary Islands in search of a tranquil and recuperative environment to help her calm a troubled mind. In February 1927, at the age of 36, she visited the Canary Islands to recover from a number of events that had taken place in her life and were having a serious impact upon her mental health. She mysteriously disappeared for eleven days in a 'fugue state', a rare psychiatric disorder characterised by amnesia of identity, memories and personality. The state is usually short-lived - sometimes a few hours, but others may suffer for a few days or even longer.

When her first marriage failed, Agatha Christie disappeared from her home and stayed at the Swan Hydro Hotel in Harrogate, under the name of the woman with whom her husband was having an affair. A young journalist, who used some of the story patterns in her books to suggest her likely moves, finally found her.

Agatha Christie's mother had recently died after a serious illness, her husband was in love with another woman and Agatha was having serious financial difficulties. Each of these problems, particularly when combined, could be a recipe for, what most of us would call, a mental breakdown. It is this series of events in her personal life that led Agatha Christie to the Canary Islands.

Agatha and her daughter, Rosalind, together with her secretary, Charlotte Fisher, arrived in Tenerife on 4 February 1927. They stayed at the Gran Hotel Taoro in Puerto de la Cruz, which was the best hotel in Tenerife and the centre of the British community. It is believed that in Puerto de la Cruz, Agatha Christie completed one of her novels, 'The Mystery of the Blue Train', which sold well and put an end to her financial worries. There is now a bronze bust of Agatha Christie and a street named after her in Puerto de la Cruz.

Having completed her novel, she decided to stay one more week in the Canary Islands to relax. Agatha longed for white sandy beaches rather than a sloping volcanic beach, and on 27 February decided to leave Tenerife and complete the remainder of her holiday in Gran Canaria, before returning to England by steamship on 4 March 1927.

Agatha Christie stayed at the Metropole Hotel in Las Palmas de Gran Canaria, which is opposite the beautiful Santa Catalina beach. Agatha described Las Palmas as the ideal place to go in the winter. Sadly, the Metropole Hotel is no more and is now part of Las Palmas Town Hall, and is where I recently paid my fine for illegal parking! The British Club and their tennis courts were nearby and Agatha Christie began to write 'The Companion', included in her collection of short stories, 'The Thirteen Problems', which has strong links to Gran Canaria.

The Canary Islands made a clear impression upon the mind of this prolific author, and feature in a number of her stories such as 'The Man from the Sea' in the book, 'The Mysterious Mr. Quin', which also takes place on an island.

Agatha Christie was a much-travelled woman who visited Europe, South Africa, Australia, North America and the Middle East. It is a compliment to the Canary Islands that it was in these islands that she found the peace and tranquillity that she was looking for. The last word, and recommendation, must go to Agatha Christie with an extract from 'The Companion':

"I had had a breakdown in health and was forced to give up my practice in England and go abroad. I practised in Las Palmas, which is the principal town of Gran Canaria. In many ways I enjoyed the life out there very much. The climate was mild and sunny, there was excellent surf bathing..."

So there we have it. If you are in need of a recuperative break, sun and relaxation, you know where to come!

The Whistle Language

I am often asked, "What are the most important things to do when planning to move to another country?" My answer is always the same, "Learn the language, and preferably before you arrive". I have learned Spanish the hard way and, because I do not find learning languages particularly easy, it has taken me considerable time and a determined effort to succeed.

I blame my early education. As an eleven-year-old growing up in rural Lincolnshire, I was forced to learn French and Latin. I did not mind Latin too much, even though I failed to see the relevance of learning a dead language. Yet, I was told that Latin was essential if I wanted to be a doctor or a pharmacist, but as I cannot stand the sight of blood that was going to be highly unlikely! Still, I liked the teacher and it could be faintly amusing chanting "amo, amas, amant" and all the rest of this ancient nonsense from my fusty textbook.

It was learning French that I really detested. Whether it was the teacher, who always seemed to exude just a hint of garlic rather than after shave, the boring pre-war edition of the text book, or the fact that I would much rather have been doing something else, as the sound of the language did not sit easily upon my ears. I became a clock-watcher willing the lesson to end. I began to dread the lessons and gave up the subject at the earliest opportunity. The experience very nearly put me off learning languages for life until I had a shot at Russian, but that is a story for another time...

There is a small and very beautiful Canary Island called La Gomera. The island has a population of around 22,000 people, and the islanders have maintained a very special way of communicating with each other. In early times, the aboriginal population, the Guanches, used a whistle language to convey complex messages across the deep valleys. As a whistle can be heard from a long distance away, it was far more effective than shouting, and much faster than travelling across the rugged landscape.

When the Romans conquered the islands, they documented this language, which in Spanish is known as El Silbo Gomero, or simply El Silbo. In the 16th century, after the islands were colonised by Spanish settlers, this language was adapted to Spanish, and it still survives today.

Silbo Gomero is not a language in its own right, but it is a way of echoing syllables of words by putting fingers in the mouth, and can be heard over distances of around three thousand metres. Pitch, intensity, length, and intermittent or continuous sounds are used to distinguish the different phonemes and syntax. I am told that the grammar and vocabulary of El Silbo Gomero are exactly the same as in Spanish. It is at the same time, both an eerie yet strangely wonderful sound to hear and experience.

Nowadays, with telephones, mobiles and broadband Internet calls, there is no longer a need to communicate by whistling. However, as we learned from the recent electrical storms on the islands, when many of us lost electricity, telephone and even mobile telephone connections, a back up alternative is always a good idea! Thanks to a local government initiative, El Silbo Gomero is taught at every school on the island to ensure that future generations will still remember and use it.

Learning Latin as an eleven-year-old? No, I still do not see the point. Even though I am told that a good grasp of Latin would make the learning of other languages easier, it did not work for me. Learning the Whistle Language? Now that is a different matter, and I wish that it had been on the curriculum when I was a confused eleven-year-old. I'm just off to practice.

Is anyone here called Juan?

I am very fond of pizza; that is if I can find one that is vegetarian. Being vegetarian, I have sometimes found it very difficult to get across the message that a 'pizza vegetal' is pizza without the inclusion of flesh of any kind. I have been presented with supposedly vegetarian pizzas laced with generous dollops of tuna, a fried egg and even a generous sprinkling of ham, which I thought was red pepper, before my stomach started heaving and I headed like a bullet for the door.

No, it has not been easy being a vegetarian in Spain and the Canary Islands, but I have now found the perfect pizzeria, or cafe bar to be more accurate. Personally, I think that the pizzas produced there are some of the best on the island - a perfect combination of a thin, not too crisp base and a perfectly cooked range of seasonal vegetables. We often have a take away pizza ready for a night in front of the television with a good film.

A few days ago I telephoned to place our usual order. Instead of the usually cheery bar owner/chef answering the telephone, came a sleepy voice. "Er, can you call back later please? The ovens have still not heated up". I thought this strange, as the cafe bar opened at 7.00pm and by now it was nearly 8.00pm, which I know is still very early for Canarians to eat. I hoped that this was not the beginning of the end for yet another cafe bar, forced to lay off staff and eventually close because of the effects of the recession.

When I finally arrived at the bar to collect my order, the chef gave me a cheeky grin and told me that he was thankful for my call, because he had overslept and my call had woken him! The bar was, by now, full of elderly and middle aged men, some with a beer in hand watching sport on the television, others playing on the gaming machine, whilst others simply propped themselves against the bar, no drink in hand, but obviously there just for the company. One younger man was cheerfully helping himself to a shot from behind the bar - after all, the bar owner was still cooking my pizzas, yet I noticed he carefully placed a number of coins by the till. It was a very Canarian scene.

Suddenly the door burst open and a small boy of about six or seven ran into the bar frantically waving a mobile phone above his head.

"Anyone in here called Juan?" he yelled (in Spanish, of course).

Suddenly the noise stopped, all the men turned and faced the small boy and three quarters of them stood up and shouted back "I'm Juan", before helpless laughter broke out in the bar. The small boy looked puzzled before he ran off followed by several of the men. I would love to have known what the urgent message was about.

Although I have not checked any surveys of the most popular names used in the Canary Islands, I would guess, without a doubt, that the most popular name for men of a certain age in my village is Juan, and the best place to find them is in our pizzeria.

An Explosive Island

The Canary Islands have a history that is, quite literally, littered with explosions. Each of the seven main islands was created by hot volcanic lava pushing through the cold Atlantic Ocean in the last million years or so. It therefore does not seem surprising that an occasional 'belch' can be heard, and seen, every few hundred years or so. One of our islands has been in a bit trouble over recent weeks, but first, a little background.

The Canary Islands are home to the third largest volcano in the world, Mount Teide, on the island of Tenerife, which is also the highest mountain in Spain. Interestingly, all the islands, except La Gomera, have seen volcanic activity in the last million years or so.

The island of El Hierro was formed over one million years ago. After three successive eruptions, the island emerged from the ocean as a triangle topped with a volcanic cone more than 2,000 metres high. Continued volcanic activity resulted in the island expanding to the island boasting the largest number of volcanoes in the Canary Islands, together with a multitude of caves and volcanic galleries.

Until recent weeks, most people had never even heard of El Hierro, also called the Meridian Island, which is the smallest and furthest south and west of the Canary Islands. However, it is a fascinating place and rich in history, customs and traditions and one, which has, mercifully, escaped much of the ravages of the present day tourist industry. It is the kind place that tourists should forget if interested only in copious quantities of booze, sunshine and discos when on holiday, because they will be greatly disappointed.

The stoic people of El Hierro are currently coping with the release of foul smelling gas, water stained by sulphur from the volcano and increased sea temperatures, which are killing fish and threatening all marine life in the area. Residents of the fishing village of La Restinga, which is the most affected area, were forced to leave their homes as the volcano just off the coast began erupting for the second time.

A string of earthquakes was registered on the island, including several tremors measuring above 4 on the Richter scale. However, in recent days villagers have been allowed to return to their homes, after scientists said they are not expecting an imminent eruption, although they admitted that the possibility of further after-shocks still exists.

Without making light of a potentially serious situation for the islanders of El Hierro, the volcanic cone that is currently pumping out magma 500 feet below the surface of the ocean is gradually heading towards the surface and experts tell us will shortly break the surface to create another Canary Island, in much the same way as these 'Fortunate Islands' were created millions of years ago. Indeed, island residents are already brainstorming names for the potential landmass, including 'Discovery Island' and 'Atlantis', amongst other suggestions. Maybe, in years to come, future generations of tourists will be heading out to holiday on the newest baby of the Canary Islands.

El Hierro has lost much of the tourist income that is the lifeblood of this beautiful and unique island. Island residents estimate that the crisis has already cost them around 4 million euros in lost earnings from the Island's restaurants, hotels and diving schools. However, according to the locals, business had picked up in the last few days with increasing numbers of people curious to see the volcano, as its underwater eruption was visible from the air.

Curiously, it is the media who are hyping the story to an extent where inaccurate reports question the very survival of the island. This is nonsense, and many islanders simply describe it as "A little local difficulty" (in Spanish of course!). Indeed, as one of our island friends put it so eloquently the other day, "Without volcanoes there would not have been the Canary Islands". It is a fair point, I think.

Gadgets and Gizmos

Technology for Expats – VOIP Telephones

It is a fact of expat life that when we move overseas we spend much more time chatting on the telephone and our phone bills soar. The introduction of new telephone services such as Skype and Voip have recently made life so much easier, and cheaper, for the expat.

My Great Aunt Gertie hates phoning me in Spain. A long distance call from Manchester to Bournemouth is perfectly acceptable, even at peak rate; however, when it comes to a call from the UK to the Canary Islands, I hear the sharp inward sucking through her false teeth and a breathless "I must be quick, dear, I am calling long distance. It is very expensive, dear." My usual response of "No, Auntie you have this number on Friends and Family…" makes no difference.

Great Aunt Gertie also complains about, "That Spanish lady. I can't understand a word she's saying…"

"No Auntie, you won't, because you don't speak Spanish," is my forlorn defence of Telefonica's automated response that Auntie will sometimes hear if I am not in. Mobile phone? I hear you say. Sadly not, as that causes an even worse problem for Auntie. "You'll have to speak up, dear. It is such a long way away."

I realised long ago that the telephone issue would have to be sorted if I was not to be banished from Auntie's will. I tried Skype, a wonderful service, but even though I bought Auntie a Skype phone, which didn't need a computer, thankfully, she still complained endlessly about the call quality. Then I discovered part of the answer. She always insisted upon putting her false teeth in when using the Skype phone, which seemed to also affect her hearing. For some strange reason she claimed that she felt naked without them. Usually she didn't bother with false teeth, following a very unpleasant argument with her dentist and a small bottle of gin, yet she can still crack a nut like a teenager. Why she had to put her teeth in when speaking on the Skype phone, I shall never know, but I suspect that it was because the magic box looked a little like a camera.

In despair, I turned to a wonderful new system called Voip (Voice over Internet Protocol). Without dealing too much with the technicalities, these clever telephones look and behave just like a normal telephone and can be easily used, as long as you have an Internet connection. You don't need to have a computer switched on; indeed, you don't even need a computer. I have a cordless version, which means I can wander anywhere in the house or outside and still be connected.

Now this is the clever part. The Voip service that I use gave me a UK telephone number; actually, I bought one with a Bournemouth code, as I used to live there and I still have a lingering attachment to that fine seaside town. I now have a UK (Bournemouth) telephone number that Auntie Gertie and all my friends and family can dial at a local call rate, or free with some telephone packages. The call is diverted to my Voip phone in the Canary Islands, and at no cost to me either. The call quality is excellent and even Auntie Gertie often comments that it sounds as if I am in the next room, and I am not shouting!

The other clever part about this system is that if I am out of the house, but in range of a Wifi or 3G mobile telephone signal, the call is diverted automatically to my iPhone free of charge as part of my mobile Internet package. I can be shopping in my local supermarket and still chat to Auntie Gertie, with or without teeth!

For me, having a UK phone number has proved to be invaluable as publishers, relatives and friends seem to be much happier calling me on my local UK number than calling my Spanish home number. I am not in the business of selling telephone services or equipment, but if you would like further information have a look at my website. Great Aunt Gertie is now quite happy with the arrangement and she assures me regularly that I am still mentioned in her will!

Rediscovering Radio

As much as many expats such as myself enjoy living in our newly adopted countries, it is strange what we miss from our countries of origin. Lemon Curd, Persil tablets and Branston pickle are just a few of the items that I know our friends beg visitors to bring when they visit. For me, it is Marmite, mince pies and 'J' cloths that ensure that our visitors receive a particularly warm welcome. I also miss BBC radio news, as well as radio drama.

I have recently rediscovered radio, bringing with it memories of the illicit thrill of listening to pop radio stations under the bed covers late at night. The breath of fresh air that these radio stations brought to the airwaves gave a new energy for youngsters such as myself growing up during those grey, and often dismal times, in fenland Lincolnshire. Later, it would be Radio 4 that I would listen to during my long car journey to school each day. This was something that I greatly missed when we moved to Spain and the Canary Islands.

Yes, I know that I can easily listen to any radio station in the world via the computer. However, sitting in front of a computer listening to radio does seem to be a very strange and uncomfortable activity and one that I soon dismissed as a complete waste of time.

One of the joys of radio is that you can do something else at the same time, isn't it? How I missed listening to radio plays that seemed to create both colour and characterisation in my imagination in a way that film and television can never do.

Just before Christmas I ordered one of the new Internet radio receivers from the UK. They are not easy to get on the island and the Roberts radio that I wanted had particular features that were unique to the product. As long as I have a Wi-Fi Internet signal, or indeed a wired Internet connection, I can now listen to any radio station in the world. Radio 4, Classic FM, local radio from the Costa Blanca, as well as from my home town of Bournemouth are now regular features of my day. How I enjoy listening to the gritty questioning when John Humphries challenges the Prime Minister about the latest budget cuts. Relaxing music and plays, as well as knowing that there are problems at the Cemetery Junction in Bournemouth yet again, as well as hearing what the Mayor of Torrevieja is up to in Spain, help me to maintain contact with places that I still love and have happy memories of.

In addition to all the thousands of radio stations that I can enjoy whatever I am doing in the house, there is also a new, very clever feature, called Last FM. This is a feature built into the radio whereby I can select my favourite genre of pop music and listen to this 'personal library' of music without the inane interruptions and burblings from would-be DJs and radio 'presenters'. It is pure bliss!

I hasten to add that I also listen to Canary Islands News as well as Spanish News, but I tend to pass on the rest. After all, there are only so many TV quiz shows and reality television programmes that any relatively sane person can take.

Expats and eBooks

I miss books! One of the most difficult things that I had to do when we left the UK for Spain was to cull my collection of books. We could neither afford to transport them all, nor was there going to be enough storage space in our new Spanish home to accommodate them. Book lovers will know the feeling, I am sure, that books become like old friends - always there to provide words of comfort and support in times of difficulty, laughter as well as endless sources of wisdom collected over the years. In the end, I had to make a decision and most of my collection of books found their way to the Salvation Army shop at the end of our road. It was heartbreaking. Even so, I just could not part with some of my earliest childhood memories and so some of my favourite children's books are still stored in a box in my elderly Aunt's garage in the UK.

How I regretted it. Somehow I felt that our home had suddenly been stripped bare of its treasures and within a few weeks I began to collect another small collection from several of the English bookshops in the Costa Blanca, or from one of the many car boot sales that were springing up in the area. Fortunately, before I had time to collect too many books we were on our travels again - this time to the Canary Islands. The cost of freight and the necessity of living in a small apartment for the first few months meant that the cruel process of disposing of books had to begin all over again.

In some ways, the lack of bookshops catering for the English speaking market in the Canary Islands has been a blessing because of the removal of temptation. Yes, I can buy books from car boot sales, charity stalls and the like, but somehow that doesn't have quite the same appeal as peaceful browsing in a bookshop. So, it has had to be browsing online from Internet bookshops and then hoping that the book ordered eventually arrives in the post, or to wait until the next visit back to the UK. My reading for pleasure days seemed almost to be over until I discovered Kindle.

Kindle from Amazon is one of a number of remarkably clever devices from many manufacturers, and is marketed as an eBook reader. These devices are able to download a large number of books via the Internet, and many of the classics are free. My own eReader will store around 4000 books; so plenty to take away on holiday! The choice of books is incredible and I personally find them easier to read on the eyes than a traditional paperback, because the size of text can be adjusted to suit personal taste. If you don't feel like reading, then an eBook reader can read the text to you! I can read books loaded into the eReader in bright sunlight or in darkness by using the light built into the case. I have already downloaded the complete collection of Charles Dickens and Thomas Hardy for the grand sum of 72 pence for each collection, as well as books from a number of modern authors, including the latest best sellers and thrillers.

As an expat living on an island, with little in the way of English language bookshops on hand, purchasing an eBook reader has been one of my best finds, and one that I highly recommend. Indeed, I have to confess to some self-interest, as I have recently published my own books in this format - a great way for me to combine my love of writing, as well as my love of gadgets!

For the traditionalists, that lovely smell of a new book is missing with an eBook, of course; neither is there that special feel of the crispness of paper, nor a shiny new book jacket, or the stiffness protecting an unopened book. However, if it is content that you are interested in, as well as the opportunity to escape into another world, then I can highly recommend it.

Expat Television

A recent announcement by the Chinese Government to axe more than two-thirds of prime time light entertainment shows and replace them with news broadcasts came as a shock to many, and was met with concern about further curbs on the freedom of the Chinese people. This law to curb "excessive entertainment" on television is designed to reduce the number of scheduled entertainment programmes from 126 a week to just 38. However, after looking at Spanish television's uninspiring offerings for the current week, I began to wonder if this was actually quite an inspired move.

The true value and quality of the UK's BBC is only really appreciated once you have left the country. Arguments about licence fees, the quality of programming and schedules disappear into insignificance once you have left the country and realise that you can no longer receive its offerings. Despite its faults, few will complain about the high quality of the national broadcaster's documentaries, news output and period dramas. It is one of those very British of institutions, like the British Heath Service, which has in many ways woven itself into the very fabric of what it is to be British. The BBC does not hold the monopoly on quality, of course, with ITV, Channel Four and even Sky TV producing some excellent programmes.

When I left the UK for Spain's Costa Blanca I resolutely decided that I would no longer care about what happened in "Corrie", or in Eastender's Queen Vic pub, for that matter. Instead, I would content myself with all things Spanish, spend lazy evenings on the terrace, a glass of good wine in my hand, reading a good book or maybe focus on those initial attempts to learn the language and maybe the Spanish guitar! It was to be a whole new way of life, and one where television would not play a part.

How wrong I was! Within weeks of arriving at our new home, I was, along with all our neighbours, trying to find out the best ways of getting British television. We were surrounded by a motley collection of satellite dishes and a kind of baking tray contraption strapped to many rooftops, designed to receive micromesh re-transmission of UK television programmes. At this point I will deftly step aside from the legal issues and arguments surrounding such contraptions, as it can lead to some difficulties. All in all, the Costa Blanca had the problem sorted. One way or another, British TV was easily available and was satisfying the needs of a growing expat population who were desperate to maintain links with 'home'.

Moving to the Canary Islands was a different matter. No longer were micromesh installations available, and satellite reception required a massive dish to receive the questionable delights of Sky TV. Indeed, I had a neighbour who filled almost the entirety of his front garden with the largest satellite dish that I have ever seen for a home installation. (I understand that the both the European Space Agency and the Island's airport are very interested in renting bandwidth!) With the advent of Internet television and the BBC's iPlayer, it is clear that British television is a must for most expats and, despite the best efforts of UK authorities to prevent receiving transmissions overseas, given a little time and effort, there are always ways around the problem.

I am often asked why there is such a demand for British television. Apart from the obvious answer of keeping in touch with our country of birth and programmes in a language that can be easily understood, the reason is very simple. In the main, most Spanish television programmes are of poor quality. With the exception of some very good news coverage, most schedules are filled with American movies, quiz and chat shows, as well that beast to be avoided at all costs, reality television. Period dramas, for instance, rarely feature in the schedules.

Maybe China's decision to axe much of the content on its channels is desirable, or is it yet another attempt by the state to control? I guess the human rights people will be discussing this issue in the weeks to come; meanwhile I am going to enjoy the next episode of Eastenders!

Go Virtual

I am often surprised that many expats have never heard of a Virtual Private Network (VPN). I have managed to watch television channels, which I am not supposed to watch as I am living outside the UK, for many years without a satellite dish or expensive television retransmission service, just by hooking up my TV to a second computer and watching by courtesy of the Internet.

Yes, the quality of reception has been very variable and I have been plagued by 'low bandwidth issues', although please don't ask me what this is, because I really don't have a clue, technically speaking. All I know is that the Internet signal is a bit like a running stream, and if you are at the end of the line or with a service provider who restricts your flow, you end up with little more than a dribble. This is the problem that I had for a number of years in Spain, until I changed Internet service providers. Magic, the flow became a torrent and I now rarely suffer from the curse of 'buffering'.

Watching television programmes from the UK, bypassing all forms of geographical restrictions, accessing blocked sites, just because you happen to be an expat living in another country, bypassing Internet 'security' monitors, unblocking access to YouTube, Skype and television channels, as well as the encryption of all of your Internet traffic, suddenly becomes possible with a Virtual Private Network.

So, what is a Virtual Private Network? If you look up the subject on Google, Wikipedia or similar, you will find very complicated explanations. In simple terms, it is basically a system that uses the Internet to connect to remote sites in another country. VPN uses 'virtual' connections that are routed through the Internet to connect to remote sites, which immediately enables access to services provided only in that country.

A Virtual Private Network suddenly provides open communication across countries and political barriers, just as the Internet was originally meant to be by its founder. Many countries and companies are constantly trying to restrict what can be seen by the general public, and based purely upon where you are. With VPN you can unblock streaming services, such as favourite television stations and gaming and lottery sites, by accessing servers in their broadcast areas, such as from your country of origin.

Internet security is also a troubling issue nowadays. I make a point that whenever I access my online bank accounts, both in Spain and in the UK, I divert my Internet access though VPN, which makes financial transactions private and more secure with encryption. Having a VPN is just another small way that you can help to defeat the all watching eyes of 'Big Brother', and open up greater enjoyment from the Internet as an expat.

The VPN service is also remarkably cheap for the benefits it offers. I have used a number of free services in the past, but these were inevitably unreliable, as many services were directed through Asian servers, which seemed to me an unnecessarily long way for the signal to travel! Instead, for a number of years, I have used a service that is based in the UK, and for which I pay about £5 per month. For me, the VPN service is worth every penny. The price too has remained constant over the years and, most importantly, has been totally reliable. Personally, I wouldn't be without it.

For further information about this and other VPN providers, as well as other useful information, have a look at the Expat Survival section of my website.

A Connection at the Mortuary

One of the downsides of living in a remote area is the problem with mobile phone signals. Although I live reasonably close to a large town, by the time that I get to the village where we live, the signal from all the major networks has all but disappeared.

It is not unusual to see and hear neighbours lurking at the end of their roads, angrily shouting loudly into their mobiles in a desperate attempt to allow the person at the other end to hear what they are saying. Needless to say, shouting does not work, but it does make life interesting for the neighbours!

As the mobile phone signal is so poor, it is easy to see that Internet data connection to send emails by using a mobile phone is almost impossible. I have tried so many times to achieve a blue flashing light on my modem in an attempt to hold a data transfer signal for more than a few seconds, with little success.

It all came to a head during the recent storms. Thunder, lightning, heavy rain and gale force winds soon knocked out our electricity supply and the telephone connection, complete with Internet broadband connection. Since leaving the UK, I have come to realise that a good Internet connection is one of the essentials of life and vital for maintaining links with family and friends in other parts of the world via Skype, email and for the multiplicity of online tasks that many of us take for granted nowadays.

There was no Internet and no electricity and I had an urgent email to send to meet a deadline for one of the publications that I write for. I thought that a journey to the nearest commercial centre would be a good idea; after all they offer free Wi-Fi access. A difficult journey across flooded roads proved to be of no use. No, their Internet connection was not working either. I tried several cafe bars in the town, as well as lurking outside a house of ill repute, which does have the virtue of an open Internet connection 24 hours a day - no doubt to meet the needs of their clients! I'm not fussy, by now I was desperate for a connection - whatever the source. Sadly, Donna's House of Sinful Pleasures was not connected either!

Finally, I had an idea! I remembered that I had once managed to achieve a respectable signal outside the local mortuary. I grabbed my laptop computer, the appropriate dongle (a clever thing that works a bit like a mobile phone to send and receive data signals) and headed off in the rain, wind and dark to the forbidding building outside my village - not a place to be on a wet, dark and stormy night. Once in the car park, I managed to climb onto a boulder and strap the dongle to a nearby post and link it with a long cable to the laptop computer in the car. After a few anxious moments, the modem burst into life, the blue light flashed and I was at last able to send my contribution to the magazine in time to meet the deadline.

I do hope that in time, the mobile phone companies will improve the strength of the signal to my village, but, meanwhile, I always have the mortuary to help me out in a crisis!

The Canary Islander

Food and Drink

The Vegetarian Expat

I have been a vegetarian for many years. I was a vegetarian when it was seen as cranky, receiving comments such as, "Are you sure you can live without meat?" to the time when vegetarianism became the thing for weight loss, or as a declaration by students, mainly to annoy their parents. It then became fashionable to be vegetarian; later, it was definitely for the health conscious, and now vegetarianism is seen as the way to conserve the world's scarce food resources. My personal reason for becoming vegetarian so many years ago was very simple; I like animals and I do not wish to eat my friends.

Living in a remote part of Lincolnshire, with few children of my own age to play with, no doubt encouraged me to develop a friendship with animals in such a way that I could not bear to eat their flesh. I shall always be grateful to my parents for having a very liberal view in allowing me to keep all kinds of animals, birds, reptiles and insects as pets. As long as I could demonstrate that I was responsible enough to care for them properly, my parents accepted most of the livestock that I brought home without putting up too much resistance. I have many happy memories of my father building hutches for rabbits and guinea pigs, as well as cages, runs and even a large aviary for a multitude of birds that came my way.

My mother was always on duty as chief nurse should one of my furry or feathered friends develop an illness of some kind, and very good at it she was too. However, even she declined to give my hamster the kiss of life, despite my insistence, when I discovered him lifeless in his cage one morning. However, I am pleased to report that with a spot of heart massage and a teaspoonful of brandy, my furry friend was soon up and about again, if a little groggy. Maybe this early encounter explains my love affair with a decent cognac after a good meal.

Moving to Spain was a shock in many ways, including the difficulties in explaining vegetarianism to many waiters. Gone were the days when the flippant comment, "I don't eat anything with a face or a mother," was a sufficient explanation as in the UK. Yes, I know all about the egg issue. The problem was that most Spanish and Canarians were, and some still are, convinced that tuna is a vegetable; it does not count as meat or fish. Despite my well practiced explanation of "sin carne, sin pescado" (no meat or fish) I can guarantee that most salads usually arrive with a generous dollop of tuna in the centre, and in some cases, the salad is liberally sprinkled with ham. I blame most of this on the "I'm a vegetarian, but I eat fish and chicken" brigade, who do no service to either themselves or the vegetarian cause.

This part of life when moving to the Costa Blanca was a culinary nightmare for the unsuspecting vegetarian, later eased by the few British supermarkets that had identified a lucrative market. It was now possible to easily obtain soya, tofu, nut roll and my old favourite, Linda McCartney sausages. We even managed to obtain vegetarian dog food via a tortuous route and, judging from the good health of our dogs over the years, this put paid to the 'special diet' syndrome that so many vets are forcing on to an unsuspecting public nowadays.

All this changed when we moved to the Canary Islands. Gone once again was the ease of availability of so many products that we had taken for granted in the Costa Blanca. British supermarkets came and went, and the reliability of a regular source of vegetable protein could not be taken for granted. Thankfully, we discovered a Canarian favourite, gofio, flour derived from maize, which is a traditional dish and served in many ways. In days gone by, farmers also used it to feed to their dogs and now we enjoy it too. If you look at the menu of many traditional Canarian restaurants, you will see it as a popular, creamy dessert. However, we bake it, fry it and grill it. We even have it sliced cold, rather like a nut roast and even barbecue it. Prepared carefully, and flavoured with the right herbs and spices, it is delicious!

Space is too short to include a recipe here, but you will find one on the Expat Survival section of my website.

Fit to drink?

A recent announcement by Thames Water in London announcing that polluted water from the River Thames is to be cleaned sufficiently to provide drinking water for the population of London surprised me. Not only is this initiative the UK's first major attempt to desalinate water, but it is also claimed to be new technology, which it isn't.

The Thames Gateway water treatment works in Beckton, East London cost around £270m to build and was brought into service in 2010. However, the company has only recently got around to testing it fully in recent weeks and during the recent 'hot spell' in the UK.

The 875 million litres proudly produced by the plant so far is said to be really clean and, reassuringly, is treated with salts and other chemicals to make it taste roughly the same as that lovely Thames tap water.

It is claimed that the technology is mostly used in the Middle East, and only after Thames Water successfully made the case that new sources of water are needed, with climate change bringing hotter, drier summers, as well as an increasing population moving into the capital.

London has less annual rainfall than cities such as Sydney and Athens, and is classified as "seriously water-stressed" by the UK's Environment Agency. However, some have claimed that water desalination is wasteful of energy and unsustainable and it would be much better to pipe water to the capital from Scotland and Wales. It also appears that if all the leaks in the Thames Water supply system were plugged, around 26 per cent of water would be saved. It seems that reducing leakage by just 1% would provide enough water for almost 250,000 people; an interesting statistic.

Meanwhile, many of my friends and relatives in the UK are complaining of hosepipe bans and restrictions to watering the garden and washing the car. Despite criticism of water desalination in the UK, there are now 15,180 major desalination plants in 150 countries, supplying about 300 million people with water each day. Many of these plants are in the Middle East, as well as the USA and Spain and, of course, the Canary Islands. After all, we are surrounded by the stuff, and plenty of wind, so it is sensible to make good use of it.

In the years that I have lived in the Canary Islands, I have never known a water shortage or a ban on using hosepipes. Yes, we have desalination plants not, incidentally, cleansing water from a grubby River Thames, but from seawater. As for wasting energy, the desalination plant near to my home in Pozo Izquierdo uses the excess electricity generated from the wind turbines to provide power for the adjacent desalination plant. How about wind and seawater? I seem to remember that there is plenty of both somewhere near the Thames.

Just a Trifle

Who likes trifle? It is strange how the Christmas and New Year period reminds us of earlier times. I guess that as we get older, incidents and memories that seemed so unimportant and irrelevant to us years ago, gain in both colour and importance as time passes. For me, one of these delightful memories is my Mum's Christmas trifle.

I have rarely thought about trifle since moving to Spain and the Canary Islands but, this Christmas, I had a craving for the one that my Mum used to make. Although my Mum died many years ago, it is true that memories of people we loved live on in so many different ways. Mum's trifle will be one those special memories, and not unique to me, that so many of us of a certain age will remember. I am not talking about one of those instant factory-made chemical concoctions that we often find lingering in chiller cabinets in the large UK supermarkets nowadays, but a real trifle painstaking made from layers of tinned fruit, sponge cakes (remember those?), red jelly and Bird's custard (yes, it had to be Bird's!). Depending upon the celebration and time of year, it would be topped with sprinklings of tiny 'hundreds and thousands' and tiny silver balls for Christmas, little sugar eggs for Easter and so on. The content was always the same and gloriously predictable, as would my Dad's comments be about the sherry. Yes, the secret ingredient was always Mum's very generous dose of sweet sherry!

As a 'non-drinker' and someone who had 'signed the pledge' as a child, Mum used to keep a few bottles of essential booze in the cupboard for "medicinal purposes only". It was strange that I never remember being offered any when I was ill, but I do remember that most of the bottles had to be replaced from time to time, which I thought very odd. Mum's special addition to the Christmas trifle would always be criticised by my father as "heavy handed", although it was clear that he, my brothers and I used to thoroughly enjoy it. I have not tasted one like it for many years.

My longing for trifle was resolved this Christmas. I happened to mention my loss to the elderly mother of a friend, Gloria, who was visiting our island for a pre-Christmas break. Her eyes lit up when I mentioned Mum's special trifle. It was clear that Gloria knew exactly what I was talking about. "I'll make you one," Gloria announced. True to her word, we visited our friend and Gloria again just before they were leaving for the UK. A dish of freshly made trifle duly appeared with Gloria watching my every expression as I ate the first spoonful. It was delicious! More importantly, it really was my Mum's trifle, made with the same ingredients and expertise that Mum had used all those years ago. Somehow, all the Christmases past seemed to merge together and in an instant I was transported back to many years earlier. Thank you, Gloria, and thanks Mum!

A Mince Pie for Christmas

It is strange how expats suddenly develop a craving for something that reminds them of life in their countries of origin. I guess it is not that surprising really, as Christmas is the time of year when our memories, particularly as we get older, recall times gone by, both happy and sad. Many of those special times have occurred, of course, over the Christmas and New Year period; many of us will have fond memories of families and friends, of precious times spent together, unique family traditions, gifts and special food that appeared at this time of the year.

Since moving to Spain, I seem to have developed a craving for mince pies. When we lived in the UK, I would not give a mince pie the time of day; similarly Christmas puddings, which I always used to consider to be a total waste of space and time. Why one would consume a hearty Christmas dinner, only to be followed by a plateful of thick brown stodge and custard was beyond me. I would only ever eat a spoonful of pudding to please my mother, who had made several during the summer months.

You see, mother's Christmas pudding making was a family tradition, a legend, and I can still see the huge copper boiler steaming away for what seemed like hours, as she prepared puddings for Christmas Day, Boxing Day and for each of my brother's and my own birthdays.

This activity took place each summer; she did not freeze them and, I am told, they became even more delicious as the months went by. I have since learned that this was due to my mother's generosity in a liberal application from the newly opened bottle of brandy that was part of the creation of this annual treat. I guess it was a basic form of embalming!

Last year, a neighbour appeared at our gate a week before Christmas, begging for help in obtaining a supply of mince pies for her Christmas party. We made a few suggestions and she went away determined to track down a few boxes. Unlike in previous years, we had also found great difficulty in locating mince pies, and we crossed our fingers that our suggestions would be helpful and that it would help the party to go with a swing. A few days later, our neighbour spotted us, waved and beamed. Yes, she had tracked down two boxes of mince pies - the last on the island, it seemed.

This year we went to our nearest branch of Marks and Spencer. Although a franchise of the UK store, stocking only a limited range of foodstuffs, we were very hopeful of finding some as we had allowed plenty of time before Christmas. The friendly sales assistant shook her head sadly, "No, we have none left," she said. She noticed our disappointment and added, "I can get you some if you like."

She picked up the phone with a flourish and called the main branch in Las Palmas and handed the phone to us. I spoke to a very helpful lady in Las Palmas, who confirmed that she had two boxes left and would send them down to our local store the following day. How's that for service?

We now have our mince pies, and very nice they are too! I can already hear some of you thinking, "Why don't you make your own?" Fair point, but have you tried getting a supply of mincemeat over here? Believe me, trying to explain such an item, in Spanish to bemused sales staff, really is not worth the trouble, but I will leave that story for another time!

Baking Bread

Expats in many countries, and particularly those in Spain, Portugal and France, will quickly discover many wonderful bakeries. Forget the plastic bread on sale in the supermarkets, but that wonderful bread baked in relatively small quantities by people who recognise that it is the taste of real bread that buyers are looking for. I like a simple, freshly baked loaf of bread, preferably white and with a dark and crispy crust. However, I still cannot quite find the taste and texture of the loaf that I was used to in the UK, despite having a wonderful bakery in the village where all types of loaves are baked.

I am pleased that I had the foresight to pack the bread maker when we left the UK. I had tried several models over the years, and all failed after a few months; it was friends who recommended a model made by Panasonic. Twelve years later, the breadmaker is still producing two or three loaves a week, with additional loaves made for friends and neighbours. The smell of freshly baked bread really is one of the most appetising of aromas, and is to be highly recommended if you are entertaining, or trying to sell your property!

Two months ago, our trusty bread-maker developed a strange grating noise. Twelve years of faithful baking was a reasonable lifespan in an age when planned obsolescence seems to be the current norm, and so I ordered a replacement machine from Amazon. A week later, a huge box arrived with the replacement machine. In many ways, the new machine looked very similar to the old one and baked a perfect loaf of bread the first time that I used it.

Before disposing of the old machine, I gave it a good shake. I heard something click inside, and I felt the need to give it just one more try. I added all the ingredients and the four-hour process began. It now appeared to be working perfectly, with no grating noise. It too made a perfect loaf of bread, so clearly a good shake was the answer!

We now have two bread-makers in our house. Some may think it strange or maybe obsessive, but I have found it to be a real advantage as I can now bake two loaves of bread at the same time. I can open only one packet of yeast and flour without any waste, and the job is done and forgotten for another week. Another advantage is that I am in control of the ingredients. There are no added preservatives and salt and sugar are kept to a minimum, unlike loaves purchased in the supermarkets. Also, bread is very cheap to make at home, which is another advantage during these difficult financial times.

Yeast has been difficult to find in Spain and the Canary Islands. Bread-making machines are not that popular over here, and most home bakers use fresh yeast from their local bakery. This is not advised for use in bread-making machines and dried yeast is hard to find. I usually rely on thoughtful friends bringing a supply of yeast from Tesco or Sainsburys in the UK, although in an emergency I can get an expensive supply from the El Corte Ingles department store. During my first hesitant attempts at bread making in the Canary Islands, I used 'levadura en polvo', which I thought was dried yeast. The dreadful result sent me heading for the dictionary, where I discovered that 'levadura en polvo' is actually baking powder. What I really needed was 'levadura de panadero', which is bakers yeast.

If you are also tempted to bake your own bread, have a look at the 'Expat Survival' section of my website, where I have included further details. Bella (our dog) and I are just off for morning coffee, toast and Marmite!

Fancy a Cup of Coffee?

One of the many things that I enjoy about living in the Canary Islands is a decent cup of coffee. Gone are the days when "a cup of instant" seemed to be the norm, and I still shudder when I return to the UK for a brief visit. A visit to one of the relatively new, and supposedly trendy, overpriced coffee shops is, for me, an ordeal best avoided. A quick visit out of sheer desperation during a frantic shopping expedition led me into one of the many branches of 'Costa Lottee' that are opening up in all of the UK's High Streets - after all, it did offer "Free Wi-Fi Connection."

My request for a cup of black coffee, no I don't like mugs, was met with a disinterested look as the spotty youth pointed to a huge variety of coffees on the board above his sentry post.

"Take yer pick," he slurped, as he continued chewing his gum and picking his finger nail.

"That one will do," I replied, "but I only want a small cup and not a mugful."

"We only do them mugs," he replied stabbing at the nearest soup bowl with a fingernail partly hanging from his index finger.

"But I only want a small cup....," I protested.

Realising that discussion with the spotty youth was pointless, I handed over my £3.50 and perched myself on a most uncomfortable stool at the side of an equally unfortunate table with three legs - goodness, they still do Formica! Maybe I should count myself fortunate that the loose fingernail was not floating in my coffee... The coffee was one of the most revolting drinks that I have ever tasted. Two sips and I was gone.

I contrast this with a cafe bar in my nearest town, Vecindario, on the island. It is a real town with real people, and well away from the expensive bars in the south of the island. Here I can get a cup of excellent coffee for 90 cents, sit in comfort and people-watch for as long as I wish. I watch Canarians, Spanish, Chinese, Russians, Germans, Scandinavians, Africans and Indians pass by, together with a variety of skin colour, clothing and headgear.

It makes me realise once again that I am living in a community where race, colour, faith and language rarely matter. It is a community where most people just get on with each other and I know how fortunate I am.

Back to my cup of coffee. Did you know that coffee is grown in Gran Canaria, as it has been since 1788 when King Carlos III issued a decree ordering the introduction of the first coffee plants to the Island?

Today, coffee is produced in very small amounts by local farmers who have kept the tradition of growing and consuming the coffee that they produce for many generations. The coffee is called Finca la Corcovada and is grown in the Valley of Agaete. This valley has a microclimate and a rich soil, perfect for growing coffee, and is grown by Juan Godoy, the only coffee grower in Europe and who is now supplying the UK market.

My memory returns to Costa Lottee in the UK, and the spotty youth who is, no doubt, still filling his soup-bowl mugs with foul-tasting overpriced coffee. I wonder if he will be serving coffee from Gran Canaria?

Marmite and Mosquitoes

Regular readers of my 'Twitters' will recognise that I am a great fan of Marmite. Yes, I readily accept that Marmite is rather like Blackpool or Benidorm - you either love it or hate it; in my case, I like all three. This 'Twitter' concerns my recent discovery about the thwarting of these miserable little beasts, mosquitoes, with a healthy dose of Marmite. No, I am not suggesting that you cover your bodies with a layer of the black stuff; although I am sure it would be highly effective, it may be going a little too far and you would not be too popular at parties.

When we first moved to Spain we lived very close to the salt lakes in the Costa Blanca. We quickly discovered that, at certain times of the year, attacks from mosquitoes were part of life and, as a result, mosquito blinds and nets were quickly installed in our home. I recall spending a miserable few months with my arms and legs covered with itching, red spots that took weeks to disappear. I spent hot summer evenings on our sun terrace, relaxing and enjoying a few drinks with neighbours - wrapped from head to toes in clothing designed to cover all parts of my body; I even wore long socks pulled over my long trousers. This was not quite how I had imagined life in sunny Spain. Despite these precautions I was badly bitten; the little 'perishers' clearly adored the taste of me.

Others were much more fortunate. My partner and many friends were rarely attacked, whilst others were, and it seemed that it was individual odour that mosquitoes were attracted to. Indeed, it seems that mosquitoes avoid around ten per cent of the human population, because they simply do not like their smell, and so I regard it as a compliment. We invested heavily in sprays and creams, whilst the usual bar chat claimed that it was alcohol in the blood that mosquitoes sensed and liked, and that they preferred some drinks to others! Well, I was certainly not going to change my favourite tipple just for them.

Moving to the Canary Islands, I was initially troubled by a few bites, although nowhere near as bad as in the Costa Blanca. However, after a few months right up to the present time, I am rarely bitten at all. This puzzled me until after listening to a recent radio programme and reading some of the latest research on the subject from a team who are designing new products to combat mosquitoes' voracious appetites. This revealed that one of the things that mosquitoes dislike is the smell, and presumably the taste, of vitamin B12. It was at this point that all became clear.

In the UK I would eat Marmite regularly. However, moving to the Costa Blanca meant that there were no ready supplies available. There were more important things to do, such as getting a water and electricity supply, and so my passion for Marmite lapsed temporarily. However, after moving to the Canary Islands, we discovered a ready supply in our local supermarket and I started eating toast and Marmite again each day for my elevenses. Our dog, Bella, enjoys it too and always demands one 'soldier' and sulks if I forget. So what was the link? Well, it seems that as Marmite is rich in vitamin B12, this is acting as a mosquito repellent.

It seems that although there are many Marmite lovers and haters around the world, our mosquito friends really do detest the stuff! Readers may have their own strategies for dealing with the problem of mosquitoes. If so, do please let me know and I will publish a selection on the Expat Survival pages of my website to share with other readers.

Political

Voting in Spain and the Canary Islands

I am no expert on constitutional affairs, but I have watched the shenanigans in the UK with increasing incredulity. I think I have missed a chapter somewhere, but I cannot see why AV (alternative vote) was recommended to voters, when it seems to be widely recognised as a flawed system, now clearly seen by voters as worse than the current 'first past the post' system. This brings me to the forthcoming local elections in Spain and the Canary Islands. Sadly, there is no Nick Clegg to wind up here, just a basic system of proportional representation, which seems to work rather well.

I have made up my mind to vote either for the male candidate who has the least facial hair, or for the woman who looks least like a poorly prepared drag queen. Another factor for me to consider is that I shall immediately disqualify any candidate who hires one of those noisy loudspeaker vans that drives past our house so fast with their distorted loudspeaker systems that I cannot understand a word that they are saying. Bella hates it and barks and cries loudly, whilst Mackitten meows pure vengeance. Those speaker vans disturb the usual tranquillity of our neighbourhood and have a lot to answer for. I am sometimes asked about the voting system in Spain, so I thought it would be useful to offer a 'Twitter' about it.

Voting here is by proportional representation, with each party publishing a list of candidates equal to the number of councillor seats available in the municipality. Councillors are elected in proportion to the total votes that they have won. If, for instance, a municipality has 17 councillors to be elected, a party that wins 65% of the total votes will have 9 councillors and be able to govern without forming a coalition because they have won a majority.

If no party wins a majority, minority parties can form a coalition government grouping that may even exclude the 'winning party'. It is therefore important under PR that everyone who believes in the policies of a particular party votes. One danger of PR is that the party that receives the highest number of votes can actually be completely excluded from government if a coalition of minority parties can be formed.

So how do we vote? On Election Day, you need to take your identification with a photo (a passport usually puts paid to any arguments about ID cards and driving licences!) and the voting paper for the party that you wish to vote for in the envelope to the polling station. Remember too that you are voting for a party and not a person, unlike in the UK.

Most political parties will already have sent voters their own voting papers and an envelope before polling day. You need to ensure that you have placed the correct voting paper in the envelope and take it to the polling station. Don't be tempted to write on the voting paper, even an 'X' will be disqualified, as will any rude comments about the candidates!

Even if you don't have a voting paper before polling day, you can still go to the polling station, go to the polling booth, and select one paper for the party that you fancy, place it in the envelope and seal it. You then go to the desk, show your passport and hand the envelope to the clerk at the desk who will put it in the box. That's it; democracy has been seen to be done! Now, no more talk of AV, Coalitions or Nick Clegg until next time!

Flamenco - the latest weapon!

Recently we have heard about protests in the UK, whether these are students campaigning against the increase in university tuition fees or anti-capitalist groups and other protestors taking direct action against what they see as injustice. Others are holding 'sit-ins' in the stores of a mobile telephone company or those owned by a government advisor, whose wife happens to live outside the UK, allegedly for the purpose of avoiding taxation. It seems that the days are gone when planned protest marches were the province of well-organised trade unions fighting for what they see as just causes for their members. Nowadays we see students and others taking direct action by attacking the headquarters of political parties, banks and government buildings. Protests organised through social networking groups have led to spontaneous protests in well-known UK shops and stores by protestors who see them as legitimate targets for not always peaceful protests.

As with many things, the Spanish do this in another way, and maybe this illustrates just one side of the Spanish psyche that I find fascinating, charming, and often amusing, in my adopted country. A new craze by Spain's anti-bank protestors is sweeping the nation. As an alternative to the angry UK's direct-action protestors that are engaged in street violence or fire bombing offices, angry citizens in Spain are calling into banks and dancing a live flamenco show, complete with anti-bank lyrics before disappearing as quickly as they arrived.

These groups of people are spontaneously called together for an anti-bank protest by an anonymous umbrella group called Flo6x8 Flashmob. The group gives the participants the lyrics and rhythms of the songs to sing and then let the protestors visit local bank branches to carry out their protests in their own individual styles.

The groups usually scatter euro cent coins on the floor in protest at the bank's 'penny pinching' approach to the recession. The umbrella group's only stipulation is that the flamenco must be 'good flamenco'. There will usually be a central dancer backed up by a rhythm group to provide the harmonisation, and by all accounts their performances are not only entertaining, but appear to make their point very effectively.

Currently, banks and police are unsure about how best to deal with these protests, but these groups seem to be getting their message across. Maybe the angry students demonstrating against increased university fees, and the anti-taxation dodger groups who are currently targeting popular stores may wish to consider this entertaining and very Spanish form of protest on future occasions?

Getting into hot water

Listening to the UK Prime Minister and the Energy Minister's attempts to help consumers with their fuel bills this year brought a mixture of indignation, amusement and cynicism from many UK consumers.

Some would say that the issue cannot truly be resolved simply by endlessly switching energy companies and tariffs, together with the odd roll of loft insulation. Many have commented that these regurgitated suggestions are akin to a sticking plaster being offered to a dying patient.

Energy experts tell us that the root cause has more to do with the rising cost of oil, greater demand for energy from China and India, diminishing oil supplies, the financial crisis, as well as the excessive profiteering made by greedy energy companies operating within a distorted market.

The problem of rising fuel bills will take much more than a one day meeting chaired by the Prime Minister, slick press conferences and bright orange publicity posters to drag this particular patient from his death throes.

So, how about green energy and renewables? Dare I even mention wind turbines for fear of middle England starting yet another petition against them and complaining in the Daily Mail?

Politicians of all shades appear to subscribe to the cause, task forces are set up to produce endless policy documents about the subject, whilst others are happily considering drilling for shale oil, together with the associated risks of poisoning water supplies, as well as having another go at blowing up Blackpool in the process. Yes, that minor earthquake a few months ago was not "natural" and was apparently due to initial drilling for shale oil in the area.

Some thirty years ago I had friends in Dorset who had the good sense to install four solar panels to the roof of their bungalow. In those days it was considered unusual, if not a little eccentric. However, our friends used the hot water provided by the sun for most of the year, topped up occasionally by an immersion heater when there was a sudden demand for consecutive hot baths when visitors came to stay. If it works in Dorset for most of the year, why not in the Canary Islands?

The Canary Islands are at the forefront of solar technology and Spain itself is a pioneer in solar power development. Our climate is ideal as the Canary Islands are one of the most highly exposed sun regions of the world. There are currently solar projects subsidised by the Canary Islands' Government and fully backed by the Government of Spain. However, I see very few solar installations on either domestic or business premises in the Canary Islands, and I don't understand why this is.

Several years ago we were interested in buying a new property that came with the option of fitted solar panels as an extra. I discussed this with the builder who, although anxious to complete the sale, was less enthusiastic about fitting solar panels. According to the builder, solar panels caused considerable problems after installation because of the high use of desalinated water on the island; he claimed that it led to corrosion. Now, I am not an expert on solar technology, but I know enough to recognise that there are different types of panels designed for different purposes and conditions, and it is merely a question of selecting the right one for the job.

Until the last few years, electricity bills were not a great concern in the Canary Islands, and energy prices in Spain were lower than in many other countries. A cooler night in February usually results in lighting a few candles for a little additional warmth, and we would think we had a harsh winter if we switched on our electric radiator for more than a few evenings. However, air conditioning is another matter, and high consumption soon results in a large bill.

Energy prices have since rocketed for all of us in recent years, and we need to take energy issues much more seriously by fully utilising our natural 'green' resources, such as the wind, waves and sun. Maybe our politicians should focus less on 'sticking plaster policies' and expensive "Switch" publicity campaigns, and much more on actually solving a developing problem.

The European Family

I admit to being a proud European. Although English born and bred, and I still love the United Kingdom, including Scotland if it remains within the Union, I do not regard myself as English or British, but European. I know it is not a particularly popular concept at the present time, but I am proud to be European.

Just mention the EU to most Brits and you will probably be greeted by a shrug or a scowl; it is often regarded as a necessary evil, at worst, and as the price to be paid for being part of one of the World's largest trading blocks, at best. Major infrastructure projects, which have received considerable funding from the EU, usually prefer to ignore that minor fact.

I contrast this to Spain and the Canary Islands where projects, both large and small, proudly announce that they are funded by the EU, and usually fly three flags, the Spanish flag, the Canary Islands flag, as well as the European Union flag.

Speaking to a British expat the other day made me realise the depth of the problem. He has lived and worked in the Canary Islands and Spain for about thirty years, but resents the fact that Polish workers, as well as other East European citizens, are now living and working in his home town in the UK.

He quite readily accepted the fact that being in the European Union as a British expat means that he can live and work in Spain, or any country within the EU, without the need for a visa or work permit, but resented that benefit being given to workers from other European countries. He could not accept the logic and we agreed to disagree about the issue.

I am also a firm believer in the euro, again a concept that is currently out of favour, even though several new members of the EU still aspire to join the euro one day. Memories are short and hindsight is a wonderful thing, but it is not that long ago when UK politicians were endorsing the project with great enthusiasm. The "I told you so" brigade are currently having a wonderful time, reminding the populace they always thought it was a bad idea. Yes, we know the euro monetary system has its flaws, and Greece is currently paying the price of a process that did not apply or stick to the rules that were established at its formation, but the idea of a currency that can be used anywhere in Europe is still, to my mind, a wonderful concept.

Now back to my euro-sceptic friend. He firmly believes that having one currency has taken the personality and excitement from travelling to other countries. He much prefers a Europe whereby he has to carry at least six different currencies for a two-week holiday. No, he doesn't mind being ripped off with high exchange rate charges, nor does he mind losing the value of the remaining currency when he returns home. After all, that suitcase of unspent pesetas, lira and drachmas would be of great interest to the grandchildren in the future, wouldn't they?

For me, this is only part of the story. The fact that I can choose to live and work in any country within the European Union, without a visa or work permit gives me a great sense of freedom, as well as belonging. Admittedly, the recession has recently led to some adjustments being made to the 'free movement' principle in some European countries, but the basic principle remains. I can benefit from healthcare, employment, trading and human rights laws that are common to all members of the EU. It comes with a form of protection; a reassurance of knowing that there is a common denominator that applies to all regardless of whether I am in a Scandinavian city or basking on a beach in the Canary Islands.

Of course, I am not naive enough to turn a blind eye to what is also an imperfect system, but it is the best we have. I have only to talk to friends and colleagues from the US and other parts of the world, to realise that we are part of something very special, which is the envy of much of the world. So, to my euro-sceptic friend, I say, of course, there needs to be continual improvement and change within the EU, because it is an evolving project that must adapt to the needs of its people. However, the post war dream of our forefathers, of a Europe, working together in friendship and cooperation for the mutual benefit of all, is an ideal that is still worth striving for.

Fluffy Tales

A Kitten in the Canaries

Regular readers of 'Twitters' may recall that an emaciated, flea ridden and sickly kitten burst into my life last year, and a number of readers have been asking about what happened to him.

Although I like all animals, maybe with the exception of snakes, I had no intention of allowing a cat to take up residence in our home. I saw myself as, first and foremost, a dog lover; I understand them and always have had at least one dog by my side. I liked cats too, but had no understanding of them. Also, I was nervous of having one because, on our island, there appears to be a policy of poisoning the stray cat population - they are regarded as vermin to be destroyed. In my own village, for example, there used to be many cats and now there are hardly any. Witnessing a child grieving over her poisoned cat in its death throws is not easy to forget.

Bella, our crazy little dog, found the kitten on wasteland during one of our walks. We took the tiny ball of fluff out of the baking sun and home to die in peace. A little water and a teaspoonful from a hastily purchased tin of cat food seemed to satisfy the little intruder, and he quickly fell asleep in a cardboard box that we found for him. I remember holding the tiny scrap of life in the palm of my hand, and wishing him to live, but doubting that would happen.

The next morning I was up early, dreading opening the box and what I would find inside. Surprisingly, two large eyes stared at me and the kitten began to lick my fingers. I gave him a little more food, which he ate hungrily and licked the water droplets from my fingers.

Each day, Mackitten, as we named the tiny, furry intruder, after my love of all things Apple Mac, gradually grew in confidence and health. On one memorable day he began to purr and it was the sweetest sound. He nestled into my hand, whilst I tickled his head gently with my finger. I began to feel some hope.

A few days later we took Mackitten to the vet for a check up, but that gave us great concern. We were told that it is the law in the Canary Islands that stray kittens such as Mackitten have to have a blood test to check for HIV infection. The vet did not say what would happen to him if the test was found to be positive. We feared the worst as we were told that HIV is common with stray cats in the Canary Islands. The week long wait for the test results were to be long and harrowing, and I tried to detach myself from my growing affection for the kitten.

It was good news! Mackitten was pronounced as healthy, but needed nourishment and a great deal of care if he was to survive and grow into a healthy cat. By then our concern was that Mackitten would not play. He showed no interest in fluffy toys, balls of wool and all the usual paraphernalia that we thought kittens adored. Phone calls to cat-loving friends began to raise concerns that Mackitten may be brain damaged; that he did not play, because he could not play. We refused to accept this possibility and began a process of teaching him to play. It took time, but we eventually succeeded.

Today, one year later, Mackitten has had his annual check up and injections and pronounced a "very fit and very healthy cat". We adore him, and even Bella seems happy to see him around, although she disapproves of him hiding and playing with her toys. He is now a much-valued member of our family and because he is a house cat, spends much of his time on my desk when I am writing. I suspect he likes the heat from the desk lamp. Annoyingly, he has a fetish for pens and pencils and is always stealing them. He is also very intelligent - far more intelligent than most of our dogs and he never ceases to amaze me with his skilful manipulation of life, as well as the people around him!

Mackitten has not only changed our lives, but also added so much to it. Little did I know on that fateful day in May last year, that a tiny worm- and flea-ridden ball of fluff could enrich our lives in so many ways.

Vets and Pets

Our little dog Bella, a lively, and slightly crazy mixture of something between a Papillion and fruit bat, recently developed a bad limp in one her back legs. We were not too concerned at first, particularly as we now also have a kitten, and Bella and Mac spend many hours playing together, and sometimes these games are a little over exuberant. The problem also tends to occur every six months or so, and I am convinced that somehow it is linked to her menstruation cycle. Usually, the bad leg returns to normal after a week or two of rest.

This time the problem continued and we took Bella to the vet for an anti-inflammatory injection or tablets, which usually does the trick. The helpful young vet gave her a thorough examination and it was clear after all the probing and prodding that Bella was not in any pain. The vet also suggested that he took a couple of X-rays to make sure that all was in order. The X-rays showed inflammation and the vet confirmed that there were no fractures and all was fine. We were to give Bella a pill over each of the next three days, and after paying a bill of 100 euros, we left.

Four days later we returned to the surgery as instructed for a check up. By then Bella was much better, she still had a slight limp, but was much improved. As soon as we entered the treatment room, the woman vet immediately declared that Bella would need an operation. We were puzzled as the X-rays had shown no signs of a problem and the first vet had confirmed this. "Oh, we get this problem with small dogs like her," she huffed, tapping on her computer keyboard, and ignored our comments about it happening twice each year. Bella was given a rather more thorough examination by a second vet and he nodded in agreement. We were then asked to see the traumatologist. When he arrived, Bella was given more prods and pokes and he confidently confirmed the diagnosis of the other two vets.

We stood in white-faced silence as the woman vet continued to tap enthusiastically on her keyboard, whilst making that sharp sucking in of breath sound that I do so detest - it always means trouble. We then entered the fantasy and frightening world of surgery - complete with anaesthetics, drugs, treatment and recovery times. "Did we also want specialist heart and blood tests before the operation?" the vet barked. We were told that this was essential in case Bella was not fit enough and would die during the operation. "That will be 800 euros, but you can pay over three months", she smiled, handing us the detailed printed estimate. "Oh, and by the way, she will also need the second leg doing as well, so shall we call it 1600 euros for the two?"

As a parting shot, we were then told that it was important for Bella to take a special, and expensive, pill lasting two weeks until the time of her operation. Each pill cost 13 euros - we bought one and drove home in silence. We both felt uneasy because what we had just heard just was not convincing and contradicted the findings of the first vet.

Two weeks later, Bella has just come back from her usual boisterous run on the field. Her leg is now fully recovered and, no, we did not give her that expensive pill nor will she be having the operations. It is now clear to us that the surgery saw us as pet-loving Brits ready to hand over 1600 euros, at the expense of Bella's well being.

Just as with human health, alternatives, therapies and drugs should always be considered before surgery. In Bella's case, the diagnosis for unnecessary surgery would have led to great expense, and treatment that would have caused her unnecessary pain and distress for several months.

Needless to say, I am concerned at this attempted exploitation of our love for Bella. We are now seeking a vet who can give sufficient professionalism, morality and decency to the care and welfare of our pets before attempting to exploit us and our furry friends.

Vets at home

Recently, there have been worrying reports in the medical journals commenting upon the revelation that visits to doctors' surgeries and hospitals increase the populations' blood pressure. No real surprises there I guess. After all, who really does enjoy a visit to the doctor?

It is the same with dogs and cats visiting the vet. All animals feel considerable stress when moved to unfamiliar surroundings, meeting unfamiliar people and smelling unfamiliar smells. Yet, we bundle Pedro and Maria into the car for their annual jabs and wonder why many dogs and cats freak out in the vet's surgery.

I was dreading Bella's and Mackitten's annual visit to the surgery this week. First of all we have disengaged ourselves completely from the previous surgery where, because we are 'Expats in Spain' and considered by some as ripe for exploitation, the vet and her cronies had decided that Bella needed an unnecessary operation designed to extract 1600 euros from our pockets. Fortunately, we discovered in time that this was a scam and Bella's pulled muscle healed naturally in a couple of weeks without operations or medication. However, it severely shook our confidence in a veterinary practice that we previously had confidence in, although it could have been cleaner and less chaotic.

A number of friends recommended their vets and we visited several. However, I was still uneasy about taking our cat and dog to one, unless it was an absolute emergency. Bella, for example, detests women vets in particular and, on the last occasion, it took four adults to pin our small dog down for a routine examination.

The distress that the event caused Bella and ourselves just cannot be right and we resolved at that time to go to a vet who had some basic understanding of animal psychology. Similarly, was it right to bundle our cat into a holdall, place him in a warm car for 30 minutes to wait in a crowded surgery with unfamiliar sounds and smells? There must be a better way.

It turned out that there was - in the shape of a mobile veterinary surgery. A mobile surgery arrived outside our door and the friendly and knowledgeable vet proudly gave us a tour of his mobile surgery. It was a converted ambulance, complete with an onboard operating theatre, equipment for blood tests, oxygen supply and all manner of equipment. It was at least as well equipped as our previous vet's surgery, as well as being much cleaner and better organised as a bonus!

The vet collected his bag, several instruments and the necessary drugs and administered them to Bella and Mac on our kitchen table. Both animals appeared to be happy and relaxed, even after insertion of the required microchip for Mac. Bella adored the new vet, and particularly after she had received several treats from his well-stocked bag. He spent time talking to both animals, as well as giving us advice about heartworm and other issues. Was it expensive? No, the price was less than the cost of a visit to our previous vet.

I am not saying that this is an answer in all situations, and in an emergency it may be quicker to travel to the nearest veterinary surgery. However, for non-essential treatment, a mobile veterinary surgery seems to be the much better option.

How to do it

Debit Cards for Expats

Many of us have fallen out with credit cards. Individually, as well as nationally and globally, we can now see that being encouraged to spend beyond our means has been a bad thing. One early catch phrase during the launch of the credit card revolution was that "Access (remember those?) takes the waiting out of wanting," which now seems rather hollow, as we now realise that our 'wanting' costs considerably more, if left unpaid on the credit card. Many people have also experienced considerable worry and illness due to increasing personal debt, particularly at a time of severe recession and job losses.

Debit cards are a useful alternative. A direct charge against our bank account helps to remove immediate temptation, and encourages us to spend within our means. However, personally, I am reluctant to use these cards online or with traders that I do not know, because of potential fraud. Now that I live overseas, I rely a great deal on purchases on the Internet; indeed eBay has been a real lifeline for items that I cannot purchase at a fair price on the island. I prefer to keep my bank debit card for cash withdrawals, and not run the risk of my card being used by some overseas scam operation to clear out my bank account. So without credit or debit cards, what are the alternatives?

Well, you could ask your bank to set up a second current account with a debit card, just for Internet transactions. However, this usually means additional charges for running the account, as well as charges for the issue of the card, which can be very expensive in Spain. Some Spanish banks issue prepaid cards specifically for use on the Internet; although useful, I have found that they are expensive and one that I tried involved a visit to the bank to top up, as this feature was not available online. Such an arrangement is not ideal if you suddenly find a good value flight online, and need to complete the transaction quickly.

I now use prepaid debit cards issued in the UK. One that I use is issued free of charge, and the other card costs around ten pounds for three years. I can transfer money instantly from my main UK bank account into the prepaid card. These funds are then converted into euros (or dollars if you prefer) and are instantly available for use. They can be used to withdraw cash from most cash dispensers worldwide, at a cost of 1.50 euros for each withdrawal (maximum 300 euros) or used for purchases in any establishment that accepts debit or credit cards in the usual way. There are no additional charges for operating the account, which is a bonus. The only downside appears to be that you have to have a UK address, but this can usually easily be overcome. (See my earlier Twitter, "What's your address?")

One of the companies that I use, FairFX, offers a particularly good rate of exchange - far better than at airports, of course, or even the Post Office. I can view the transactions online, top up from my mobile phone, as well as operating a second card for my partner. Best of all, it is a secure way to do business online, and it is reassuring that, should the worst happen, I would only lose the top up amount on my card, which I deliberately keep at a low limit and top up only when needed.

Prepaid debit cards are also a good idea if expats have children living in the UK, or maybe attending university. They can be given a card linked to the main account and then their card can be topped up as and when they need, or deserve, some additional cash! It is ideal for Christmas and birthday presents too!

There are now a multitude of such cards available, but, as an expat, only a few meet my criteria of being either free or cheap to run, offer a good exchange rate, online access and choice of currency. I have a card that I operate in euros only in Spain and the Canary Islands, one in dollars for purchases from, and when visiting, the US, as well as one in sterling for UK purchases and visits.

I hope this information helps. Further information about the cards mentioned is available on the Expat Survival section of my website. If you come across some better deals that are suitable for expats, do please let me know and I will share the information with other readers.

Complaining in Spain

One of the worst things that the newly arrived expat quickly faces is the sudden inability to complain if things go wrong. Spain may well be a member of the EU family, but when it comes to complaining, the expat would be wise to remember that it is a very different culture and pace of life. After all, isn't that why we left the UK in the first place? Forget shouting, being abusive and banging your fist on the table, because, at best, you will be completely ignored or possibly sent to the end of the queue to sulk, or, at worst, you may see the inside of a prison cell for a few hours.

One of my first experiences of trying to make a complaint in Spain was about our new home in the Costa Blanca. We had no water and the electricity was on builder's supply, which meant that it was very erratic. Most of our neighbours had similar problems, and after endless weeks of waiting, breakdown of electrical appliances, unfulfilled promises and several freezer loads of food destroyed, we had enough.

At that time I had very little Spanish to help me, other than the ability to order a bottle of wine and basic food items. Staff in the builder's office could speak English; after all we had bought a property from them in English a few weeks earlier. However, when it came to after sales it was strictly Spanish speaking only. Out of desperation one morning we went to the sales office to complain, and it was a true eye opener.

We joined the queue of angry people. Two harassed young women were trying to do their best to calm angry clients. It was a painfully slow process and involved many telephone calls, long, tedious explanations and much sharp sucking in of breath - a mannerism which I detest at the best of times, because it usually means that there is no likelihood of anything being done - ever.

After about half an hour in the queue we noticed one unshaven man in a grubby vest and an unpleasant disposition, who had arrived in the office before ourselves; he was clearly very angry and could hardly contain himself. When he reached the counter, the young woman smiled and asked what she could do to help. His response was to bang on the table and shout considerable abuse at the poor woman. Although we were angry too, I found myself feeling very sorry for her having to deal with this thug of a man. He snarled and growled about his problems, which I gather was something to do with a faulty water heater. The young woman watched and said nothing as she pressed the buzzer beneath the desk. After what seemed like several minutes of abuse, two police officers burst into the office, pistols bristling at their side and duly handcuffed this protesting lump of foul-mouthed humanity. We all cheered as our countryman was bundled into the waiting police car outside. It was several days before we saw him again, greatly subdued. I believe that he became a much better person after his night in the cell.

In contrast, other neighbours took a very different approach. An attempt at speaking Spanish in a calm manner, together with the occasional box of chocolates worked wonders. I also recall these neighbours taking the office staff for a meal on one occasion! As a result, our wise neighbours were connected to the mains water and electricity supply very quickly, as well as having many of their other problems attended to promptly and courteously. We very quickly realised which was the most successful approach when complaining to the builders.

Customer service in Spain is good overall, but you have to be patient, polite, prepared to give up a full morning and persevere. The golden rule is to remain calm and cheerful, despite the surging feeling of anger inside. Remember too that whoever is trying to help you also have their own problems and issues to deal with, and they will get around to dealing with your problem eventually. Yes, basic good manners and an attempt at the language go a long way in Spain, as it does in most other countries.

Paternity leave

The UK's deputy Prime Minister, Nick Clegg, recently announced government proposals for revising the paternity leave arrangements for new dads. This proposal could see dads getting up to ten months paid leave after their babies are born, by allowing parents to divide the existing year's maternity leave between them. Unless you actually run a small business, I can see a lot of merit in these proposals, and it should help our youngsters to get off to a better start in their young lives, as well as helping to ease the stress of having a new baby in the home for both mum and dad.

Babies are the hope and future of any society and, as a teacher, there were few things more exciting for me than to help and watch very young children grow and develop in confidence, gain knowledge and understanding and an awareness of other people and their environment. After all, whether we have our own children or not, all children are the hopes and dreams of our futures.

Over the years, these values have been recognised and supported in most civilised societies, who have felt that a collective investment in children is an investment in society as a whole. Sadly, as we have seen with the increase in tuition fees in the UK and the erosion of the principles of 'free education for all', these values appear to be under threat or, depending upon the colour of your politics, are requiring "readjustment to meet changing fiscal needs."

'Baby Bonds' and grants that used to be given to newly born babies in both the UK and Spain have been withdrawn in both countries in recent months in response to the global recession. Although some may not need these grants, it was an indicator of the value and hope that we place upon all children, and symbolic of a collective hope and determination that all children should have a good start in life.

However, all is not lost. The Canarian government has announced economic assistance for parents expecting more than one child, which can financially break a family. Parents will be given up to €1,200 for each child per year until the children are 10 years old. The actual amount given will depend upon the number of children born and the family's earnings. Maybe both new schemes do not answer all the need, but at least it is better than nothing, and continues to recognise the value of children to society.

So what has all this to do with the new arrangements for paternity leave in the UK? Contrast these recent developments to the birth of babies in the Canary Islands just a few generations ago. After the birth, mum would be expected to resume work and normal household duties right away, whilst dad took to the matrimonial bed for a few days 'to recover from the birth' and to receive relatives, friends and neighbours who were no doubt anxious to meet the new baby.

This local custom was seen as an important step for dad to bond with the newly born baby, as well as a social occasion to welcome the new child into the world and was, no doubt, an excuse, for quite a few toasts, and whilst mum was scrubbing the floor, no doubt. Somehow I don't think modern dads would get away with this kind of behaviour nowadays, even if it is called 'paternity leave'!

What's your address?

As soon as the initial euphoria and exhaustion of a move to another country has evaporated, many expats quickly discover that they also need to have an address in the UK. Even if, at first sight, with a new home and address in a newly adopted country it no longer seems necessary, most expats quickly find that a UK address is almost essential.

Many UK expats will, for instance, continue to quote their old UK home address to banks, credit card companies, driving licence authority etc., even though it is not strictly legal. In my experience, financial institutions in particular, often became rather nervous when told of my impending escape to a country in the sun; for example, would they mind sending on policy renewal forms and replacement bank cards to my home in the Canary Islands? Sometimes, the response to such a request was met either with a curt reply that smacked ever so slightly of jealousy, or as if I had decided to move somewhere off the planet.

"Oh no, Sir, we have no procedures for sending post overseas. We will have to close your account", or "Please do not tell me that, it may cause problems with your licence, insurance policy...", have both been responses that I have received to such a relatively simple request. After all, we are still talking about Europe and not a move off Planet Earth aren't we?

When it comes to ordering items from the Internet or mail order catalogues, you will be met with much the same response. Notable exceptions are Amazon - both UK and USA, who are terrific, as well as QVC who will take a 'foreign address' in their stride. Similarly, with eBay orders; some traders will send overseas and others will not. I won a beautiful camera at a knock down price recently on an eBay auction, only to be informed by the seller that he did not ship overseas. The Orkneys were somehow most acceptable, but not the Canary Islands. Had he heard of registered post overseas, I mused?

If you are fortunate to own or rent a home in the UK, maybe a relative or helpful neighbour would be willing send on your post from time to time? Expats that I know often quote their son's or daughter's address, or that of a close friend or neighbour, but, over time, this well-meaning arrangement often ceases to be efficient, and important post can be left unattended for many weeks. Teething babies, flu and appalling weather, making a trip to the Post Office impossible, are some of the more likely excuses, although I did hear of one case recently where a newly arrived puppy chewed up, and was sick on, three months of bank and credit card statements for one unfortunate expat. Be warned, there are other ways!

Personally, I use a UK mailing service. I have tried several such companies over the years, and most have been very good, but the one that I currently use is excellent. It gives me a UK street address, sends me an email or text message whenever a letter or parcel arrives at their office. I then log on to their very clever online system, and tell them if the item should be sent on to my home in the Canary Islands, stored, opened and scanned (which saves postage costs) or shredded. This company will send mail to anywhere in the world and makes ordering items online very simple. I can see a photo of the envelope online and can easily determine if it is yet another promotional leaflet to be shredded, or something important that I should ask to be forwarded. This service is not particularly cheap, but it is reliable and blisteringly efficient and gives me peace of mind. With this service under your belt, expats can focus on what they do best - relaxing, and enjoying the sun!

I also use a similar service in the USA that allows me to order electronic goods at particularly good prices, which can then to be forwarded to my home. Again, this is not a cheap service, but some goods can be purchased at particularly advantageous prices and sent on, whilst still making a substantial saving.

For more information about these services, have a look at my website, under the section 'Expat Survival'. I hope these suggestions help.

Learning the Language

I am often asked what I see as the main priority when planning to move abroad. In my experience, planning to be an expat doesn't work quite like that; it is more often a spontaneous reaction to events, maybe a new job or a response to sudden ill health or maybe an unexpected windfall.

Learning the language and remaining open-minded to the culture that you find yourself in, is my usual answer. Even a basic knowledge of the fundamentals of the language will make life much easier in a newly adopted country. If nothing else, it is usually appreciated by the locals, who realise that you are making an effort and, in my experience, most will go out of their way to help you.

I well remember a small, but vociferous group of expats in Spain, endlessly demanding that Town Halls, police stations, doctors' surgeries, hospitals etc. should offer a free translation service for expats. They resented paying the 50 euros or so fee that private interpreters charged. I used to point out that if such services were offered in English, why not also in German, Russian, French, Norwegian and all the other languages represented in the country?

You could imagine the outcry from taxpayers in the UK if such a service was demanded by the multitude of nationalities now represented in the UK. In my view, the responsibility remains firmly with the expat to make an effort and, in doing so, enriching their own experiences and culture of their newly adopted country.

It is easier said than done, I hear several readers muttering. Yes, I agree, and as someone who has never found learning languages easy, I tend to dismiss the view that languages can be taught to anyone of any age. Maybe, with an effective teacher, one-to-one tuition and plenty of time for regular lessons, good progress can be made. However, the reality for most expats is that they are either working too hard to make time for lessons, or are not working and do not have enough spare cash to pay for them!

When I arrived in Spain, I knew very little Spanish. I enrolled for one of the free Spanish classes for expats offered by the Town Hall. The intention was good, but when I arrived for my first lesson I realised that the lesson would be with one teacher and forty students at all levels of ability for only 45 minutes a week. This was hardly the stuff for effective learning, and could do far more harm than good.

I tried one of the popular courses on CD. It was very well constructed, but very boring. I lacked motivation and quickly gave that up. Meanwhile, my partner, who had to learn Spanish quickly in order to get a job, enrolled on a four-week intensive Spanish course at a local language school. It was for two hours a day, five days a week for a month. This approach was on a one-to-one basis with a well-qualified and experienced teacher, and with plenty of homework. The lessons were very expensive, but it was highly effective.

I was fortunate to find a local teacher with whom I had twice-weekly lessons. This arrangement worked well until I moved to the Canary Islands. However, I was able to continue my lessons twice a week for one hour by using the Internet and Skype. The teacher was still in the Costa Blanca, but was flexible in his approach and this meant that I could arrange the lessons around my own busy schedule. These lessons worked very well for me, because they were mainly conversational, about real issues that interested, as well as motivated, me.

In addition, I accepted a language course that was offered free-of-charge by the Canarian Government. This course was a computer-based distance-learning course for English speaking expats, and monitored by a tutor who also gave feedback and assessments. I was very pleased to achieve the diploma offered after just a few months. The course also had the advantage of adding a firm vocabulary and grammatical structure to what I had already learned from other methods.

I have learned to take my language learning less seriously than in the early days. I used to worry that my mistakes could cause great offence to the listener; I have had a few of these experiences! However, I no longer worry if I make a mistake. I do the best that I can with what I know, wave my hands around a lot and speak clearly; I am also very good at mime. Usually, the recipient of my antics understands me and knows that I am making an effort. The only exceptions that I make are in cases relating to legal, financial or medical issues, which have potentially serious implications, and when I would also take along someone confident in the language.

I am told that the best way of learning a new language is take on a lover who speaks the language of your choice. However, that can cause some problems, but whichever method of learning you choose, just enjoy it!

"You need new track rod ends, Sir"

This seemingly endless refrain used to greet me whenever I collected my Mini from an MOT service station in the UK. No, my Mini was not one of those lovely BMW look-a-likes, but a genuine Mini - just as its creator Alec Issigonis had intended, and by all accounts complete with poor track rod ends, even though it was not a particularly old vehicle.

If it wasn't track rod ends, it would be new brake pads, suspension, bearings or sub frame. I am not talking only about my Mini, but a whole range of vehicles over the years that I was driving in the UK. A failed MOT meant that often owners were unable to drive their vehicle away from the garage, as the car was deemed unroadworthy; and was therefore held as captive for the garage to do whatever it wished to both the car and owner's wallet. It was a classic open cheque book scenario, and one where I and many others were left with the distinct feeling that we were being 'ripped off'.

In later years, I would have my annual service and pre MOT check just before the official test was due, but I rarely survived the MOT inspection unscathed. Like so many UK consumers, I would challenge the bill, eventually pay up and look for another garage to use in the future. Of course, there were some good garage experiences too, but on reflection I have to say that these were rare.

Moving to Spain and the Canary Islands was a breath of fresh air, in more ways than one. Over here we have a system of government inspections of vehicles. The tests are called ITV tests (Inspección Técnica de Vehículos), which take place at approved centres. These centres are not garages, but a network of testing stations approved by the state to focus solely on vehicle inspections. The centres can be easily located by going to the website of the Dirección General de Tráfico. An appointment may be made in person, by telephone or on line.

The owner of the car is present when the vehicle is tested and, indeed, takes part in the testing process, such as applying brakes and switching on headlights when required. This process can be a little disconcerting the first time a non Spanish speaker takes part, but the staff are usually helpful enough and it is easy to get by with a mixture of Spanish and English, together with quite a lot of arm waving. The vehicle's registration document (permiso de circulación), technical papers (ficha technico) and proof of valid motor insurance must be taken to the testing centre and shown when the vehicle is tested.

The test is thorough. The vehicle is placed over a pit, on rollers; it is prodded and shaken, seat belts are tested, lights are switched on and off, tyres are checked, exhaust emissions tested and recorded, and brakes and shock absorbers checked for efficiency. Cars are also checked for the condition of the bodywork and mirrors, windscreen and wipers. During my last ITV, the vehicle in the neighbouring test lane to mine was failed, because the passenger door would not open and this was rightly considered to be a safety violation.

When the tests are complete, a document is issued detailing any faults found (Infracciones Graves & Infracciones Leves). Any fault listed in the section Infracciones Graves (serious fault) must be repaired before an ITV can be issued.

If a vehicle fails the test, the owner is given a document listing the faults. The repairs must be completed within two months of the test. However, if the repaired vehicle is returned to the ITV centre within 15 days, the owner will normally receive a discount on the cost of the repeat test. Should the car not be retested during the two-month period, notification will be sent to the Jefatura Provincial de Tráfico, and the car may be deregistered.

The inspection process is usually completed in about 20 minutes when, if successful, a new sticker will be stuck to the windscreen to prove that the car has been inspected together with a reminder when the next test is due. The process is relatively cheap, efficient and effective.

New cars are first tested after four years and must be inspected and tested every two years thereafter until the age of 10. Any car over 10 years of age must be tested annually. More information about the ITV testing process, and requirements for cars, motorcycles and caravans are available on the Expat Survival section of my website.

No process is ever perfect and I am sure that some readers will have had negative experiences. However, my experiences have been pleasant ones; I know that my car has been checked thoroughly, as I have been part of the process, and do not feel that a 'get rich quick' garage is exploiting me.

Complaining

"I just wanna be OK, be OK, be OK..."

Our move to Spain and the Canary Islands has not been without some stress. However, few things have given me as many problems, anger and, very occasionally, amusement as my endless dealings with that big beast of a telephone company, Telefonica. Love 'em or hate 'em, I dare say that very few of us have escaped their clutches.

My first encounter with 'The Big Beast' came shortly after moving into a new housing development in the Costa Blanca. Obtaining a reliable electricity and water supply were both considerable challenges, but none more so than getting a telephone. I recall standing in endless queues with other equally frustrated expats of all nationalities, and sometimes the shop closing before anyone was available to attend to our needs.

I have witnessed grown men cry with anger and frustration at the sheer incompetence of trying to get a telephone line installed. I joined the waiting list for connections, only to be told one year later that my name had been removed from the list. This apparently was the procedure if a connection is not available within six months! Sadly, no one had thought to tell us of this ruling. We managed to get a connection just before we left the area.

As a reporter, I quickly became aware that I could supply an entire week's submissions based purely on horror stories about 'The Big Beast'. I remember visiting one terminally ill lady with a heart condition who was unable to leave her home. Her husband had tried in vain for months to get a telephone installed.

The mobile signal was poor in their area and it was essential that the couple had a form of communication for an emergency, as well as a modem link for a new form of electronic gadgetry linked directly to the hospital. When I visited the couple, I enquired if there were technical reasons as to why they could not be connected. The couple shook their heads and pointed to the telephone junction box just a few metres from their home.

Now living in the Canary Islands, I continue to face similar incompetence and unreliability. Rarely a month goes by without some kind of problem rearing its ugly head. I find that I become even more irritated by the endless rendition of that inane song, "I just wanna be OK, be OK, be OK..." when I am put on hold for twenty minutes or so. A few weeks ago after the alarm company reported that my landline was not working, I called 'The Big Beast'.

I was given a twenty-minute rendition of "I just wanna be OK, be OK, be OK..." before a very cross-sounding woman advised me that I had been disconnected, because I had not paid my bill two months earlier. As I have had a direct debit set up for a number of years, I was puzzled. The conversation with the señorita ended abruptly when she enquired if I would like their television service added to my account. Somehow I thought not.

Eventually, after several days of calls and complaints, and a reconnection charge of 25 euros, the line was eventually reconnected. Enquiries with my bank revealed that a direct debit was set up and there were sufficient funds available to pay it, yet the debit had not been presented. I was also told that the company had changed their trading name during the month in question, and there were many customers in the same position as myself. However, even after filing a formal complaint, my claim for a refund of the reconnection charge was denied.

Last month the line failed again. I was told that there was nothing that they could do for 48 hours, but would I like to consider having their new television service added to my account? Er, presumably I would need a working telephone line?

A few days later an engineer appeared and agreed that the line was not working. He disappeared, only to reappear a few minutes later, having driven to the telephone exchange, to announce that the line had been disconnected in error, as there was some confusion about whether we had an ADSL connection with Telefonica or not. Wisely, we did not! The line miraculously started working again.

Two weeks ago, the connection failed again. I called "I just wanna be OK, be OK, be OK..." and was told, "There are technical problems in your area. Can I interest you in...?" she began. Six days later the line started working again. There was no prior warning, no reason given, no apology and no refund of line charge.

As I write this, I am happy to report that we have finally broken free from 'The Big Beast'. My mobile phone contract with the same company has finally ended, we have ADSL with another company, and we have just transferred our line away from "The Big Beast". I'm not saying that my telecommunications life will be problem free, but at least I no longer have to listen to that inane rendition of "I just wanna be OK, be OK, be OK..." I really am OK now, thank you.

A Tortoise called 'Aduana'

Despite all the positive aspects of living in the Canary Islands there are, as in all things in life, a few negatives too. One of my main irritations is the Aduana (Customs) process. Even though the Canary Islands are part of Spain, and within the European Union, we are outside of both for the purposes of taxation. This state of affairs is of great benefit to residents and visitors alike, who can buy all the luxury goods they can afford whilst on holiday, and pay only 7% IGIC (local tax) instead of IVA or VAT in Spain of 21% and in the UK at 20%. However, there are downsides too.

If, for example, I wish to purchase an item from outside the Canary Islands, I invariably end up paying both the tax from the country of origin, as well as the local Canary Islands tax, plus a delivery surcharge of around 15 euros! Fortunately, those very good people at Amazon have now seen the error of their ways after I challenged them recently. I was surprised and delighted to receive a hefty refund for all the VAT that I had paid on items delivered to the Canary Islands over the last few years. Yes, if you contact them after delivery they will refund your VAT!

Now back to the Aduana. This organisation does seem to move at the pace of a tortoise on Prozac. They appear to be totally unaware that we have a global economy nowadays and that many of us also like to shop globally. After all, there are some things that cannot be purchased in the Canary Islands. Take, for example, Amazon's very clever new device - the Kindle eReader. I do confess to having some interest in the success of this product as I have several publications in this format. However, if you live in Spain and the Canary Islands, the only realistic option, until recently, was to purchase the Kindle from Amazon.com in the US.

On the face of it, this was not a problem. Ordering from Amazon.com is quick and simple, apart from having to deposit an additional sum for local tax to be paid to the Aduana upon arrival. The tracking information was fascinating; my Kindle left Kentucky in the US and arrived in Germany the following day. The package arrived in Madrid the next day and was in Las Palmas the day after that. I think that four days for a package to get from the US to the Canary Islands is rather good. However, my box of goodies sat in the office of the Aduana in Las Palmas awaiting release for around seven days, and without any attempt to contact me.

Some time ago, my publishers in the UK sent me a box containing copies of my latest book, 'Letters from the Atlantic'. One month later I was still waiting for the box to arrive when I received a telephone call. The publishers had just received the box of books back in their offices, undelivered. Undaunted, they tried again. Three weeks later, the same thing happened and the box was returned to them. No reason given, and was just returned. "We send all over the world, even Oman despite the recent troubles, and the books always get there. It is always the Canary Islands that are the problem," commented one irritated member of staff.

The whole episode was just a little embarrassing. I had been receiving messages from friends, family, readers and the media in the UK commenting and asking me about my new book, without having actually seen a copy myself. Out of desperation, I ordered a couple of books from Amazon - they were delivered five days later. Now, I am not suggesting that all this is the fault of the Aduana, but I do have my suspicions!

How big is your gnome?

I have to confess that I am not a great lover of gnomes. No, I don't mean the 'real' ones that appear in fairytales, but the depraved garden variety. Toadstools, seagulls, fairies and wishing wells I can accept quite happily, but the grinning garden gnome, wearing that totally impractical, ostentatious and irritating red hat really makes me see red (if you excuse the pun).

A garden is meant to be a thing of beauty, an extension and reflection of our own personalities; so why is it that some people fill their gardens with these malevolent, desperate looking creatures?

Many people think that garden gnomes are quite innocent, sitting quietly with their fishing rods dunked into a sea of concrete that will never catch any fish. Do they really think that they are sitting on a toadstool for their benefit? No, they are planning their next attempt to undermine the human race. Besides, most gnomes are far too plump and well fed for any self-respecting toadstool to survive under their weight.

I am not quite sure why I react in this way. Maybe it was some horrific tale that I read in childhood - after all, some fairy tales actually are not at all fit for children (the authors are not called the Brothers Grimm for nothing!). Maybe they remind me of a much-detested Sunday School teacher from my early years or, as I have long suspected, the uncanny likeness between them and the much disliked Great Uncle Gilbert.

I used to think that gnomes were a 'Brit thing' and I recall many quite attractive gardens in the UK ruined by rows of these miserable creations. I recall another uncle who had dozens of things, which he brought into the garage each winter and spent his spare time repainting them ready for the next season. As a child, I always had the desperate urge to pull the communication cord on a fast moving train. Similarly, I also had the desire to blow the heads off as many of these evil creatures that I could find in Uncle's garage. No, don't worry, I never did either, but I wish I had.

I thought I was safe in Spain, and maybe more so in the Canary Islands. Don't believe a word of it. Today, I walked past a neighbour's house - they are a nice old couple who spend a lot of time developing their small garden. It has moved on from being a stony desert left by the builders into a thing of beauty, a delight on the eye and full of colour for most of the year. Neither is there a prickly cactus in sight, which is remarkable - given where we live.

As I walked my dog Bella past the garden gate, we stopped as usual to peer inside at the latest development. Horror upon horrors! As I peered over the gate, the gaze of another being met my eye. The evil gaze that met me was from the largest and most malevolent looking creation that I have seen for some time. It was the tallest, plumpest gnome that I have ever seen! He grinned and, I thought, winked at me. Bella growled menacingly and I walked smartly on. Bella seemed relieved to get away too.

So there we have it. Our early nightmares come back to haunt us in later life, it seems, wherever we are. Mine lives just a few doors away and is a constant reminder of the nightmares of childhood.

We also have other neighbours, well known artists, who have a passion for drawing, painting and designing naked gnomes. The first time that I saw them I was rather taken aback, but at least they had hung up those silly red hats. As with humans, it is rather hard to look intimidating without wearing a shred of clothing. Apparently the pictures sell rather well in a specialist market and I was given a free sample, but that is a story for another time.

The Sunshine Expat

One thing that amuses, intrigues and sometimes irritates me as an expat in Spain has been a small, but vocal, group of expats who have been fortunate enough to escape to the sunshine, yet spend their time complaining about life back in the UK. The 'sunshine expats', as I call them, sit on their sun drenched terraces, gin and tonic in hand, philosophising on what they see as the failure of Britain to somehow justify their move, and good fortune, to another country.

The Government, Health Service, state of the roads, young people, the weather, Nick Clegg, Jeremy Clarkson, and the economy are all likely targets for ridicule. "Britain is dead," or "We had to get away because of the weather" or "There is no future for anyone in the UK" are all comments to be heard on many expat balconies and British bars, and particularly during those first heady months of an escape from Britain.

Is it really an escape? It is interesting to note that many of these expats, who are so keen to criticise the country of their birth, still wish to maintain their UK voting rights, driving licence, UK address, dentist or doctor (if they can get away with it), even though they no longer visit the UK and have no real experience or understanding of current issues.

On a sadder note, it is interesting to see how many of these 'sunshine expats' quickly desert their adopted country as soon as they hit trouble and return to the UK. Unemployment, relationship break-up, illness and bereavement are all deciding factors in a decision to "return home". It is understandable, of course; during times of great stress we need to be with our families, friends, in a country whose systems we can understand and have the fluency in language to deal with the things that frighten or worry us.

Recently, I have been reading some of the comments and questions on several expat blog sites, which are often best avoided if you wish to keep your blood pressure down. Many of the current questions and comments currently relate to money held in Spanish banks. Questions are usually along the lines of "Is it safe to keep my money in a Spanish bank?" "Should I transfer my money back to a UK bank?" or "Should I move my savings to an off shore account?"

An urban myth is creeping into expat bar chat that, should the worst happen and the euro collapses, investors in Jersey or the Isle of Man would somehow be at less risk than if they had left their savings in a Spanish bank account. As for transferring funds back to the UK, just remember Northern Rock! Such advice tends to overlook the fact that security guarantees for deposits in Spanish banks are similar to those offered by UK banks.

If all such government guarantees fail, then a few quid in Jersey is hardly likely to make any difference as we will all be heading for the lifeboats! Meanwhile, quite a few offshore banks and investment brokers are making a tidy profit by encouraging expat panic and the transfer of funds to offshore bank accounts, so be warned!

For me, and many others like me, being an expat is all about taking the rough with the smooth, and I am not about to bail out as soon as the going gets tough. Learning more about the culture, making an effort with the language, getting to know local people and customs is what being an expat is all about. It is one of life's real adventures and, taken in the right spirit, can be a life changing and wonderful experience, as many have already discovered. Yes, sunshine and cheap booze is a bonus, but it is not the only reason to move and, for many expats that I know, life in their newly adopted country is where it feels right to be, it is from personal choice and not just the result of an accident of birth.

Expat Life

Beware of Submarines and Drug-smuggling Grannies

I am not sure why, but a recent news item from Columbia set my mind racing about submarines. The story was all about Colombian soldiers seizing a fully submersible drug-smuggling submarine capable of reaching the coast of Mexico, and reminded me of how determined and devious drug smugglers can be. The story is even more astonishing because previous drug-carrying vessels found in Colombia were only semi-submersible, with part of the structure always remaining above the surface. However, the submarine recently discovered could operate completely underwater, and was estimated that it could hold eight tons of drugs.

Apparently, the submarine could submerge up to three metres deep and was equipped with a five-metre periscope and had the ability to travel to the coast of Mexico without surfacing, a journey taking eight to nine days. It was a heavy investment for the drug smugglers, as the submarine had taken six to eight months to build at a cost of about 1,500,000 euros. Colombia has seized at least 32 semi-submersible vessels designed to smuggle drugs over the years, including a dozen last year.

All this puts into context the number of pensioners who have been caught smuggling drugs from the Canary Islands in recent months. Apparently, drug smugglers prefer to recruit elderly and disabled people to carry out their drug running operations, because no one would suspect an elderly, innocent-looking granny of carrying drugs in her bra, or that smart looking elderly gentleman of carrying a supply in his colostomy bag! Maybe a submarine is the next logical step for the determined smuggler?

Talking of submarines, the recent Wikileaks revelations suggest that the US Government approached the Spanish Government via their embassy in Madrid with the suggestion that Las Palmas could be developed as a useful port for the American fleet, and with a view to an increased US presence in Africa. In addition, it seems that there were also suggestions that the current military cooperation agreement was adjusted to include Las Palmas on the list of ports authorised to host nuclear submarines. Understandably perhaps, the Spanish government has refused to comment on such revelations.

Can you imagine nuclear subs ducking and diving off our islands? Well, maybe they do already. Finally, if you do enjoy deep sea diving or scuba diving, just be very careful where you put your flippers!

The weather influences walking

Sometimes, if I am in the right mood, I get a rather warped pleasure from reading recent research papers. I know that researchers will have worked long and hard over many months, if not years, to complete their work, and many of these research papers are extremely valuable. However, some are just plain silly, are totally irrelevant and, in my opinion, do not justify a research grant. Some of the worst offenders are published and often misinterpreted in the tabloids as space-fillers and can be highly amusing, particularly if they will make good headline grabbers such as "Eating fried cockroaches adds ten years to your life!"

A recent study by researchers from one university in the US examining obesity has just come to the enlightening conclusion that climate affects our walking habits. Indeed, people will walk more if the weather is right. No argument with this so far.

Researchers observed pedestrians in nine cities around the world - Santa Cruz in the Canary Islands; Kilmarnock and Glasgow in Scotland; Rousse in Bulgaria; Gliwice in Poland; Oulu and Jakobstad in Finland; Sion in Switzerland; and Ithaca in the United States over 170 days from late autumn (I refuse to use that ghastly Americanism, 'fall') to early summer.

Living in the Canary Islands, I am not too keen of walking when the temperature is over 40°C, nor is my dog, Bella. Mindful of government health advice, as well as words from Noel Coward's "Mad dogs and Englishmen go out in the noonday sun", I tend to walk for a short distance when it is hot and walk for longer distances when it is cool, or preferably in an air conditioned shopping centre.

Similarly, would you really set foot outdoors for pleasure if you happened to live in Glasgow or Kilmarnock? I think not. How about a nice stroll outside during winter in Finland? I suspect you would need an ice pick to prise your mouth open.

The researchers came to the staggering conclusion that a 5-degree temperature increase led to a 14 per cent increase in pedestrians on the streets and a shift from snow to dry conditions was associated with an increase of 23 per cent in pedestrian traffic. Now, would you believe that people actually like walking when their feet are allowed to move?

"Now, let's ban snow and the cold weather and heat our pavement areas. Forget global warming, let's just get them walking," I can hear the Mayor of London booming to the policymakers at City Hall.

The authors concluded that more people would walk if town planners would design neighbourhoods that counter extremes of temperature and use surfaces that help people to walk. Prompt removal of snow and efficient drainage would also encourage people to walk. How about council staff out on the pavements with shovels, salt and grit early in the morning? Didn't they used to do that when Grandad was a boy? What a good idea!

The study concluded with the insightful comment about how people will walk more if they are prepared for the weather. Hmm, given the recent debate in the UK about the relevance and quality of degree courses currently offered by UK universities, with poor old media studies and computer games degree courses being considered as "irrelevant", I recommend the 'Walking in the right weather' course as an ideal candidate for the budgetary chop.

Mowing the lawn

So, what exactly is the point of grass? One of the household jobs that I used to hate in the UK was the weekly chore of cutting the grass. It was a job that seemed to last all Saturday morning, if the weather was decent enough, and I seemed to spend most of my time trying to get the mower to work and collecting up the grass clippings afterwards.

Edging the lawn, removing moss, clover and daisies seemed such an unnecessary and time-consuming chore. Worse still, two days after I had cut the grass the job really needed doing again.

Then came the blissful luxury of patio tiles! Creating a tiled patio area around our homes in the Costa Blanca, and later in the Canary Islands, seemed such a sensible idea with no more cutting of grass ever again!

Once the design has been chosen, the site levelled and the tiles firmly stuck down on the cement that would be that - forever! Hmm, red rain? Surely that would be an easy matter to sort out with a hosepipe? Sadly this was not the case.

I have watched neighbours struggle and become obsessed with the after effects of red rain in the Costa Blanca. At first it was rather amusing to watch the frenetic activity on neighbours' patios after a rainstorm. Patio furniture, tiles, steps, banisters and balustrades all had to be carefully washed and scrubbed within minutes of the rain stopping. After all, this red dust from the Sahara was pretty powerful stuff and it seemed to get into places, cracks and crevices that you would not think possible.

Then of one our neighbours discovered the idea of using Agua Fuerte - an acid that when diluted with water would bring back the showroom shine to the newly laid tiles. What a find that was! Word soon got around the neighbourhood and we were all soon busily washing down our patio tiles with a solution of this potentially dangerous mix.

Here in the Canary Islands we have just finished washing our patio after a heavy storm. Fortunately it was not of the red rain variety, but after weeks without rain it has certainly brought with it a fair amount of dust and dirt.

Grass is a rare sight in this part of the Canary Islands. I read in one of the trade journals recently that artificial grass is a growth export business with hundreds of rolls of the stuff being sent to the Canary Islands from the UK and Germany. Indeed, we realised just a few months ago that our dog, Bella, had never seen grass, let alone chased a ball or rolled on it as our dogs in the UK used to. For a treat we drove her to a park some distance from our home and watched her cavort, roll and play in this green paradise with the greatest of pleasure. Sadly, she also peed with excitement several times and so my sincere apologies go to the Town Hall for the brown patches that no doubt appeared on this carefully manicured lawn a few days later.

Sitting on my patio chair enjoying the last of the day's sunshine with a glass of wine, I hear the familiar sound of a lawnmower. It is from the neighbours who live just behind our property. They have a small patch of grass, which is about the size of a large tablecloth. This little patch of Britain is carefully nurtured, watered, fed, fertilised and regularly cut with tremendous pride and the greatest pleasure. They even use a rotary lawnmower to cut the grass when a large pair of kitchen scissors would be more than adequate and the event is over in seconds. I breathe in the faint smell of newly mown grass and my mind goes flooding back to those years of battling with a lawn mower in our Dorset garden.

Do I miss it? Well, maybe I do feel a little nostalgic.

The Lollipop People

I do apologise if you thought you were about to read something about people selling ice cream products. No, instead I am talking about the gallant men and women who see our children safely across the roads each day in schools all over the UK.

The correct term is School Crossing Patrol and most are kindly souls, often retired, who are happy to give up a couple of hours each weekday to help children to cross busy roads safely, in return for a small salary cheque at the end of the month. I am sure that we all remember many happy lollipop people from our childhood, films and in picture books.

However, the reality is very different. As a busy head teacher, I have to confess that Lollipop Persons (in reality most were women of a certain age, but I guess I have to be politically correct) were, in reality, the bane of my life.

Along with caretakers, cleaners and lunchtime persons (more commonly known as Dinner Ladies), they often filled my day far more than dealing with curriculum issues, discipline, teachers and children, as well as actually teaching from time to time.

I would sometimes receive calls at 7.00am to tell me that one of my 'Lollipops' had a chiropodist appointment, in-growing toenail or broken false teeth that needed immediate attention. Consequently, 8.30am would often see me clad in startling luminescent overalls, usually in the pouring rain, ushering the little darlings and their parents across a busy road.

The task was not a pleasant one, because in addition to trying to avoid the children and myself being spread liberally all over the road, many parents would tackle me as they crossed, determined to question me about the latest homework policy decision, a problem with their class teacher and did I know that we had head-lice in the school again?

As the traffic roared past, I was only comforted by the thought that after little Gary had finally stopped picking his nose and decided to cross the road, I had precisely three minutes to dash back to school, park the lollipop, change, grab a cup of coffee and be prepared to take school assembly - no doubt kicking off with "All things bright and beautiful' sung through clenched teeth. How I hated the Lollipop role!

So why was I doing the job, you may ask? Well, in short, no one else wanted to do it. How I dreaded the latest resignation or retirement of the present incumbent. It usually meant weeks of advertising, interviews, police checks and training followed by two days on the job and a determined knock on my door. "I really don't think the job is for me..." the conversation would begin. This inevitably led to me being back to square one. "Anyone living and breathing out there who is desperate for a job?" I felt like announcing in the next 'Jobs Vacant' page in the local newspaper.

How envious I am of schools in the Canary Islands. They actually have a real police officer, complete with gun at the ready, to guide children safely across the road. Do vehicles stop and take notice? Of course they do. Do parents stop them and chat about homework, curriculum and the school disco? Of course not. Over here one does not argue with the police and busy head teachers can get on with the real job.

The Collapse of the Euro?

Spotting a new, repackaged bank account being offered in Spain earlier this week reminded me of an unhealthy trend that was very familiar in the UK a few years ago, and now appears to be arriving here.

"The imminent collapse of the Euro! The Euro is about to implode, but that doesn't mean you can't make a profit" screamed the advertisement on one web page that I spotted today. "The collapse of the Spanish housing market is good news for many! Make sure you profit!" was the good news announced on another site. Good news for whom exactly? Certainly not, the young Spanish couple who can no longer afford the mortgage and whose home has been repossessed by the bank, or the middle aged British couple who have been forced to sell their dream home in the sun for a song, because both have lost their jobs and they no longer have an income. Good news for some indeed.

Rest assured, I am not about to develop an argument in support of the euro: disaster may strike, but then again it may not. Remember the scare story a few years ago that a great chunk of rock on the Canary Island of La Palma was about to fall into the sea and create a tsunami that would destroy most of the east coast of the USA?

Urban myth would suggest that this was a scare story invented by some of the US insurance companies, to 'encourage' householders to take out or increase their insurance cover. Whether or not an insurance policy would really be of help in such a national emergency is open to debate; the tsunami may or may not occur in the next few million years or so when, I guess, most of us will no longer be concerned anyway.

As far as I am concerned the only real certainty, other than death and taxation, is that most financial advisers and banks look after themselves, and hang the consequences for the general public. Why is it that so many speculators, investment companies, financial advisers and traders are salivating at the very thought of the "imminent collapse of the euro"? There is a quick profit to be made, of course. Indeed, there are a number of examples of very wealthy individuals and corporations that have made substantial sums of money from similar currency collapses of the past.

I have always objected to the 1980s and 1990s phenomenon, when banks and insurance companies began to launch 'financial products'. For me, the definition of a product is something that has been created or made, not merely a repackaging of an existing financial service. A newly crafted chair, a shiny new car, a new novel or MP3 track are products that have been created by someone, or manufactured for sale.

One example is the ordinary current bank account, which has now been 'repackaged' with membership to a motoring organisation, together with a free electric pop up toaster, into an exciting new 'product', heavily promoted by slick advertising, for which the grateful customer now pays £15 per month. Is this really a 'product'? Who pays? Well, we all know the answer to that one. For me, the trend of "new financial products" was the beginning of the 'easy talk' about financial services, easy money to be made and making a fast buck, and the debt that individuals, companies and much of the world fell into, and for which we are all now paying the price.

Who remembers endowment mortgages? I recall being told by 'financial advisers', and I use the term loosely, that this would be the answer to our mortgage, and that 25 years later, our home would be fully paid off and there would a rather handsome lump sum to go with it. Like so many others, I took their advice and took out policies with two companies, such as Equitable Life and Standard Life, which later collapsed, despite both being heartily endorsed by Which? magazine (The Consumers' Association) at the time. In short, endowment policies made a lot of money for the 'financial advisers', banks and the insurance companies, but the rest of us were told to "seek compensation". Fortunately for me, it was early in the life of the policies and was not a critical situation, but I do wonder what happened to those who were nearing retirement when the news of their failed investments broke.

When it comes to money, one thing that I have learned, is that should you make a handsome profit from an investment, it has usually come at the expense of another poor soul, who has been less wise and less cautious. After all, isn't that what capitalism is all about? So, back to those advertisements, I suggest that expats give them a very wide berth and enjoy a round of golf, or take the dog for a walk, instead.

Maybe I want to go home?

No doors or windows!

The World recession has claimed the hopes and dreams of many expats, as well as local people. Many expats who finally achieved their dreams of a new life and home in the sun have packed their bags and the few belongings that they have managed to salvage and returned to their home countries. Many cases that I know of have been little short of tragic, although there are some that have left me wondering whether the intending expat should ever have been allowed to leave their home country in the first place!

James and Charlotte moved into their new home full of the usual excitement and hopes for the future. Both had good jobs and hoped to shortly start a family. As with so many, they overstretched themselves and their mortgaged home required two incomes to pay the hefty mortgage bill, credit card bills and new car, as well as the usual day-to-day living expenses. The couple were already deeply in debt before the young woman lost her job followed by her partner a few weeks later. Unless you are very fortunate, most banks in Spain are not tolerant of mortgage arrears and, rather quicker than in the UK, owner occupiers are soon forced out of their homes and the property is repossessed by the bank, and resold at a knock down price or, more likely in these difficult times, auctioned for a song.

The young couple were given notice to leave, but before they left, they decided it was 'pay back' time for the bank and they decided to take with them whatever they could salvage. They removed kitchen units, cupboards, and the bathroom suite and shower cubicle. This was followed by removal of the wooden staircase, all windows and doors and metal railings from the front of the house. One thing that did astound me was that they also took all the external patio tiles, as well as indoor floor tiles! Anyone who has tried to remove tiles will know that it is backbreaking work and it is, in my experience, almost impossible to remove tiles without breaking them. One can only imagine the heartache, bitterness and anger that lay behind these actions.

Another young couple, Grant and Sue, wrote to tell me of their difficult situation. Grant and Sue had lived in their new home for a couple of years, but when both lost their jobs they could not pay their mortgage. The bank was unsympathetic to their plight, and so they decided to rent out their property and move away from the area to live with friends until better times came, when they could move back into their home. Grant talked about their problem in a bar one night when he was drowning his sorrows, and soon found a Spanish couple that agreed to rent their home for six months or so. It seemed like an answer to his prayers, or was it?

Foolishly, Grant made the mistake of revealing that unless the rent was paid then they could not pay the mortgage and the bank would repossess the property. The Spanish couple moved into their home and, being well aware of the law, failed to pay any rent at all. The house was duly repossessed by the bank, the Spanish couple were allowed to remain in the property, as they were now sitting tenants and had a child attending the village school; a situation that provides tenants with additional rights. Grant and Sue's home was then sold to the sitting tenants for a very low price, and Grant and Sue were left with nothing. Indeed, they still owe a considerable sum of money to the bank, as not all the debt was repaid.

Renting is a strategy that many expats consider if they cannot sell their property and still have to pay the mortgage. However, this can be fraught with difficulties and may lead to heavy fines being imposed if the property is not registered correctly as a property for rent with the Town Hall. My best advice is to avoid doing this at all costs unless you are absolutely clear about the law in your adopted country. If you should go down this route, you need a good local lawyer and a well-established lettings agency to support and advise you.

Lightning Strike

It is a safe bet that few people living in the UK and Northern Europe will have little sympathy for poor weather conditions in the Canary Islands. At the time of writing we see people facing horrendous weather conditions in the UK with reports of temperatures plummeting to minus 20°C in parts of Scotland, and little better in most parts of the UK. Daily lives and routines are all thrown into chaos, and the health and safety of the young and elderly in particular are put at risk by the excessive cold, as well as very dangerous road conditions.

As I sit on my sun lounger tolerating a slightly cooler than normal temperature of around 23°C I admit that we have very little to complain about. However, a few days ago many of us witnessed one of the worst electrical storms on these islands for many years. The islands' government had announced a rare 'Red Alert' warning several days earlier. Schools and many public buildings were closed in readiness for the torrential storms that were heading towards the Canary Islands from the Atlantic Ocean.

After being flooded, within two days of moving into our new home several years ago, we quickly learned the hard way of the necessity of fitting external shutters to windows, as well as attempting to fit thresholds to the bottom of door frames, which are virtually non-existent over here.

I had always taken door thresholds for granted in the UK, but this simple addition to door frames in Spain and the Canary Islands would make such a difference during heavy rainstorms. Without them, water will pour into any room with an external door during rainstorms, and particularly when accompanied by heavy winds.

I started the day with a throbbing headache - a rare, but always a reliable, telltale sign of a heavy storm to come. Dark, black and threatening clouds appeared over the mountains, the town fell silent and even the dogs stopped barking in anticipation of what was to come. The sound of rumbling and flashes of lightning began, as the rain and wind started and we reached the safety of our home before the torrent that would later turn into a flood.

At three o'clock in the morning we awoke to the most horrendous thunder that I have ever heard. The house shook as lightning shot across the sky, lighting it up rather like it does with fireworks on fiesta days, but this was not to be from the joy of fireworks. Rain beat down and the wind blew violently against the closed shutters and doors with a mighty force that seemed not to be of this world. I tried in vain to switch on a light, but the power had failed.

As we take a break from cleaning the patios and repairing some of the damage, we hear that at one period during the night, the islands were at the receiving end of more than 7000 lightning strikes and that between 5.00am and 10.00am there were another 8249 flashes of lightning. At around 6.00am, 1539 negative rays were recorded - these are the ones that go from earth to the sky. I would just like to know which obsessive soul sat and counted them all!

The sun is shining again; the sea is calm, children are on their way to school and the dogs are barking. Lives are quickly returning to normal. The first of the flights from frozen Europe are heading towards Las Palmas airport, full of mostly pasty white and hopeful passengers longing for a week in the sunshine and an escape from worry and all the talk of recession back home. They will not be disappointed. Apart from some ground water, muddy roads and some clearing up to do, it is difficult to reconcile this calm, everyday scene with the nightmare of the previous night.

Too much of a good thing...?

"Ooo, lovely! 45 degrees in the shade!" exclaimed our friend, vigorously tapping our outside thermometer, as we were desperately trying to keep cool during yet another heat wave. High temperatures such as this are great if you are on holiday, have nothing to do but drink refreshing liquids in the shade of a palm tree, or can sit in an air-conditioned room all day. However, all this can get a bit much for normal day-to-day activities, if such extreme temperatures continue for too long.

Admittedly, these high temperatures are unusual in the Canary Islands, and often only last for a few days as the hot winds are blown from the Sahara. Yet the excessive heat is often uncomfortable for many, not only because the heat disturbs sleep, but also for the associated eye irritations and infections that my ophthalmic surgeon tells me often accompany the hot winds. Don't misunderstand me, I am not suffering from the usual Brit disease of endlessly complaining about the weather; I left that little bundle of misery back in the UK many years ago, but merely pointing out that adjustments to extreme temperatures do take getting used to.

It has been a strange year on an island that rarely sees such wide variations in temperature. A few months ago, temperatures on the island plunged to around 10 degrees, which some of our elderly neighbours told me was the coldest for 30 years, yet a few days ago temperatures were in excess of 45 degrees, and higher in parts of the south of the island.

During spells of high temperatures, medical alerts are issued by the islands' government and, unlike some holidaymakers who attempt to go trekking during periods of excessive heat, often with disastrous consequences, most people attempt to follow the Canarian way of doing things. Such changes in day-to-day living include getting up early to complete necessary physical activities and household chores before it gets too hot, having a siesta during the hottest part of the day (a sensible idea at any time of the year anyway), not taking the dog for a walk during the heat of the day, drinking lots of fluids (not alcohol!), as well as shopping in one of the many air conditioned shopping centres late into the evening.

Visitors to the island often ask me about our energy bills and are envious when I tell them that we have no central heating, other than switching on a fan heater occasionally during the coldest parts of the year, or maybe the negligible expense of lighting a few candles on a really chilly evening, remembering that it is all relative to what you are normally used to. However, the flip side of the coin does mean that many homes on the island now have air conditioning units installed, and these are now used much more frequently now than in previous years, when they were a rare sight in all but the most expensive properties. These units are expensive to run, and mean that what is not spent on heating during the winter months tends to be spent on air conditioning during the summer; so we do not escape high energy bills completely.

Island living means that many of us spend most of our time outdoors. Other than periods of very low or excessively high temperatures, we tend to eat breakfast, lunch and dinner outdoors and, again, with just a few candles for company, which also helps to reduce overall energy consumption.

"What about lack of water?" is another question that would be expats and visitors often anxiously ask. Despite the lack of regular rainfall, sometimes occurring only for a few days in February in the south of the island, I have not known a time when we cannot use hosepipes to wash our cars, hose our patios or to water the plants in the garden. Underground reservoirs, as well as occasional rainfall in the mountain areas, together with an endless supply of water from the desalination plants, means that this is rarely an issue. After all, we are surrounded by the stuff. As for washing the car? No, it is far too hot for that. I'm off for a siesta!

Hypertension in the Canary Islands

"You are living in the Canary Islands now. You cannot be stressed; it is impossible. No one is stressed over here!" I recall one doctor declaring confidently to the weeping young woman in his surgery one morning. Actually, it was quite clear that this poor woman was suffering from postnatal depression and that she had reached one of the lowest points of her life. Well, I have news for this doctor, who maybe should undergo a period of retraining, there are many stressed people living in the Canary Islands, just as there are in most other parts of the world. A glorious climate cannot compensate for all the ills of the world and are, no doubt, made more acute by high unemployment, repossession of family homes and relationship breakdowns.

In the last few days, I have seen a friend lose his job, his relationship collapse, as well as having his home repossessed. Each one of these events is, in itself, a trauma of such magnitude and achieves the highest rating on the stress factor tables. Having all three events happen in one week is potentially disastrous for the individuals concerned and not surprisingly results in an acute level of stress and often much worse. My friend went to the doctor, had his blood pressure taken and, surprise, surprise, was diagnosed with hypertension. As a result he is now on a considerable quantity of medication, which I suspect he will be on for many years to come.

Few people would argue that this individual needed help and support and that, in the short term, medication is part of the urgent help required at a time of crisis. However, there are many people who visit their doctors with relatively minor conditions and return home clutching a prescription for drugs to ease their hypertension, which they do not need.

Recent news from the National Institute for Clinical Excellence (NICE) in the UK revealing concerns about blood pressure tests taken in doctors' surgeries were inaccurate, leading to misdiagnosis of high blood pressure, has confirmed what has long been suspected by many. After all, who enjoys visiting the doctor's surgery or hospital?

For most people it is a period of deep anxiety, not surprisingly leading to a natural rise in blood pressure. Wise doctors recognise this and make allowances, and possibly arrange for a retest. However, this is still likely to be an inflated reading and usually results in increased profits for the drug companies.

I knew one sincere young woman when I lived in the UK who worked briefly as a salesperson for one of the major drug companies. It was her job to persuade doctors to prescribe a certain brand of drug.

The disturbing news was that the orders for supplies of certain drugs came with the carrot of a new laptop computer, 'study trips' to Switzerland and the Bahamas, as well as many other luxury items. Clearly, it was in a minority of unscrupulous doctors' interest to prescribe and keep patients on these drugs for as long as possible with drugs to deal with hypertension and cholesterol at the top of the list. My friend quickly decided that the job was immoral and resigned.

According NICE, this misdiagnosis of blood pressure has led to as many as 25 per cent of patients being treated for hypertension, who should not have been treated with these expensive drugs. The report has concluded that new technology should be used to confirm a diagnosis of high blood pressure by using a device that measures a person's blood pressure throughout the day. The new system has been evaluated as being more accurate and better value-for-money when compared to blood pressure readings taken in the surgery by harassed doctors and nurses.

All this sounds like a common-sense policy that, no doubt, the drug companies will hate and hard-pressed governments trying to balance health budgets will applaud. However, I doubt this will really help my friend. What he really needs is a steady job, a stable home and to be reunited with his family.

Embalming anyone?

The unexpected phone call from the mortuary in Las Palmas immediately took my attention. Was I in a position to pay the outstanding account at the mortuary? This really was not the kind of call that anyone would wish to receive first thing in the morning, and particularly when one is struggling to make sense of the world before coffee.

I assured the very pleasant lady at the other end of the line that I had no previous knowledge of their service and that, no, I did not have any kind of account with them, nor did I have one that was due for payment. However, I assured her, that I would keep her number on file - just in case I needed a spot of embalming in the future. One just never knows when such services might be required. The very nice lady even offered to send me a brochure about their range of services...

The early morning telephone call reminded me of a series of articles that I wrote as a newspaper reporter several years ago about 'Death in Spain'. The series of articles were intended to be a helpful guide in managing one of most traumatic times of our lives, and to assist expats in making the right choices in a country with different customs and traditions in dealing with death. The articles were not exactly a bundle of laughs and not ones that would, at first sight, encourage advertisers to promote their new restaurant or estate agency on that particular page; however, the series was very popular with readers.

I recall one elderly gentleman who shuffled into the newspaper office to ask for back copies of the newspaper. He was asked why he wanted them. "It's those Death pages", he muttered, "my wife reckons she'll be needing them soon."

Although it is not really a subject that is often discussed over dinner, or over a gin and tonic on the balcony, thoughts about our passing and those of our loved ones should be considered seriously, particularly when living as an expat in another country. Do we have a will in the country that we are residing in, for instance? I know of many expats who are relying solely on wills made in the UK many years ago. However, lawyers assure me that this arrangement is potentially fraught with difficulties and that all expats should also have a Spanish will, as well as their UK one.

What about bodies? It is traditional, and good sense because of the heat, that bodies are cremated or buried very quickly in Spain, and often within two or three days. This is in contrast to the UK where bodies can be waiting for two or three weeks before funerals can be arranged. Over here, the final departure is quick, which adds more pressure to be clear about the wishes of the deceased.

In the event of your demise would you prefer to be flown back to the UK at considerable expense, cremated in your newly adopted country and then sent back in a pot, or popped into one of those filing cabinet tomb arrangements that seem to be popular in Spain? What about costs? Has provision been made to cover the cost of repatriation, for instance? Do you have a funeral expenses insurance policy? These are all very serious issues, I know, but ones that need to be considered carefully and wishes made clear to dependents.

Now, back to that early morning telephone call. I am still wondering why that very nice lady at the mortuary called me.

There is further information on the 'Expat Survival' section of my website. If you have additional information to add, do please let me know.

Expats and Recession

It was not that many years ago that Dot and Bert from Wigan, and others like them, managed to achieve their life-long dreams of opening a bar or a small business in the Spanish Costas and the Portuguese Algarve. They, and many like them, discovered that a pound went a long way in the countries where the peseta and the escudo were king. It was also a time when the equity locked in many British homes was substantial, and could be released to fund a new lifestyle and a new home in the sun.

As well as the silver entrepreneurs, thousands of British pensioners, many nowhere near the UK state pension age, realised that they too could have a healthier and more comfortable life in the sun, either as 'winter birds' enjoying the delights of an all inclusive hotel in Benidorm during the winter months, at a much lower cost than surviving the UK winter, or making a full time commitment with a new life in the country of their choice. Low fuel and food costs and comfortable pensions meant a huge improvement in the quality of life for many.

How things have changed. Even though the UK Government, exporters and economists welcome the weakening of sterling to correct the UK's trade imbalances, it is not good news for expat pensioners, who have fixed incomes.

Many British expat pensioners are now facing real reductions in the purchasing power of their UK state pensions, with some analysts citing that their average monthly pension income has dropped by over €250 since the start of the global recession, with British pensioners living overseas having lost out on over €13 billion of their income since the global recession began.

However, the global economic downturn has meant belt tightening for everyone and most expat pensioners are far better off than many Canary Islanders. I know a number of people whose monthly income is less that 600 euros, with many surviving on around 400 euros, which is the subsistence level provided by the Spanish state to those who are entitled to seek help.

I saw an Italian woman on television the other evening complaining, in response to the Italian Government's latest austerity measures, that an income of 1000 euros each month is insufficient to live on. I know many Canary islanders who would be very grateful to receive anywhere near half that amount.

I know times are hard for most people, but a recent Canary Islands' Government survey of more than 500,000 homes surprised and shocked me. The survey shows that around 95,000 households in the Canary Islands survive on an income of less than €350 each month. About 16,000 households survive on much less: just €180 each month.

Complaints about reduced spending power and reductions in the standards of living that we are used to are certainly justified, but it seems that many expats are still in a better position than many locals.

'The Seven Year Itch'

'The Seven Year Itch' is often a term applied to relationships between people that have begun to fail. The early excitement and romance of the first few years of a new relationship have soured, and been replaced by mistrust, disappointment and betrayal.

New responsibilities, work pressures, children and financial difficulties are often the root cause of many problems within a relationship. In many cases, talking over issues, counselling, medical help and realisation that no problem is unique will hopefully avoid leading to the cliff edge and total relationship breakdown. However, in other cases, separation and divorce may be the only answer to such serious problems.

Similar problems also face many expats. In many cases during my time living in Spain and the Canary Islands, I have seen the initial excitement and challenge of a new life in the sun being replaced by anxiety, bitterness and a desire to return to the expat's country of origin at all costs. Often the drive to return 'home' has been forced upon the expat by an inability to find a new job, or losing a job, financial and relationship pressures and sadly, too often, following a lifestyle that may encourage the increased consumption of alcohol.

Often it is a realisation that living in another country means a disconnection from friends and family in the long term. The unintentional 'out of sight and out of mind' syndrome sets in, with previous good friends and family becoming even more distant. After all, in time, the expat begins to have little in common with the folks back home.

Living on an island, the situation can become even more acute. The recession and the highest unemployment in Spain have meant that many expats living in the Canary Islands have lost their jobs and, as a consequence, also lost their homes. Regular travel to mainland Europe can be expensive and it is not easy to regularly visit family and friends. Island living is not for everyone either. The romantic idyll can soon turn into a nightmare of missing certain foods, television, entertainment and, most of all, friends and family.

Even for those who have taken the trouble to learn Spanish, and many do not even make the effort, quickly realise that however long they study or however hard they try, complete mastery of the language will never be enough to share jokes, innuendo and relaxed communication that they enjoy in their native language, unless of course, they manage to find a native partner - and many have!

Seven years appears to be the time that many expats begin to re-evaluate their original decision of making a new life for themselves in the sun. Rather like a marriage, questions begin to be asked and particularly in the case of those with medical conditions and those reaching old age. It is after seven years or so that I see many expats beginning to pack up and move back to their country of origin. Hopefully, these expats will realise that nothing in life is ever wasted and it is always better to have tried and failed than not having even made the attempt in the first place.

During my time in Gran Canaria, I have known many people who have enjoyed their time on the island, but reached a point in their lives through work, relationships or finances that they are forced to return to their country of origin. This can be unsettling for the rest of us, as the expat community is a small one and each departure can make a significant difference. Strangely, I have also noticed that many people who leave the island tend to return a few years later, or certainly have expressed that it is their intention to do so. These islands are wonderful places to live and returning expats often quickly realise their mistake and make every effort to return once again, older and wiser.

I recall discussing this issue with a visiting psychic several years ago. She listened with interest, retrieved some charts, and pointed out to me that Gran Canaria is at the crossroads of ancient ley lines and, because of this, it is a place of increased spirituality. This has created the unlikely phenomena that the island draws certain people that it wants to its shores, rejects those it does not want, yet continues to draw back those that leave and the island wishes to retain. It all sounds like a good plot for a future Doctor Who series. Cynics will, of course, immediately reject this explanation as non-scientific rubbish; however, from what I have observed over the years, I do not easily dismiss the explanation.

The beginning of the end, or the end of the beginning?

The British have always been keen explorers and travellers. A glance through any British secondary school history textbook reveals countless accounts of adventurers and explorers who left the islands that they called home in search of new adventure, new experiences, a new life and, in some cases, a hearty profit. In many ways, the British expat is merely following in the footsteps of these adventurers and explorers.

Maybe it is something to do with living on an island that makes one want to get off it. It could be down to the climate; after all, lack of sunlight, endless rain and cold temperatures can have negative effects upon even the most resilient of people. The rising cost of living and an increasing feeling that our islands are quickly running out of space, also add to the appeal of relocating to another country. However, I suspect that the real issue has more to do with escaping from an ever increasing frenetic pace of life, and a growing realisation that there is more out there to live for and enjoy.

Being an expat is not always 'a bed of roses', and I hope 'Expat Survival' has gone a little way towards exploding this myth. Living in another country, even the English-speaking ones, brings with it many challenges and frustrations. These can quickly destroy the dream of living in another country and sharing a different lifestyle. However, the true expat will see these challenges as merely a temporary setback, and sees the bigger picture, and learns from negative experiences.

Some expats do not make it and, after a few years, decide to pack their bags and return "home", wherever that may be. "Home" is a word that I use very loosely and, to me, it usually means the place where my loved ones are, and that, for the present, is the Canary Islands. I recall asking one expat why he had decided to return home to Manchester. "To be honest, I really do miss the rain beating on the windows when I am warm and cosy inside, and sleeping in a bed with a thick duvet over me," he said, almost apologetically.

You see, it takes all kinds of people and sometimes the things that we miss are trivial yet, over time, grow in importance. For me, I miss friends and family. Not all of them, I might add, and a reasonable distance between some of them is often very helpful! Over time, I confess to missing things that I had never thought of as important before; for me, such things include daffodils and bluebells in springtime, the smell of newly cut grass, Dorset cream teas and mince pies at Christmas.

I have come to realise that being successful as an expat has something to do with being part of something much bigger, being aware and appreciative of other languages and cultures, learning from people representing other faiths who have something significant to say about life, as well as giving something back when I can. Over the years, I have come to the conclusion that the least successful expats are those who see expat life as one bathed in endless sunshine and cheap gin and tonics, and where the euro stretches further than the pound did in the UK.

I have met and corresponded with many bitter and resentful expats over the years who continually complain that expat life was not as they thought it would be. Much of it usually boils down to misplaced priorities, sometimes greed and a failure to integrate into a different society. Many such expats also have one thing in common, the ability to take, but rarely to give. Many have not made the overall 'profit' that they had originally sought, because of wildly fluctuating exchange rates having a negative effect upon their pensions. They fail to realise that being a successful expat is not about profit, but involves giving something of yourself to your new country, and I do not simply mean in taxation.

I have also met many successful and happy expats who play a significant part in helping local charities and good causes, such as animal rescue, feeding the homeless, visiting prisons, teaching English or comforting the sick and dying. Many such people give selflessly, without pay or recognition, and it is their way of giving something back.

Although much of 'Expat Survival' relates to Spain and the Canary Islands, there are many common factors relating to expats everywhere, be it in the South of France, Argentina, Canada, South Africa or Australia. Wherever you are, enjoy your new life and remember to give generously of yourself too!

MESSAGE IN A BOTTLE

The Canary Islander

History and Culture

A Queen Calls...

The launch of the new Cunard Queen Elizabeth caused considerable interest, not only in her new home port of Southampton, but also in Las Palmas de Gran Canaria, which was one of the first ports of call during this super liner's maiden voyage.

Appropriately, the Queen Elizabeth, which is the same length as 36 London buses and holds 2,092 passengers, started her maiden voyage on a 13-night cruise to the Canary Islands on 12 October 2010. This maiden voyage was fully booked within 29 minutes after it went on sale, and more than 50% of its remaining 2010 cruises were sold within one and a half hours.

Little was been made in the press that the official launch of the new liner by Queen Elizabeth took place on 11 October and the maiden voyage to the Canary Islands started on 12 October - Columbus Day. The day itself always causes some dispute each year, because Columbus Day in Spain is always celebrated on 12 October. However, in the United States, Columbus Day is always celebrated on the second Monday in October, which in 2010 was 11 October. It was not the first time that a vessel of intrigue, excitement and anticipation had docked in Gran Canaria's famous port of Las Palmas...

Back in 1485, Portugal refused funding to Christopher Columbus. It took him seven years of lobbying to get funding from Ferdinand and Isabella of Spain. Initially, Queen Isabella turned him down and sent him away. Later, King Ferdinand called him back and granted the funding. Half the financial support also came from private Italian investors. Columbus set sail and made it to the Canary Islands in August 1492.

Columbus arrived in Gran Canaria's port of Las Palmas, where he restocked the provisions and made repairs, and on September 6, started what turned out to be a five-week voyage across the Atlantic Ocean.

The five-week voyage across the Atlantic by Columbus actually started from La Gomera, one of the smaller of the Canary Islands. La Gomera has a fascinating association with Christopher Columbus. Popular legend, speculation and contemporary reports all indicate that Columbus was in love with one of its most infamous of residents, the aristocratic Beatriz de Bobadilla, by reputation a vicious medieval nymphomaniac, and by all accounts, a great beauty.

Having said goodbye to his beloved, Columbus sailed for five weeks before land was sighted on October 12, 1492 and Columbus called the island (in what is now the Bahamas) San Salvador, although he continued to believe he had reached Asia until his death in 1506. He also believed the peaks of Cuba to be the Himalayas, which says little for his sense of direction!

Columbus Day has been celebrated as a holiday in Spain since 1958, as 'Día de la Hispanidad'. Well, it is an excuse for another fiesta!

Size Does Matter

It is rare to see Americans visiting these islands nowadays, which is probably due to the long flight and some similarity to the Caribbean Islands.

However, until the horrors of September 11, many tourists from the USA visited the Canary Islands regularly. Concerns about long air flights and security meant that flights from the USA were more or less halted and, until recently, these islands have seen a much-reduced number of visitors from the other side of the Atlantic.

This state of affairs is about to change once again with recent meetings between the President of the Canary Islands and the American Government with a view to extending and developing business links to these islands. After all, the Canary Islands are situated in an ideal strategic position for easy access to all parts of the European Community, as well as Africa and Asia and recent improvements to telecommunications have opened up considerable trading and business opportunities.

Trade and business links aside, these islands mean a great deal to many American citizens, many of whom have ancestry firmly based in the Canary Islands.

This fascinating story begins in 1778 in Louisiana, then a Spanish colony, when 700 men were recruited to increase the size of the Louisiana Regiment. The Spanish Crown had held Louisiana since 1762, and the possibility of an invasion by Great Britain was becoming a worrying threat.

Spain looked to the Canary Islands for recruits to increase the size of the army in Louisiana. Despite initial attempts to recruit single men, there were insufficient volunteers. Finally, the Spanish Government had to settle for married recruits with the dual role of defending the territory, as well as populating it. After all, as history tells us, there is more than one way to win a war and colonise a territory than using guns alone.

The new recruits from the Canary Islands had to be aged between "17 to 36 years old, healthy, without vices, and more than five feet tall". Recruiters were paid extra for every half-inch that each recruit stood in height above the minimum of five feet specified, so size was an important factor in their selection. These men were recruited on the understanding that they would be staying in Louisiana permanently, although there was no written agreement.

By the summer of 1779, 352 families and 100 single men had arrived in Louisiana, where the Governor, Bernardo de Galvez, settled them in four areas that he considered to be major invasion routes planned by the enemy.

The men were formed into militia units led by Galvez in his conquest and occupation of British territory on the lower Mississippi River. In those days Britain was Spain's mortal and historical enemy, and by doing this Spain supported the Americans in their revolution against Britain.

A total of 2,363 men, women, and children from the Canary Islands had been sent to colonise Louisiana by the end of 1783. Living conditions were difficult in a flat, wet, undeveloped land and vastly different from their volcanic island homeland in the sun.

It is easy to understand the fascination of many Americans with these small volcanic islands just off the coast of Africa. More than two hundred years have passed since the arrival of the Canary Islanders in Louisiana. However, Spanish surnames are plentiful in Louisiana as well as in other states, and their descendants still treasure the unique heritage of their brave ancestors from the Canary Islands.

The Baby Sellers

Living in present-day Spain and the Canary Islands, it is often hard to remember that Spain has only relatively recently emerged as a successful and fully-fledged democracy after years of fear and repression under the hated Franco regime. As the last remaining statue, erected by Franco during his dictatorship, was recently removed from Barcelona, most Spaniards look to a time when a thick line can finally be drawn under this black period of the country's history. It is credit to the strength of personality and character of its people that Spain has achieved so much since the dictator's death, and although not always a popular concept with the British, it must be said that membership of the European Union has also been instrumental in the country's transformation from fascist dictatorship to a highly successful democracy.

Anyone following the TV programme, Eastenders, will no doubt be aware of the much publicised and over hyped 'outcry' to the soap's desperate storyline about a stolen baby over the Christmas and New Year period. Christmas just wouldn't be Christmas without a grim Eastenders' story line to go with the Christmas pudding would it? Do we care anyway? Sadly, there are echoes of the drama currently happening in Tenerife, as well as elsewhere in Spain.

In Santa Cruz, police recently arrested one man and five women, who were offering €10,000 to pregnant, homeless women in exchange for their babies. Police had been watching the suspects for some time after hearing about a person in charge of finding homeless pregnant women who were prepared to give up their babies for cash. Fortunately, the gang have now been detained and charged with crimes against family relationships, as well as attempting to alter the paternity of a child.

Sadly, this tragic story is not new to Spain. Currently there are demands to open a national investigation into allegations that babies were taken away from their mothers at birth and sold to other families for many years, under a law approved by Franco's dictatorship. It is thought that as many as 300,000 children were stolen in this way during Franco's 1939-75 dictatorship and continued until the late 1980s.

This ongoing human tragedy was the result of a 1940 decree that the Spanish state was allowed to take children into custody if their "moral welfare" was at risk. This left the way open for the dictatorship to take children of jailed left-wing opponents from their families, with state approval and often with the blessing of the Roman Catholic Church, in an attempt to purify Spain of Marxist influence. Historians now reveal that many of these stolen children were given to religious orders and eventually became monks and nuns, whilst others were adopted illegally by families and given changed identities.

Currently, legal cases are continuing against doctors and nurses who participated in the policy and also continued with this illegal business by providing babies for childless couples. One heartbreaking side of the story, which in so many ways follows the much criticised Eastenders' storyline, was that new mothers were told that their babies had died within hours of birth. The hospitals told mothers that they had taken care of their burials when in fact the babies had been given to another family.

Fortunately, the story is now fully in the open and an association acting for the victims is now pressing for a full national enquiry into the allegations. Maybe the Eastenders' storyline isn't so far fetched after all?

Lighthouses and Lime Kilns

There are many lighthouses in the Canary Islands, and locals and many visitors will know that there is a particularly fine one at Maspalomas in Gran Canaria. The lighthouse, or Faro in Spanish, helps sailors to navigate their ships and is an integral part of sea-life.

Usually, lighthouses are cylindrical towers with a light on top, and emit a fixed sequence of beams that is unique to a particular lighthouse. Built in 1980, the Maspalomas lighthouse is still operational and, for those who like full details, provides 3 white flashes every 13 seconds. Before lighthouses were invented, sailors were warned of hazards by the lighting of fires along the coastline.

Since visiting these islands for the first time many years ago, I am often amazed to discover the strategic and important place that these small islands and its people have in history. Indeed, these islands pack a far greater punch than their size would lead most to believe. The development of the lighthouse is just one of these intrigues.

Let us now visit Plymouth in Devon, and stand on Plymouth Hoe, looking out to sea into the impressive expanse of Plymouth Sound...

About 14 miles from the coast stands the Eddystone Lighthouse, which is the fourth lighthouse to be built on the treacherous Eddystone Rocks. Earlier attempts had either caught fire or were washed away, with the exception of one. This was the lighthouse called Smeaton's Tower, which now stands proudly on Plymouth Hoe and was once used to guard against those treacherous rocks.

In 1756, an engineer called John Smeaton was asked by the Royal Society to design the third Eddystone Lighthouse. His inspiration was to be an oak tree - a tall, natural object that could withstand gales without breaking. He used 1,493 blocks of stone, rather like the rings of a tree, dove-tail jointed together with marble dowels and oak pins. Now this is the clever part, Smeaton also pioneered the use of hydraulic lime, a form of concrete that would set under water. This lime came from Arinaga, in Gran Canaria.

Since ancient times, the small coastal town of Arinaga, operated a small cottage industry for the extraction and burning of lime. Quicklime from the Arinaga furnaces was sold throughout the islands and beyond its shores, which led to increased prosperity and economic expansion. It was this quicklime from Arigaga that made the building of Smeaton's Tower possible.

In the early twentieth century, the first cement plant in Arguineguin opened and demanded a lot of hydraulic lime, as well as being needed for agriculture, buildings, ports and roads. Most of the lime produced in Gran Canaria came from Arinaga, where dozens of workers worked in this industry. The industry is now long gone, but some of the old furnaces have been carefully restored and preserved and can still be seen at the end of the beach in Arinaga, as a memento of its proud contribution to the building industry on the island and beyond. It is inspiring to think that a combination of Smeaton's inspired design and highly advanced engineering skills still required the contribution of Canary Islanders over 2000 miles away!

Smeaton's Tower protected shipping in Plymouth Sound for 120 years and when it was finally replaced in 1882, and was dismantled stone by stone and rebuilt on Plymouth Hoe. It still stands as a permanent reminder of the very clever engineer who created it, with just a little help from the lime workers of Arinaga!

The Ship that Died

I am not a great lover of things nautical; after all I tend to get seasick when having a bath if the water is too deep. However, the recent announcement of a new ferry service from Las Palmas in Gran Canaria to Huelva in Peninsular Spain, with a journey time of just over one day, as compared to nearly three days on the alternative service, set me thinking about a once-beautiful ship now lying off a beach on our neighbouring island of Fuerteventura.

This is the story of SS America, a luxury liner that was launched the day before Hitler invaded Poland and brought the world to war in 1939. It was not an auspicious start for a cruise liner that had to be immediately converted into a troop carrier that would not carry the planned 1200 passengers on a luxury cruise, but was destined to become a troop-carrying vessel that would carry up to 8000 troops to war.

The ship was renamed, West Point, and she carried troops around the world. Later, she was confined to the North Atlantic route where her speed and manoeuvrability were ideal to outwit German U boats, gale force winds and the treacherous sea. Troops were carried from the USA to Europe and wounded soldiers, as well as prisoners of war, shipped back to America.

After wartime duties, the SS America resumed life as a cruise ship and was seen as one of the most beautiful of the American fleet. After 24 years of service, the ship's career came to an abrupt end due to labour disputes and the growing popularity of air travel. The SS America was sold to a Greek shipping company, renamed Australis, and began a new life transporting British passengers who were emigrating to a new life in Australia, as part of a campaign to increase its population. Later, the assisted passage scheme was gradually phased out and long haul flights made air travel more attractive than a long voyage at sea, and in 1977 the Australis made her last voyage to Australia.

There were attempts to reinstate the ship for cruises once again. The SS America was given her original name and intended to resume life as a floating casino. The first voyage in 1978 was a disaster and angry passengers forced the ship to return to port. The shipping company was sued for $2.5 million and the SS America was held as a surety against debt; the ship's fate was sealed, and the SS America was to be auctioned.

The vessel was then repurchased by her previous Greek owners and was intended to be used as a Mediterranean cruise ship. Italis, as she was renamed, never put to sea. She was sold again in 1980 and renamed Noga, and this time destined to be a floating hotel in Beruit.

This plan did not materialise and so this once proud ship was due to be returned to the USA to become a prison ship, but that fell through too. She was sold again and renamed Alferdoss, which means 'Paradise' in Arabic. Sadly, it was nothing like paradise and for ten years the ship rotted until damage to her bilge pipe meant that she had to be beached to prevent sinking.

Finally, a consortium bought her and gave her yet another new name, the America Star. A star she was no longer and, as she was being towed to Thailand to be converted into a floating hotel, the towrope broke in stormy weather off Fuerteventura. She broke into two pieces and what little remains has been slowly disappearing into the sea, leaving part of the bow remaining above the water. This once proud vessel is waiting to be finally claimed by the sea.

Camels and Cauliflowers

I remember once being told by a zookeeper that there is nothing tastier for a camel to eat than a nice fresh cauliflower. I doubt that many of these grow in the desert, and remember thinking at the time that it was a tall story intended to satisfy the curiosity of child's endless questioning. I suspect camels will eat anything that they can get their teeth into.

These majestic yet strange creatures look almost out of place in today's world, yet still continue their role as a beast of burden in many countries, because of their ability to travel great distances across hot, dry deserts with little food or water. They are perfectly designed to walk easily on soft sand where vehicles could not travel, and to carry people and heavy loads to places that have no roads.

I was looking at some old photographs of life in the Canary Islands a few days ago. I felt a certain déjà vu as I was looking at the old sepia coloured prints, because they reminded me of some old family photographs that I had seen in my mother's photograph album many years ago. These were of my grandfather and great-grandfather ploughing a field in rural Lincolnshire, with the help of some magnificent looking horses. The photographs of men and animals working the land in the Canary Islands looked remarkably similar, except instead of horses they were using camels. Until relatively recent times, it was camels and not horses that were used as the beast of burden on these islands.

The first camels were brought to the Canary Islands from Africa in the late fourteenth century, and these creatures were essential for the European colonisation of the islands. Being so close to Africa, the camels adapted perfectly to the hot and dry conditions in the Canary Islands, and particularly in the south of Gran Canaria and Tenerife, as well as Lanzarote and Fuerteventura. As well as having an important role to play in agriculture, they were perfect for carrying people and goods.

The Canarian Camel, or Camello Canario, is a dromedary, which as I recall from my early school days, has one hump and can be remembered because of the shape of letter 'D' in dromedary. Its cousin, the Bactrian camel has two humps, as in the shape of the letter 'B'. There are around 1200 camels still on the islands and the indigenous population of the dromedary are the only breed to be recognised as a breed in its own right in Europe and has been recently included in the official Spanish records of livestock breeds.

Nowadays, of course, the Canarian camel is mostly used in the tourist industry as a means of transport on excursions in the islands' national parks and nature reserves, as well as Maspalomas beach. The islands' camels are also very busy on the night of the Three Kings in January when they are paraded through the streets of many towns on the islands.

As for camels and cauliflowers, I have since found out from a very knowledgeable camel keeper that desert camels are usually fed dates, grass, wheat and oats. In zoos, camels are fed hay and grain, which is about 3.5 kilograms of food everyday. However, if food is very scarce, a camel will eat anything and even its owner's tent!

Admiral Nelson and the Canary Islands

You may remember Horatio Nelson from school history lessons as the jolly little man with the big hat and equally inflated ego; his costume goes down a treat at fancy dress parties. In pictures, Nelson is instantly recognisable as the semi-blinded, one-armed naval officer who destroyed the French and Spanish fleets; he also had a fascinating ménage à trois with the rather interesting Lady Hamilton. So what is the real story of the man whose statue dominates London's Trafalgar Square, and how does it link with the Canary Islands?

I am often surprised to discover that these lumps of volcanic rock, known as the Canary Islands, punch well above their weight when it comes to links with famous and interesting people, as well as key moments in history; the links with Admiral Nelson are yet another example.

According to the history books, Nelson lost his right eye capturing Corsica and his right arm whilst attacking the Canary Islands. He captured six and destroyed seven of Napoleon's ships at the Battle of the Nile, trapped Napoleon in Egypt, assaulted Copenhagen and dealt with Napoleon's combined French and Spanish fleets off the coast of Spain. This defeat of the French navy stopped Napoleon's power at sea, and with it, his dreams of world domination. Nelson is, of course, best remembered for winning one of the greatest naval battles in history, the Battle of Trafalgar, on 21 October 1805.

The Battle of Santa Cruz de Tenerife was launched by Nelson on 22 July 1797, and was heavily defeated. British soldiers who succeeded in reaching the beach were riddled with bullets fired by the citizens of Santa Cruz; indeed, these citizens were so closely involved in repelling the attack that many were given honours and medals. Three days later, the remains of the British landing party withdrew under a truce, which allowed the remaining British forces to return to their ships with full military honours. Part of the truce included an undertaking not to burn the town, or make any further attacks on Tenerife or the Canary Islands. The British fleet had received a painful defeat and would never again attempt to capture Santa Cruz, yet Nelson was given a hero's welcome back in England.

The Spanish suffered 30 dead and 40 injured, whilst the British lost 250 and 128 men were wounded. Nelson had lost many men and ships and so the journey back to England was going to be a problem. In a generous act of chivalry, General Gutiérrez let Nelson borrow two Spanish ships to help the British to get home, as well as allowing the British to leave with their arms and war honours. These acts of chivalry led to a friendly exchange of letters between Nelson and Gutiérrez. However, Nelson would later comment that Tenerife had been the most horrible hell he had ever endured. Nelson's letter, offering a tasty cheese as a token of gratitude, is on display at the Spanish Army Museum in Toledo.

Nelson himself had been wounded in the arm, which resulted in partial amputation. Nelson's operation was quick and the limb was thrown overboard, despite the admiral's wish to keep it, presumably as a macabre souvenir. Or was it?

One of the parts of this story that intrigues me is that during the assault against Tenerife are claims that Nelson's arm was kept as a souvenir and later stored behind the altar in Las Palmas Cathedral in Gran Canaria. Whether there is any truth in this story seems unlikely because it would have been against Roman Catholic rules, as only the relics of saints are kept under altars. Nelson may have been a great man, but a saint he was not. Maybe his arm was an exception to the rule?

Interestingly, Canarians also regard Nelson as a great man, and the date of Nelson's defeat, 25 July, is still a public holiday in Santa Cruz de Tenerife where he is described as, "The most gallant enemy we ever had."

Although some sections of my old school history book are questionable, Nelson was certainly an outstanding naval commander. However, he did say, "Kiss me, Hardy," and Captain Thomas Hardy did kiss him, twice. Sadly though, Nelson never wore an eye patch, so do remember this minor detail the next time you hire a costume for a fancy dress party.

Slavery in the Canary Islands

The horrors of slavery remain a blot upon the human conscience and collective human history. However, even in modern times, despite being outlawed many years ago, slavery still continues in various forms, such as prostitution and trafficking, around the world, including in many 'civilised' European cities. The Canary Islands have a story to tell about this perfect example of "man's inhumanity to man".

The Spanish occupation of the Canary Islands coincided with the massive deportation of the native Guanches from these islands, many of whom were sent as slaves to Spain and other European countries. The Guanches who remained on the islands were forced to work on the estates and businesses run by their new masters.

The ownership of the Canary Islands had been the subject of a long running dispute between Portugal and the Kingdom of Castille for many years. This period of instability and effective rule resulted in periodic raids on the islands to acquire slaves.

The Catholic Church developed an early form of an anti-slavery policy in the 15th century that, to its credit, attempted to rescue many Canary Islanders from the horrors of the Atlantic Slave Trade.

A papal decree, known as Sicut Dudum, was issued in 1435 by Pope Eugene IV, and sent to the Bishop of Lanzarote, which was intended to prohibit Portuguese traders from capturing and incarcerating slaves from the Canary Islands, and shipping them across the Atlantic.

Sadly, this decree only applied to those who had recently converted to Christianity or were, more likely, tricked into baptism, and threatened much dreaded excommunication to those who failed to return the newly processed Christians to the Canary Islands. This decree appears, at first light, to be an enlightened step during those turbulent times to protect Canary Islanders from the evils of this horrendous trade in human lives. However, although African converts to Christianity were now protected by the papal decree, the same did not apply to Muslims, Jews, heathens or atheists who were still considered to be 'fair game' by the Vatican.

Whatever the truth behind Pope Eugene's original intentions, his successor, Pope Nicholas V, as part of the fight against Islam in 1452, gave the Portuguese king the right to enslave people who were not Christian. Indeed, this agreement was used by the Portuguese to enslave Africans for many years to come.

Needless to say, there have been many attempts over the years by Christian academics to credit the Vatican as taking the first steps towards the banning of slavery and crediting Pope Eugene 1V, in particular, with enlightened views about freedom and morality, which many present day historians and academics say he simply does not deserve.

Sadly, the truth in the Canary Islands seems to be that you either converted in a manner dictated by Pope Eugene IV or risked being rounded up by the Portuguese and sold into slavery - not really much of a choice, was it?

The religious concept of free will appears to have been forgotten too, and due to be repeated many times in the future, with Jewish and Muslim converts joining the ranks of Christianity to avoid the violent machine of the Spanish Inquisition.

Still, as we all know, the rewriting of history is a popular pastime, as well as a strategy much loved by some politicians, historians and newspapers. Maybe some things will never change.

Wear White and Throw Talcum Powder!

I am not a violent man, and I detest violence of all kind. However, I do make an exception for just one day each year in the Canary Islands - Dia de Los Indianos (Day of the Indians).

As many Canary Islander residents and visitors already know, Carnival is celebrated with a passion in every major town in each of the seven main Canary Islands, with the main celebrations taking place in the capital cities of the islands. These celebrations take place between January and April each year with the actual dates changing according to when Easter is celebrated; this is most annoying for holidaymakers, but take that issue up with the Vatican! The forty days before Easter, known as Lent, have always been marked by the Catholic practice of giving up meat. So the fiesta of Carnival that takes place just before Lent begins on Shrove Tuesday or Mardi Gras. Carnival means 'goodbye to flesh' in Latin and became a time for a wild party, and yes, I do mean wild!

There are references to Carnival in island government records as far back as February 1556, but the fiesta has grown from strong influences from South America and the Caribbean, as many Canarians left the islands after the Spanish Conquest seeking work or their fortunes in the newly discovered lands of the Americas. Some islanders were forced to leave their homes in the Canary Islands by the Spanish government, as it wanted more people to settle in the Spanish colonies in the Americas.

Later, many Canary Islanders returned home, having made their fortune, dressed in Cuban-style white panama hats, and carrying large suitcases full of money. These newly wealthy emigrants were so full of their own self-importance, bragging about their riches, that they became the target of Carnival jokes.

On the small Canary island of La Palma they hold a unique fiesta called Fiesta de Los Indianos - The Festival of the Indians - and now often called the White Party. On the Monday before Shrove Tuesday or Mardi Gras, the city of Santa Cruz de La Palma celebrates Los Indianos Fiesta. This is a celebration of those who emigrated from the island many years ago, particularly for islands in the Caribbean and South America and then returned having made their fortune.

The fiesta is a representation of people wearing white suits and costumes of an earlier colonial period; some portray the wealthy and some are their servants. The parade takes place through the streets of the capital to the sound of Latin American music. The main event of the day is the Batalla de Polvos de Talco when bags of talcum powder are thrown at anyone standing nearby. So, by the end of the battle, most people have white hair and faces, as well as white clothes.

The traditions of this important part of La Palma's Carnival have been 'borrowed' over the years and now play a full part in the Carnival activities of the other Canary Islands.

On Carnival Monday, the streets of Santa Cruz de La Palma, as well as Las Palmas de Gran Canaria, will fill with thousands of white-clad revellers and huge clouds of talcum powder in this eccentric celebration.

Now, that is what I call a real fight and, hopefully, no one gets hurt! Maybe I should suggest this to the United Nations as a way of settling international disputes.

Living on a Volcano

Shortly after moving to the Costa Blanca, we discovered that an earthquake had destroyed a small town close to the urbanisation where we had made our home in the nineteenth century. Nowadays, we live on a volcanic island in an archipelago where there are still several active volcanoes.

One of the very first pieces of advice that we received when we arrived in the Costa Blanca, and one that we quickly learned to be particularly valuable, was "Never believe what you hear from bar gossip; always find out the facts for yourselves."

Bar chat is easy and, like Chinese Whispers, often varies significantly from the truth, and particularly if it is bad or disturbing news. However, many expats, desperate for information and advice in their own language, often readily fall for misleading information.

The current topic in many of the Brit bars in the Canary Islands is the issue of seismic shocks currently underway in one of our neighbouring islands, El Hierro. This island paradise is quickly becoming the source of overreaction and potentially dangerous gossip causing concern. So what exactly are the issues?

Over the last few weeks, seismic shocks on El Hierro, which the experts call 'swarms' have been mostly of low magnitude since they started in early July, and most of the seismic activity has been limited to about 9 to 16 kilometres below the surface. The question on everyone's mind is, "Is El Hierro heading for an eruption and, if not, what is going on beneath the surface?"

We need to remember that the Canary Islands are volcanic in origin and a wide variety of lava has erupted from Canary Island volcanoes over the years. This is what makes the islands what they are, and without the volcanic eruptions in the past there would be no Canary Islands. Experts tell us that they are similar to the volcanoes found in Hawaii, and that they share many similarities in that they can grow very large and that the style of eruption and lava flow are similar.

Should we be surprised by this seismic activity at El Hierro? The answer seems to be: No. Although the islands' volcanoes are nowhere near as productive as Hawaii or indeed Iceland, the Canary hotspot is one of the more vigorous on the planet. Does this seismic activity automatically lead to an eruption? Not necessarily, and this activity might not even lead to an eruption.

However, now that we have many of these volcanic systems so closely monitored, we notice this subtle activity as it happens, rather than waiting until we can feel the seismic activity on the surface, which usually means that an eruption is highly likely. In other words, there are plenty of warning systems and the monitoring of seismic activity is constantly taking place. These incidents should remind us that El Hierro is an active volcano and that these signals are a warning of an eruption sometime in the future.

It is always a good idea to be prepared, especially when living on a volcanic island. Over 10,000 people live on El Hierro, and emergency planning will tell residents what to do and where to go if El Hierro does decide to erupt. However, most eruptions produce lava flows and ash that are not likely to be a major threat to the island's residents unless they are caught unaware, which is highly unlikely.

People on Hawaii have been living with a constantly erupting volcano for over 30 years, Mount Etna in Sicily performs a regular firework display, as do the volcanoes in Iceland; so any activity on El Hierro should be impressive to watch, but not a catastrophe for the residents of the island, nor indeed for the rest of the Canary Islands. So back to your gin and tonics and the sun beds; you now have the facts and not just the bar gossip.

Live and Let Live

One of the many things that I love about our island in the sun is the 'live and let live' attitude of most of its people. No, I don't mean the thousands of tourists, but the true Canarian people, those who were born here and have stayed in this little corner of Paradise. As long as it is broadly legal and does not interfere with anyone else, in the main, anything goes. For many of its present day expat population, with its heady mix of faith, culture, colour and sexuality, it takes time to get used to not being judged. Maybe this stems from the time, it is said, when Spain's General Franco, intolerant of gay men in the military, would ship them off to Gran Canaria, which became a kind of penal colony for homosexuals. Whether there is real historical substance to this claim or whether it is an urban myth, I do not know for sure, but it sounds reasonable enough to me, although I am quite sure that the Yumbo Centre wasn't there then!

For me, one of the real unsung heroes of the Second World War was the code-breaker, Alan Turing. 23 June 2012 saw the centenary of his birth and it was thanks to this mathematical genius that the war against Nazi Germany ended two years earlier than it otherwise would have done. He managed to intercept and crack ingenious coded messages that gave detailed information to the Allies about the activities of German U-boats. However, in the eyes of many, there was only one problem with Alan Turing - he was gay.

Alan's reward for his pivotal role in cracking intercepted messages was quickly forgotten when, in 1952, he was prosecuted for 'indecency' after admitting a sexual relationship with a man. As an 'alternative' to imprisonment, this unsung war hero was given 'chemical castration' - a newly devised treatment for such 'disorders' at the time. In 1954, at the age of 41, he killed himself by eating a poisoned apple, which was apparently inspired by the story of Snow White. Needless to say, as with much of history, this version of events is currently being challenged and massaged for the financial gains for another film, documentary or book. However, I rather like the original version of the tragedy, agreed by the coroner at the time; it is just so dramatic!

Or was this the end of Alan Turing? This amazing man is also credited with creating the beginnings of computer technology and artificial intelligence, which led to the development of one of the first recognisable modern computers. Alan Turing's brilliance and personal life came to the attention of present day computer programmer, Dr. John Graham-Cumming, who began a petition asking for a posthumous apology from the government. Many thousands of people signed it and a previous UK Prime Minister, Gordon Brown, finally apologised for how Alan Turing was treated in the 1950s.

Whether it was through political motivation or genuine compassion for this brilliant man, and I like to think it is the latter, he said that "on behalf of the British government, and all those who live freely thanks to Alan's work, I am very proud to say: we're sorry, you deserved so much better."

My thoughts also go out to the many thousands of gay men and woman who have been persecuted over the years - just for being themselves.

All this serious stuff brings me back home to Gran Canaria. Spain's General Franco certainly had his faults, but I cannot help thinking that being shipped off to a life in the sun in the penal colony of Gran Canaria, just for being gay, was a far preferable alternative to 'chemical castration'!

Mystery, Awe and Wonder

Do you suffer from Paraskavedekatriaphobia?

We have a lot to thank the Greeks for and, no, I am not being sarcastic about the level of Greek debt. I am referring to the ability of the Greek language to make something quite ordinary sound rather special, and particularly, if there is a phobia attached to it for good measure. So, in this rather splendid word, **Paraskevi** (or Paraskeve) is Friday in Greek, Dekatria is thirteen, and phobia is a word that we all know. Paraskavedekatriaphobia is the fear of Friday 13th.

So what is it about Friday 13th? This day has been associated with market crashes and other disasters for many centuries. It is also believed that Jesus was crucified on a Friday and, in Britain, Friday the 13th was execution day and later Hangman's day, or the 'Witches Sabbath'.

Hindus believed that it was unlucky for thirteen people to gather in one place and perhaps the best known symbolism of this is the biblical 'Last Supper'; if thirteen people dine together, one will die. However, it is not always Friday that is the day of bad luck. In Spain, and other Spanish speaking countries, the saying "Martes trece, ni te cases, ni te embarques, ni de tu casa te apartes" has particular relevance. When translated it means, "On Tuesday the 13th don't marry or board a ship, or even leave your house".

In Spain and Greece, Tuesday 13th is thought to be an unlucky day and in Italy it is Friday 17th that is considered unlucky. While the origins of these unlucky days are debatable, the impact of them can be disturbing and cause considerable stress to may people around the world. Research from the USA alone considers that 21 million people have a genuine fear of this unlucky day.

What about the Chinese? They have to be careful to avoid occurrences or reminders of the number 4 during festive holidays, or when a family member is sick. Similarly, 14, 24, 34 etc are also to be avoided due to the presence of the digit 4 in these numbers. In China, these floor numbers are often avoided in hotels, offices and apartments. Table numbers 4, 14, 24 etc are also missed out in wedding receptions or other social gatherings. In Hong Kong, some apartments have missed out all the floors from 40 to 49. Immediately above the 39th floor is the 50th, leading many who are not aware of tetraphobia to believe that some floors are missing.

In cities where East Asian and Western cultures blend, such as Hong Kong and Singapore, it is possible in some buildings that both 13 and 14 are skipped as floor numbers along with all the other 4's and so it goes on. Indeed, the Finnish telecommunications firm, Nokia, also observes this superstition and try to avoid releasing any phone models that begin with the number 4, except in some rare cases, "as a gesture to Asian customers."

Am I superstitious? Certainly not. However, I would rather not walk under a ladder, I am not sure about black cats, and I do think a shamrock is a rather good thing to have... Well, it is always better to be safe than sorry, isn't it? I had better come clean about one thing though - I was born on Friday 13th, so I am not paraskavedekatriaphobic.

Imaginary noises?

I wonder if any readers have been plagued with a strange noise that they cannot find or understand? I had such an experience last week that troubled me greatly. Try as I may, I could not trace the origin of the squeaking noise in my study. At first, I thought it was a mobile phone or a gadget that needed recharging. Maybe it was a clock that needed oiling, or maybe it was a mouse? I called in our local expert on such matters, Mac our cat. He listened intently, but then paid no further attention and wandered off. Clearly it was a sound that was not coming from vermin, and he was not interested. I had to investigate further myself.

The problem reminded me of another incident some time ago. A retired couple were deeply concerned about their coffee table that had suddenly developed a ticking sound. Brenda thought that she was hearing things. Every time she entered part of the living room, she heard the strange sound, and she was certain that it was not a clock or an electrical device.

Maybe it was from next door? The ticking went on all day and all night – only it was much louder at night. Sometimes when she came into the room at night it sounded more of a scratching – was it mice or maybe rats? Colin, her husband, also heard the strange noise.

Eventually, the couple, through a process of elimination, traced the sound to a coffee table in their living room. It was a rather lovely wood coffee table, purchased over two years ago from a furniture shop in Spain, and was part of a traditional dining suite. It was made of pine, but stained a darker colour in true Spanish style. The table was silent for the first six months, but had since found a voice of its own.

Since the scratching/ticking/clicking noise started, friends were invited in to listen and they too confirmed that the strange noises were coming from the table, and that the sound appeared to be coming from one leg in particular. Many solutions were offered. Maybe the leg could be cut off? What about fumigation? How about painting it with a drop of alcohol? All the ideas were rejected because, it appears, that Brenda and Colin had become rather fond of the creature within – and they wanted to see what would happen next.

Brenda had also recently spotted a small amount of dust around the table leg and was anxious that the creature did not infest other furniture in the house. Brenda was convinced that it was not just woodworm, and that the eggs or larvae of the creature were already within the wood when the table was made.

Later, the couple happened to meet an entomologist on holiday and discussed the problem with him. He visited the couple's home, and identified 'the bug' as 'Spondylis Buprestoides' and explained about the creature's life cycle.

Apparently, the creature starts off life as one of many eggs hidden behind the bark of a pine tree. The incubation period is between one and five years, but may be as long as ten years – dependent upon climatic conditions.

Presumably, once it has been made into furniture and moved into a warm, sunny room in Spain, this hastens the process. The creature then eats its way out of its woody incubator, goes through three stages as a chrysalis and then finally emerges as a beetle. The beetle is then ready to do what all beetles do to ensure continuation of the species.

I cannot help but to feel some admiration for this creature and for its determination to survive. Brenda and Colin's furniture had been through a manufacturing process of dipping and staining before they purchased it, yet these creatures survived even these toxic processes.

So, what about the noise in my study? Sadly, it was nothing quite as exciting or as exotic as Spondylis Buprestoides, but a UPS unit (used to provide a buffer of power to my computer during our regular power cuts), which had reached the end of its useful life and was telling me that it needed to be replaced.

"The Stars Smile Down on You"

Those who have easy access to BBC television may have seen the recent series, 'The Wonders of the Solar System', hosted by the equally wondrous Professor Brian Cox, which has inspired me to take much more notice of the night sky. After all, the Canary Islands are very well placed for stargazing. During these programmes, I also wished that such a passionate and enthusiastic teacher as Brian Cox had taught me during those interminably boring physics lessons when I was a pupil at school.

Apart from one memorable experience, my studies were a very boring diet of what seemed like useless information and regurgitated facts that had no relevance to the world that I lived in. Why were we not told more about the wonders of the universe and information that related to our very being? No, the highlight of my career in physics was a pinhole camera that I made after one lesson about light, when I was suddenly and surprisingly inspired. This happened to be the beginning of my interest in photography and so possibly those boring physics lessons were not completely wasted on me after all.

My pinhole camera experiment was a revelation in more ways than one, because in the process of testing the quality of focus, a friend and I decided to photograph the rear of a teacher's car in the staff car park thinking that we could use the vehicle's number plate as a test card.

It was after we had spotted that the parked car was swaying gently from side to side that we realised that we had discovered a passionate relationship between a member of staff and the pretty French language exchange student in the back of the Morris Minor that we were photographing. Needless to say, for two curious eleven-year-olds, the whole experience was an interesting revelation into the ways of the world and made for an interesting physics lesson after all.

Returning to the television programme and the wonders of the Solar System where our own small planet Earth was both celebrated, as well as placed into the much wider context of the solar system and beyond. From this programme, I began to understand one of the sayings about the Canary Islands, possibly used far too much by travel agencies, as a place where "The stars smile down on you". Physics now, at last, began to make some sense.

Sky watching is at its best in the Canary Islands where the night skies are mostly crystal clear thanks to the efforts of successive islands' Governments over the years to reduce light pollution. The location of the Canary Islands also means that we can see all the constellations of the northern hemisphere throughout the year and mostly without the help of a telescope.

As our eyes become accustomed to the night sky, we can get a flavour of the vastness of the universe and suddenly thousands of stars seem to appear and form a glittering blanket; if we are really fortunate we can sometimes see shooting stars as well. A high position away from the main centre of population gives the best view or, in my case, a quick stroll to the seashore is usually good enough for a spectacular viewing.

It is wonderful how new information and earlier gained knowledge sometimes just falls into place when inspired or we are somehow reminded at a much later time. For me, stargazing has been a revelation, although I do still wonder how two grown adults managed to do anything of significance in such a small car! Mind you, they may just have been conjugating verbs!

Environmental

Energy Island

We hear a lot about global warming, renewable energy and climate change nowadays. The need seems to be clear enough but, as yet, only around 12.9% of the energy supply required by the world comes from renewable sources. Of that, about half comes from the burning of wood for heat and cooking in developing countries, which causes other problems. In addition, these sources are not always renewable, because they depend upon new trees being planted, which is often overlooked.

The fastest growing technology is solar electric power, yet this continues to be among the most expensive option and will continue to be so for several more years. The good news is that a recent report on climate change says that renewable technologies could provide 80 per cent of the world's energy needs in the next thirty years or so. However, there is a solution closer to hand than we may think, and that solution is just a few hops across the water to one of our beautiful islands - El Hierro, once known as 'Fire Island'.

El Hierro gained its original name of 'Fire Island' from its origins of volcanic eruptions many years ago, and although volcanic activity has decreased, the natural Earth forces of water and wind remain. These power sources are now due to be harnessed so that by 2012, this small island in the Atlantic will be the first to be able to generate all of its electricity needs from sources that are renewable.

There is plenty of wind on El Hierro and visitors will have noticed that the reason that most plants and trees seem to be suffering from osteoporosis is that they have become bent by its force. There is enough rain to meet the needs of the 10,700 inhabitants of the island, and the five wind turbines in the north east of the island will produce enough electric power to supply all of the island's energy needs, as well as pumping water from a reservoir near the harbour to a bigger reservoir at a higher level within a volcanic crater.

What if there is no wind? Well, in that case, water is released from the higher reservoir through these pipes that will drive hydraulic turbines to create electric energy. Therefore, electricity can be produced by wind or water power. Clever stuff!

This project in El Hierro is the first that does not use electricity produced from traditional methods, and contributes to moving the island towards being totally self-sufficient. When the project is completed in 2012, this renewable energy project will produce three times the island's needs for electricity, including electricity for 60,000 tourists who visit each year. Also, when there is a surplus of electricity produced, this will be used for three desalination plants to convert seawater into fresh water for irrigation.

In 2012, the oil-fired electricity power station that currently produces electricity for the island will close, reducing carbon emissions and saving on the cost of importing 6000 tonnes of oil each year. Although this renewable energy project will have cost €65 million, future income from this energy source will eventually repay this investment, cover future maintenance and replacement costs, and still make a profit.

This project alone means that the island will meet 100% of its energy needs by 2015, but El Hierro has launched other sustainability projects too. The island is mainly agricultural, and is a leader in organic farming, as well as in projects that convert sewage into fertiliser and methane.

Even more energy savings are planned after 2012 by replacing all the cars on the island with electric vehicles, and although the investment costs for charging terminals and purchasing the vehicles will need a similar investment to the wind energy project, this would be repaid in ten years, assuming that drivers are charged the same price as for petrol. Yes, there is always a catch!

Lizards Prefer Islands

One of Bella's favourite pastimes is lizard hunting. Bella is unlike any other dog that we have known, and her terrier nature is certainly one of her very prominent features. If it moves she will chase it, whereas Barney, our self-willed corgi, would just look at something thrown for him to fetch, stare back at us with a "fetch it yourself" look and wander away for yet another snooze in the sun. On our walks, Bella loves to run on the sunny sandy or rocky wasteland areas where she knows that she will find many an unsuspecting lizard peacefully sunbathing. Fortunately, they are all far too quick for her; they hear us coming and scurry away before Bella can catch them.

These creatures fascinate me, and when I am walking on my own without Bella, I watch them carefully. I have the same feeling about lizards as I do tortoises, crocodiles, elephants and camels. They represent an age long gone, and seem almost stranded in the modern day world.

I am told that lizards in the Canary Islands are harmless and do not attack people. They often live in the gaps between rocks, as well as in walls, and I know of tourists in some areas who have fed them when they have appeared in their holiday accommodation.

Apparently, they like to eat crumbs, cactus flowers, grapes, biscuits and fresh fruit, as well as fresh hibiscus flowers. It is the females who are the friendliest of the species and may even jump on your hand for a while, whilst the males are very territorial. Tourists often spot them basking in the sun on a really hot day on their stomachs and with their feet off the ground. They are certainly fascinating creatures to watch.

Several species of lizard exist uniquely in the Canary Islands, including the Canary Gecko, which is found nowhere else on earth, and thrives on the smaller islands. Indeed, it seems that lizards prefer islands. Scientific research has shown that this is because limited areas and isolation on islands reduces the number of likely predators and competition pressures.

As a result, island lizards are able to reach exceptionally high population densities. I am not a lizard expert, but I am aware of a fascinating story about lizards that relates to one of the smaller Canary Islands, the island of La Palma and the La Palma Giant Lizard.

The La Palma Giant Lizard disappeared about 500 years ago. It was one of countless species that was thought to be extinct. It was believed to have gone into decline with the arrival of humans on its native home in the Canary Islands.

In 2007 one La Palma Giant Lizard was discovered alive and well on the island. Little is known about these lizards, but the one that was found measured about 30 centimetres long - a size that Bella would not approve of.

Researchers hope to revisit the island over time in an attempt to find a breeding population. Two other species of giant lizards have been rediscovered in the Canary Islands in recent times such as in 1974 and 1999, the El Hierro Giant Lizard and La Gomera Giant Lizard.

As I chase across the rough ground with Bella in the hunt for yet another phantom lizard, I try to tell Bella that she will never catch one, so why bother? It would be much more fun to chase her ball instead. She ignores me and I suspect that she lives in the hope that one day her opportunity will come.

Daring to dream the impossible

Teachers have a responsibility to ensure that their pupils can read and write, and are numerate. It is a stated aim that they should do well in their SATS and achieve good grades in their GCSEs and beyond. However, education is much more than this and wise teachers place learning about life, learning to being happy and fulfilled human beings, as well as daring to dream the unthinkable at the very top of their priorities. By this I mean that creativity, and the ability for clear thinking, as well as original thinking, are all necessary for the process of 'real education' to be successful and for the ultimate survival of the species.

I like to hear stories of people defying the odds, achieving the unachievable and daring to be different. When faced with crises and potential disaster the human race has always had a remarkable capacity for daring to dream the impossible to get out of a tight corner. Over the years, explorers, wartime leaders, artists, philosophers, musicians and sportsmen and women have all contributed to the feeling that the impossible can not only be dreamt about, but can also be made real. History also teaches us that we are often at our best when faced with a crisis.

Many of us will have witnessed the horror story of drought and famine in Africa unfolding daily on our television screens. Charitable appeals and harrowing stories are now the nightmare of television news. We want to help, but we often feel helpless against such odds.

However, one man may just have an answer to some of the current problems facing the world. Georges Mougin, often dismissed as a crank, recognised some 40 years ago that 70 per cent of the world's fresh water reserves are locked in the ice caps, yet thousands of people are dying of drought and famine in Africa. To Georges, the answer is simple - tow giant icebergs thousands of miles from the polar ice caps to Africa or, more precisely, to the Canary Islands.

Georges initially received backing from a Saudi prince; however, experts told him that the project was unworkable and it remained as an idea at the back of his mind for decades. Computer technology has since demonstrated that his imaginative project to tap into the 'floating water reservoirs' is both achievable and affordable. 3-D computer simulations show that a single tugboat could transport a seven million ton iceberg from Newfoundland to the Canary Islands in less than five months without the iceberg melting.

After a suitable iceberg has been chosen, it is lassoed and an insulating skirt wraps the submerged section of the iceberg. This skirt acts rather like a wetsuit, holding in the melted water and insulating the iceberg. A tug, assisted by sail and ocean currents, then drags the iceberg, at one knot per hour. 141 days later, the tug and its cargo of ice should arrive in the Canary Islands - considered to be an ideal holding location from where the water can be directed to drought spots in Africa.

Tests indicate that just 38 per cent of the 525ft-deep iceberg would melt during its journey - with plenty of fresh water remaining for drought-ridden areas. It is calculated that a 30-million ton iceberg could provide 500,000 people with fresh water for a year. Daring to dream the impossible could mean that Georges Mougin, armed with the latest evidence, will be able to fund a trial run next year. I bet his class teacher would be very proud of him.

Solar Rubbish Bins

A recent visit to the UK, after a break of several years, prompted a number of comments from family and friends about the things that had changed during our time away, along the lines of "Have you noticed many changes?"

Well, the weather was still damp and cold; I was struck by how green and beautiful the countryside looked and there was not a cactus in sight. I was interested to see how many rather ordinary secondary schools, that I had previously known, now proudly announced that they were 'Academies', although apart from the new signs, I cannot comment whether anything inside these schools had actually improved, or whether the pupils were more academically successful or not.

I did notice that people seemed to be behaving in a more frenetic manner than usual; they looked more troubled than I remember, and most conversations were about "The Recession", "Nick Clegg" or "the demise of the NHS". The homes of relatives and friends also seemed much colder than I recall, apart from one of my nephews who lit a real log fire to warm us up. Scarily, a few friends and relatives were wearing body-warmers and hats - inside the house! Maybe after several years of living in the Canary Islands our blood really has thinned, or maybe our families and friends have just turned down their thermostats, because of the horrendous gas and electricity bills.

What really did make an impression upon me were the solar rubbish bins in Bournemouth Gardens. First of all, I was impressed that solar energy was at last being taken seriously by a borough council that is not usually given credit as being particularly forward-looking, but also that any such devices appeared in the UK at all; after all, they do require frequent sunlight. This very clever machine, affectionately known as the "Big Belly Solar Compactor", looked like many other large metal rubbish bins, but a solar panel provided all the power it needed to compress the rubbish as it became full.

One of the gardeners who was planting seedlings nearby, assured me that the bin now needed emptying every two weeks rather than daily as previously, which I found very hard to believe, given the size of the bin. Even so, this device should represent a significant saving in manpower over time, assuming that the sun does its bit too. Why do we not have these bins in the place where the sun shines to order, the Canary Islands?

Bearing in mind that the Canary Islands are now home to the largest solar power station in Europe (at Granadilla in Tenerife) and there are many companies dedicated to the development of solar power in the Canary Islands, the lack of solar installations on domestic and commercial properties always surprises me.

Given the heavy increases in electricity bills that all Canary Islanders have had to face in recent years, one would imagine that there would be a huge demand for solar panels, yet I see no evidence of this. In contrast, our small neighbouring island, El Hierro, is already well known for its recent headline grabbing volcanic eruptions, but less well known for its achievements over a twenty-five year period in making the island fully self sufficient with 100 per cent renewable energy, which is a clear example of what can be achieved with determination, as well as inspiring leadership.

El Hierro, which means "island of fire" – has an abundance of wind and water and, thanks to the combined forces of the two, will shortly be able to provide a supply of clean energy for the islanders. Until then, most of the electricity needed is from diesel fuel shipped to the island in oil tankers. The new renewable power sources will lead to a reduction of around 18,000 tons of carbon dioxide emissions every year. Given this result for a small island, just think of what could be achieved for larger communities worldwide - solar rubbish bins for all!

Are we bothered?

"What the British can't see won't bother them" was the response from the British Ambassador to Spain when asked about the recent news of the authorisation of an oil company to explore for oil off the Canary Islands.

Although mindful of the creed of most Ambassadors to be "All things to all men" (such is the world of diplomacy), it is understandable that the Ambassador was not in a position to criticise the decision of the Spanish Government. However, to many Islanders, as well as environmentalists in Spain, his inappropriate and ill-timed comment at the time of the announcement was regarded as unhelpful at best, and insensitive at worst. The islanders are bothered.

It is certainly true that the British like their holidays in the sun, but many are also concerned about environmental dangers facing the world, as well as in an area so rich in marine life as the Canary Islands. Holidaymakers flock to the islands each year in search of sunshine and beautiful beaches, to enjoy fresh fish and to explore some of the more remote areas in the mountains. Will they really continue to do so with oil platforms scattered around the area and polluting our ocean? Holidaymakers are bothered.

Most holidaymakers are well aware of the issues surrounding the dangers to the fishing industry and local population should another disaster occur, as in the Gulf of Mexico.

Warnings from Greenpeace too highlight the immense dangers to the environment from all forms of deep-sea exploration. Of course, the irony is that fuel from oil is required to bring holidaymakers to the islands in the first place. Do we really have to see the dangers before we are aware of them, and become concerned about their impact to ourselves and future generations? Most British holidaymakers are bothered.

The Spanish Government needs more revenue and, in theory, a reduction in oil bills would significantly help the economy in time. The Spanish Government also maintains that their decision will bring much needed revenue and jobs to the islands, as well as Peninsular Spain. This is indeed tempting, as the islands have one of the largest unemployment statistics in Spain, and the lack of opportunity for its young people is heartbreaking. However, this claim is disputed by many politicians in the Canary Islands, who comment that most jobs in the new oil industry will go to people from outside the Canary Islands, and its largely unskilled workforce will not be needed and neither, in time, will there be a tourist and fishing industry to sustain them in the traditional manner. Many island workers and young people are bothered.

Ironically, the British government has just given BP the go-ahead to drill a new deep-water well in Scottish waters off the northwest coast of the Shetland Islands. The issues to be faced in Shetland are very similar to those in the Canary Islands, and environmentalists were outraged with the announcement, quoting the potential risks to the climate and threat of an oil spill.

Is deep-water drilling really worth the risk? Should we not be phasing out our use of oil instead of chasing ever more difficult sources? These are some of the comments that are currently echoing in both the Canary Islands, as well as the Shetland Islands. Are the Shetland Islanders bothered about the risks to their beautiful and unique islands? Of course they are.

Only last week, investigations began into a large oil spill from a platform in the North Sea that was "allowed to disperse naturally" into the ocean. The spill of 23 tonnes of crude oil came from the Tern oil platform 100 miles north east of Lerwick, the capital of the Shetland Islands. The oil company stated that the spill was a result of "a temporary upset in the production process whilst cleaning up a new well", and the spill was stopped quickly and posed no risk to either crew or the platform. This one incident is a taste of issues that could seriously affect both island archipelagos for generations to come.

I have no answer to the twin dilemmas of the demand for oil balanced with environmental and climatic impact. However, I do know that warnings about the environment and climate change should be taken seriously and that we do need to reduce our dependency upon oil. Meanwhile, a clear debate about all the issues involved, as well as alternatives to the current proposals are what the inhabitants of both the Shetlands and the Canary Islands require. Dismissive comments such as those made by the Ambassador about the current proposals are unhelpful. In the words of comedienne, Catherine Tate, yes, we are bothered.

A Prickly Issue

My Great Aunt Gertie sent me a present by post for my seventh birthday. How pleased I was, until I opened it. The package contained a small book, 'The Observer's Book of Cacti'. Now anyone who really knew me in those days could see that I was besotted with adventure books, books about animals and islands. Indeed, two of my favourite presents were 'The Observer's Book of Dogs' and 'The Observer's Book of Cats', and I really wanted the one about reptiles. My disappointment was such that I wrote the obligatory thank you letter to Aunt Gertie under sufferance, and as instructed by my mother, and tossed the book ungratefully onto my bookshelf and forgot all about it.

Many years later, I was doing what many would-be expats do before leaving their country of origin, which is the painful decision of what to take and what to leave behind. My collections of books, records, CDs and cassettes all had to go to the charity shop, and I contented myself with the thought that if there was something that I really wanted in the future, I could buy it again. In the end, giving all my childhood memories away was just too painful, and I secreted a small collection of books from my childhood in a relative's disused garage.

Recently, I had to return to the UK, and I was drawn to my elderly relative's garage, and discovered the box of books, still languishing where I had left them, but now dusty and covered with cobwebs.

As I sorted through the books, memories came flooding back like old friends. Rupert Annuals, Sooty Annuals, Robinson Crusoe, Swallows and Amazon, The Famous Five and The Secret Seven all brought back happy memories of, what I seem to remember, as endlessly long and hot summer evenings, when I went to bed early and read for hours. Suddenly, I spotted a book that I did not recall ever opening, 'The Observer's Book of Cacti'.

I sat on the corner of a dusty old bench and flicked through its contents. It was not such a bad book after all. The shiny, printed-paper revealed some good quality photographs, and the text was quite revealing. I had never realised what very adaptable and hardy plants cactus are. I popped the small book into my rucksack, and was determined to read it in further detail when I arrived home.

It was on the long and tedious flight home to Gran Canaria that I opened the book once again, and suddenly realised an answer to an ongoing problem. Like so many expats, I miss the greenery, trees and flowers of the UK. I am not a skilful gardener, but I do know what I like. Occasionally, impulse buying gets the better of me and I am tempted to buy plants that are totally unsuited to the desert conditions in the part of the Canary Islands where I live. Hydrangeas, rhododendrons, magnolias, azaleas and orchids all suffer the same fate during the hot summer months on this island. Suddenly, it came to me. I knew what I would grow in my garden - cactus, and lots of them!

I have since read The Observer's Book of Cacti in detail, and purchased dozens of flowering cactus for one euro each. These fascinating living gems have beautiful and dramatic flowers, and not the stuck on plastic flowers that adorn the overpriced cactus for sale in UK garden centres. Several months on, the cactus plants are growing fast and my garden is now full of colour. Finally, I have learned to appreciate cactus and to grow plants to suit where I live, and not to attempt to copy the plants that grew in my previous garden in the UK. In a way, it is another expat lesson; it is all about recognising and fitting in with where we live, and not trying to make our new surroundings fit around our own limited perspective of life. Thank you, Aunt Gertie.

What a load of old rubbish!

Visitors to smart, upmarket Meloneras and the agreeably tired Playa del Ingles often comment about how well the gardens, roundabouts and public facilities are maintained and that the area is mostly free of litter. In the main, this is true, and so it should be given the huge amount of tourists that visit the area each year, together with accompanying revenue. Basic cleanliness and tidy, litter free areas are the least that we should be offering our visitors.

Sadly, all is not 'smelling of roses' in some of the outlying areas of the municipality of San Bartolome de Tirajana (often referred to as Maspalomas). Some of the outlying areas and villages are sadly becoming increasingly neglected, refuse collection has been reduced, and rubbish allowed to run riot. One example is in the village of Castillo del Romeral, a pleasant village, which is mostly ignored by tourists. A central rubbish collection point adjacent to a very pleasant beach and an open air swimming pool has rarely been emptied in recent weeks, and a huge amount of litter including old sofas, cookers, garden furniture and builders' rubble has been allowed to accumulate. Although the massive skip is compressed and emptied from time to time, it is not frequent enough, and the municipality appears to have given up on removing the larger items and the rubbish that has collected adjacent to it.

The problem is exacerbated by local vagrants who gather, argue and fight for the honour of climbing into the skip and sorting through the rubbish in the forlorn hope of finding something useful to sell and yes, often to eat. Such desperation is a sign of very difficult times, yet many cannot be bothered to throw unwanted items back into the skip, preferring to strew the area with plastic bags, unwanted fruit, vegetables, left over meat and fish instead. As a result, vermin, cockroaches and flies are having a wonderful time, and the smell is appalling for local residents and visitors. Even the motor caravans that gather nearby each weekend now give the area a wide berth. Village locals do not help the situation either. Building rubble, bottles and boxes, broken furniture, unwanted electrical items and broken furniture do not appear miraculously by themselves. On several occasions I have seen young children and dogs with cut hands, feet and paws from the shards of broken glass strewn nearby.

Our nearest town of Vecindario in the neighbouring municipality of Santa Lucia appears to deal with the issue in a much more practical manner. Instead of open skips, vulnerable to the wind, vermin and vagrants, neat stainless steel hoppers are installed in the streets, complete with cavernous hoppers hidden beneath, which are regularly emptied by the municipality. It is impossible to dump large furniture, builders' rubble and garden rubbish in these bins, which instead has to be taken elsewhere, presumably to dump in Castillo del Romeral or another forgotten village in a neighbouring municipality!

Cutbacks, recession, holidays and staffing levels are just some of the excuses that I hear for this current lack of attention to basic refuse management. For goodness sake, basic hygiene and security are the hallmarks of any civilised society, and it does not require a huge amount of funding to achieve a minimum standard. Let's make a start by cleaning up our own mess.

Cleaning the floors

I rarely hear the irritating sound of vacuum cleaners coming from neighbouring homes in the Canary Islands, where I live. I often hear that relentless drone from British, German and Scandinavian homes, but rarely from Canarian or Spanish homes. It is something that I have noticed, yet has remained at the back of my mind until recently when one of our Canarian neighbours asked us to her home for a coffee.

Her home was spotless, and knowing what a busy lady she was, I commented upon the gleaming floors. "Oh, just a daily brush and a mop and bucket," she answered, with a smile. I thought back to our own home, complete with marble floors, which we had so foolishly been taken in by when we purchased.

Believe me, marble floor tiles are a complete nightmare and unless they are treated very carefully, always tend to look as if they are in need of a good scrub. Marble tiles absorb red wine stains too, which is not good and they mark very easily. We regularly use a steam cleaner to bring them back to their original shine. It is a painstaking process, but well worth the effort. Next time we move, it will be to a home with the usual ceramic floor tiles, not marble.

Our neighbour went on to tell me that she has a vacuum cleaner, but only uses it to clean the inside of her car occasionally. She had always used a brush, just like her mother and grandmother, which still remains the preferred choice for many Canarians and Spanish families. She gave me a few tips on how best to maintain our marble floors in pristine condition, and I promised that I would give them a try.

I will not be forsaking our beloved Dyson though! I thought back to the days when we were living in the UK. Heaven knows what a forensic investigation would have revealed in all those fitted carpets! A Dyson with truly impressive suction really was the only answer to ensure a basic level of cleanliness in those days, and particularly with dogs as part of the family. After all, it was the development and widespread use of the original 'Hoover' that virtually wiped out human fleas in the UK population, almost overnight, so vacuum cleaners do have a lot going for them.

Whilst on the subject of cleaning, our young road sweeper still sweeps the paths and roads in our village with the branch of a palm tree. He claims that it is much more effective than a commercially produced brush, and the results that he achieves would certainly seem to bear that out.

I have recently been tempted by the new electronic floor cleaning robots that are currently available in many electrical stores. The demonstrations look highly effective and, as a dedicated gadget lover, I cannot wait to try one for myself. I will let you know how I get on.

Places to Visit

Head for the Mountains!

I had a 'significant birthday' a few days ago. Birthdays are strange things, and I guess I now take the view that if we are lucky enough to celebrate one, it means that we are still alive which, I guess, is something of a plus. However, what to do and where to go was initially something of a problem.

Frankly, I didn't fancy the idea of a party, dinner and the like this year, but really wanted to go somewhere, and well away from the tourist route, where my partner and I could both relax, enjoy a change of scene, eat good food (we are both vegetarians, which can still be an issue in the Canary Islands) and would, hopefully, provide a stimulus for my next novel. I really didn't want to travel too far, and have the hassle of flying, nor did I want to leave the fluffies (Bella and Mackitten) in their respective kennels and cattery for too long either. All in all, it was a tall order, but one which we resolved remarkably easily.

We finally headed to the Parador at Cruz de Tejeda, billed as being in "the heart of Gran Canaria". What a treat! Not only did this Parador offer the most spectacular views in the most peaceful of settings, but the food was exquisite, the service remarkable, and facilities second to none. Best of all, this Parador was only about 30 kilometres from home - although it seemed much further, because of the winding mountain roads.

The whole experience was a delightful, as well as an enriching experience that I would happily recommend to anyone, but it has set me thinking about exploring more Paradors in some of the other islands, as well as in Peninsular Spain too.

In the UK, I was a member and supporter of the National Trust, and we would often enjoy time exploring some of the magnificent buildings and gardens open to the public. In many ways, the Paradors in Spain fulfil a similar purpose - that of both preservation and accessibility.

Paradores de Turismo de España is a chain of luxury hotels that was an idea initiated by King Alfonso XIII, as a way of promoting tourism in Spain. What a good idea it was too. It is now a profitable state-run enterprise and the hotels are situated in palaces, palaces, convents, fortresses, monasteries and other historic buildings throughout the country.

There are 93 Paradors in Spain that operate from Galicia in the north-west to Catalonia and Andalusia in the south of Spain. There are five Paradors in the Canary Islands, as well as in the Spanish cities in North Africa. They are not particularly cheap to stay in, and prices vary according to room, region and season. However, there are often special discounts for residents (as in the Canary Islands) and other offers from time to time.

There is an equivalent organisation also operating in Portugal. These are called, the 'Pousadas de Portugal', and were founded in 1942, and I am told that these are very similar to the Spanish model.

During our stay, I spoke to one gentleman who has visited many Paradors over recent months. Both he and his wife are truly hooked on the experience. Sadly, he has a life threatening condition, but both he and his wife are determined to make as much of the time that they have together as possible. They have the financial resources and, as a result, they visit Paradors throughout Spain for part of each month throughout the year.

It seemed to me a very good way of spending your money, if you can afford it, and to enjoy it whilst you can. As for cost, they actually compare very favourably to the price of a night in a Premier Inn in the UK, particularly if you take advantage of the special offers, and the food is much better too.

As for my next book? Yes, it did the trick and I am sure that the influence of the Parador in Cruz de Tejeda will make an appearance in a future novel.

Just 27 Crossings!

At around four kilometres long, the Avenida de Canarias in Vecindario on the island of Gran Canaria is billed as "the longest shopping street in Spain". It is not difficult to believe such an awesome statistic, particularly when you have spent a good part of the morning trying to drive from El Doctoral, where it begins, to its end. On a good day, I have managed the journey in about twenty minutes, but on a particularly bad day it has taken me nearly two hours. If you are the type of driver that suffers from a lack of patience, or high blood pressure, I suggest that you do not undertake the experience.

Without doubt, the Avenida de Canarias is one of the worst roads that I have driven through, and when I first arrived I used to ask why it had remained so. Surely, traffic could be diverted around Vecindario and leave this nightmare of a shopping street to take its chance with the locals? Of course, now that I know the town, I realise that this is not the answer. Diverting traffic would immediately destroy it as a shopping centre and shoppers would instead drive to one of the many soulless shopping centres nearby and desert a once thriving shopping centre, leading it into decay and eventual ruin.

When I lived in the UK there were often complaints that, "All high streets look the same". Partly, this was true because each high street usually consisted of a Boots the Chemist, WH Smith, maybe a Debenhams, HMV, Dixons, Marks and Spencer and Woolworths (remember those?).

On my recent visit to the UK, I noticed that in many high streets, familiar stores had either closed, gone into receivership or moved into the new out-of-town shopping centre. The previously well known shops in the high street were now replaced by empty boarded up units sporting "For Sale " and "To Rent" notices, often with some very attractive graffiti. A general air of depression replaced what were once very busy and successful high street shopping centres. As they say, be careful what you wish for.

Back to the Canary Islands and the Avenida de Canarias. In this street there is no picturesque, historical quarter, or indeed anything vaguely historic, so cross it off your list for sightseeing. However, what it lacks in cultural antiquities it certainly makes up for in shopping. This very busy street has all manner of shops and businesses; there is very little that you cannot purchase if you have the time, an empty credit card and the energy to wander its length.

Here, you will not find the faceless chains of clothing and electrical stores, but real shops run by real people whose livelihoods depend upon selling merchandise and services that customers want. A mix of Spanish, Canarian, Hungarian, African, Indian, Pakistani, Chinese, Argentinean, Cuban, Polish, German and Swedish traders makes for a heady, yet healthy, mix of language, culture, faith and wares on offer.

Despite my earlier reservations, I now enjoy exploring this street. It is a place to sit in one of its many bars and restaurants and pass the time 'people watching'. The buildings are not particularly attractive or architecturally relevant, but it is a place where real people live and work. The street employs many traffic wardens, for want of a better name. These men and women not only allow you to park your car along the length of the street for 50 cents, but also most are friendly and polite, happy to give local information, and will often stop the traffic to help you reverse out of your parking space, if things get a little tight!

There are 27 zebra crossings from beginning to end, although I am convinced that more have been added since the last time that I counted. This high number of zebra crossing are genuinely needed as there are always many people attempting to leap across the road, usually without looking or waiting for the traffic to stop. This is a street where, despite the heavy traffic, the pedestrian reigns supreme.

So, if you want to escape from the busy tourist centres in the south and take a glimpse at what the locals get up to during their time off work, head to Vecindario for the day. By the way, in the Avenida de Canarias you can still get an excellent cup of coffee for just 90 cents!

Small, but beautifully formed

A special anniversary and the need for a break away recently led us to El Hierro, the smallest and most westerly of the Canary Islands. As we live on one of the larger islands, Gran Canaria, it seemed strange to many of our friends that we should chose to spend our holiday on one of the other islands on the archipelago.

However, each of the seven inhabited Canary Islands are very different in character, scenery and tradition to each other and, being a relatively short hop away, made an ideal break.

El Hierro is within the sphere of influence of Tenerife, but is nothing like its bigger, brasher brother. This island is quiet, very quiet and, at times, I had the feeling that maybe only half a dozen people actually lived there! In reality, it is more like 10,000 residents, but where they all hide, I really cannot say.

If you are only really interested in bars, clubs and entertainment then forget El Hierro. If you are interested in beaches with golden or white sands, then El Hierro is certainly not for you. However, if you are interested in spectacular, long walks, a healthy sea breeze and breathtaking scenery, I can highly recommend it as a place to relax and unwind. The real world seems a very long way on El Hierro.

This island makes little allowance for the tourist. Although maps are relatively easy to find, and obtaining a guide book in English, or even Spanish, was a challenge. Finding one in German was easier! Even the tourist information office in the island's capital, Valverde, seemed politely disinterested in tourists, and despite a visit when we first arrived in the town, it took a second visit to extract information from the tourist office that there was actually a museum in the town, quite close to the Tourist Information Office, but hidden from view and considered unworthy of a mention, it seemed!

Visitors travel to El Hierro to walk, photograph and relax. There is also considerable interest in the island's volcanic activity, which may explain why many houses appear to be boarded up. It was fascinating to overhear groups of seismologists talking earnestly over their laptops at breakfast, examining charts and graphs of recently recorded volcanic activity.

Whilst we were on the island, a visiting party of elderly men and women visited from Lanzarote, another Canary Island, complete with their folk music group. It was only a day visit, but they were certainly out to enjoy themselves.

I didn't really want to hire a car on this holiday, as I see quite enough of them during the year, and so we decided to make do with local buses! Needless, to say, that was our greatest mistake. The microbus to our hotel, which also delivered newspapers, ran only once a day, and links with other routes were almost impossible to work out and it was not the most reliable of services. A hire car is essential if you want to make the most of your holiday and see all that the island has to offer.

I left the island determined to return again one day, but next time it will be with a car and preferably a direct flight from Gran Canaria, as a stopover in Tenerife North Airport is not particularly pleasant due to the strong crosswinds!

The Canary Islander

Reminders of Home

A Mini in the Canaries

Did you have a love affair with a mini? No, I should clarify, I did say "with a mini" and not "in a mini" or "on a mini" - that is the stuff for a different publication. I read somewhere once that around seventy-five per cent of the British population of a certain age, have had a love affair with a mini at sometime in their lives. I am not talking about the expensive BMW version, as superb as they are, but the original Alec Issigonis design, much loved in some of the British comedies and many other films; indeed, it was a true car of the people.

My first mini cost the princely sum of fifty pounds and, to be honest, was a little rough. The colour was supposed to be 'Snowberry White', but the exact shade had long since disappeared under layers of grime and red rust. However, after fitting a couple of new wings, the use of a generous supply of filler and a complete paint re-spray, which my father and brother did at home, new seat covers, a padded steering wheel, a new cassette radio and a set of remould tyres, it was more or less ready to take to the road. It certainly looked the part, although you wouldn't want to rub your hand over the bodywork - it felt like sandpaper, because Dad hadn't quite got the hang of the new spray gun and carried out the process on a windy day in a dusty Lincolnshire garage! My mini took me from Lincolnshire to Dorset many times during my student days, and I lost count as to how many people and luggage I managed to stuff into it at any one time.

I haven't seen a 'real mini' for many years, either in the UK or in Spain, and I have to admit that I do have a real craving for one. It was the first vehicle that I had that had so much character, manoeuvrability and was, to use modern parlance, seen as exceedingly cool - at that time anyway. On the downside, I seemed to be forever paying for new track rod ends (whatever they were), a new sub frame, as well as endless supplies of tyres and brakes. Rust was always a problem, but my Dad was always on hand with his spray gun and revised techniques, which never quite worked out, because it always felt like sandpaper, although I didn't complain. Nowadays of course, it would never have been allowed on the road.

I spotted my first mini for many years in the Canary Islands the other day. It sat proudly on an industrial estate in Arinaga. It gleamed in the sunshine and the only thing that ruined the effect was a Honda sunshade in the front windscreen. New seat covers had been fitted and the metal work shone. It was the much-loved car of an enthusiast. The little car seemed to be beautifully cared for and was painted in a dashing shade of blue. I didn't rub my hand over the bodywork, because I thought that might lead to an arrest, but I can guarantee that it would not feel like sandpaper. How I craved to drive it!

The Grandfather Clock

I have a grandfather clock in my home. It is not antique, nor is it particularly valuable, but it is priceless to me. It is a clock made by and given to me by my father many years ago. My father was not a carpenter by trade, but when he retired, he spent much of his leisure time in his shed at the bottom of the garden indulging his love of carpentry and wood turning. I used to tease him that it was only to get away from mother for a few hours; he would smile and say nothing.

Over a period of ten years from his retirement to his early death, my father made four grandfather clocks, one for each of my two brothers and myself and a larger one for my mother, which I have now; with the one originally given to me now passed on to my nephew for safekeeping. My father imported high quality timepieces direct from a clockmaker in Germany, but all the cabinet work was his own design and craftsmanship.

I often look at the clock with admiration, knowing that it took many hours of painstaking, detailed craftsmanship and remembering that it was made with love. I often rub my hands over the highly polished surface, and feel the finely turned carvings. I listen to that stealthy reassuring tick that makes our home feel a home. It makes me feel relaxed and I sense a very strong link with the past.

All expats have to make serious choices once they opt for a new life in another country. Many sell or dispose of the family possessions that they may have collected, and make a financial and personal decision to buy new furniture and household goods in their new country; this is often the cheapest and wisest option. Others, like myself, decide to take their memories with them, in the form of books, records, personal items, family heirlooms and furniture. This is by no means the cheapest option and I have paid a lot of money to furniture removers over the years to transport items that mean a lot to me, but are of no particular value, to my home in the Canary Islands.

Is it worth it? Yes, for me it certainly is. I look at a highly polished coffee table in our living room knowing that it was purchased at a time when money was short for the very first home that my partner and I set up together so long ago. A pinewood dining table and chairs that have mellowed to the most beautiful golden colour over time sits in our dining room, and I remember many meals shared with family and friends; the broken and lovingly repaired swivel chair in the hallway that my brother, now deceased, sat on and broke. I still remember the initial embarrassed silence and the subsequent guffaws of stifled laughter that is still the stuff of family memories. It still makes me smile to remember the incident.

Every Sunday evening I open the door to my grandfather clock to reset the time and to pull the heavy chain that will rewind it for another week. Although it has been many years since it left my parents' home, that unique smell of polish and the 'family home smell' that most of us will recall from childhood in our own family homes, hit me when I open the door. For a brief moment, it is like stepping back in time; the memories come flooding back.

Was it worth the expense of transportation to an island in the Atlantic? For sentimentalists like myself, yes, it was worth every penny.

Reclaiming the flag

Visitors to the Canary Islands and Spain will notice that the flying of flags is a popular pastime. Public and government buildings, as well as many private organisations, usually proudly display three flags in the Canary Islands: the Spanish flag, the Canary Islands' flag and the flag of the European Union, and we even have another that is specific to the island of Gran Canaria. Yes, despite the usual negativity and cynicism of many Brits, the European Union is still a popular and welcome concept in many European countries. Spain's recent victory in the European Cup has also seen a flurry of Spanish and Canarian flags adorning the homes, cars and bodies of many islanders, and has been a delight to see.

Flags are important; they are a symbol of unity and pride. Although I personally find flag waving and adorning myself in the Union flag embarrassing, I respect and admire those who do. However, this is not the case throughout the world; we have only to look at the example of Northern Ireland, where flying a Union flag, or indeed the Republican Tricolour, is seen as provocative, and is one of the reasons why UK driving licences do not include a Union flag, but only the European Union flag, for fear of upsetting the sensitivities of some in parts of the United Kingdom. This is a position that I understand is soon likely to change with the inclusion of both the Union flag and the European Union flag on UK driving licences, with the exception of those licences issued in Northern Ireland.

As a child, I was always taught that the national flag was called the Union Jack. In later years, we were told that this should only refer to the flag when being flown on warships, and that Union flag was the correct terminology. I understand that the position has changed once again and we can call it whatever we wish. The idea that the Union flag should only be described as the Union Jack when flown from the bows of a warship is a relatively recent idea. The Admiralty itself frequently referred to the flag as the Union Jack, whatever its use, and in 1902 the Admiralty declared that either name could be officially used. Parliamentary approval was given as long ago as 1908 when it was stated, "the Union Jack should be regarded as the National flag". Therefore, I am going to return to using the original terminology that I learned at school, the Union Jack, from now on.

It recent years there has been a noticeable reduction in patriotism and pride in the UK, matched by a significant decline in 'flying the flag'. Much of this seems to have come from the idea that displaying, waving and celebrating with the Union Jack was, in some ways, endorsing the racist and distorted views of a right wing, political party, which claimed the Union flag as the symbol of their own obnoxious organisation. Thankfully, the balance has now been corrected and it has been good to see many ordinary people enjoying and celebrating the Queen's Jubilee, Wimbledon, Euro 2012 and the Olympic Games with their own national flag once again. The Union Jack has been reclaimed and renamed!

Hats, umbrellas, jackets, dog leads, boxes of chocolate, mugs and even slippers are now happily adorned with the Union Jack. No longer has it anything to do with allegiance with a particular political party, but is part of belonging, identity, celebration and pride. The Union Jack has been around since 1606 and it is good to see the flag being reclaimed by ordinary people who feel pride in their country and wish to celebrate with it. Indeed, it is good to see the flags of any nation being displayed with pride anywhere in the world. It is perfectly possible to feel pride in being English, Scottish, Welsh and Northern Irish, a member of the United Kingdom, as well as also being a good European.

Something for the Weekend, Sir?

Walking past a new hairdressing salon in a Las Palmas commercial centre made me stop and briefly retrace my steps for another look. There was something just a little unusual about this salon and its clientele. Instead of the usual rows of salon chairs, hair dryers and display stands revealing the latest expensive hair products, were small red fire engines, delightful rocking horses, fabulous open top cars in shocking pink, and red velvet thrones fit for any aspiring King or Queen. There were no perms or blue rinses in sight, nor were there any ladies with their hair adorned with tin foil or cling film awaiting the next stage of the colouring process. No, this establishment was strictly for kids only.

The owners of this attractive and brightly coloured salon had spotted a great business opportunity clearly aimed at those parents who have a little extra cash to spend on their children, and want them to look good. Many children that I see here are dressed in fashionable, and I assume expensive, designer clothes and so a designer cut and style is the next obvious step.

After all, the family dog goes to the pet parlour for a cut and trim, so who can begrudge Carlos or Maria from having the best possible hair styling in a place that understands children, which is also a happy and non-threatening place to visit?

Seeing this wonderland for children, complete with a vast array of drinks, ice creams, sweets and designer accessories, made me think back to my own childhood and the times that I dreaded going for a haircut at the barbers in the Lincolnshire village where I lived.

How I hated visiting Potter's, with its heavy door, dark wood panelled walls and strange smells. The queues of grumpy, smelly old men, many of whom were smoking cigarettes or pipes, sat on wooden benches waiting their turn for a shave or haircut. The heady, sickly smell of Brylcreem, combined with tobacco smoke made for a heady, vomit-inducing mix for a young child.

It was always a mixed blessing when my turn finally came, and I was beckoned forward and strapped into what look like a dentist's chair and shrouded in a huge white sheet. Mr Potter continued talking to the smelly, grumpy old men whilst he operated, cut and fiddled with my hair with his enormous pair of scissors and comb. Mr Potter was probably a very nice man, but as he never spoke to me, I really cannot say for sure. The final insult was the thick globule of that ghastly, sticky Brylcreem ladled out of its white pot into my hair before I escaped from the chair and was directed to a bench to wait until someone came to collect me. The strange thing is that I cannot remember being taken or collected; I just remember being there.

It is a memory that haunts me to this day and one of the reasons why, as soon as I became responsible for my own hairdressing actions, I refused to set foot in another barber's shop, and much preferred unisex salons. Well, at least they had no Brylcreem on the premises! This was until a few weeks ago when my own delightful hairdresser was on holiday and I needed a quick cut. I foolishly entered a barber's shop in the town where I live.

As I walked inside the dark panelled shop, memories came flooding back of troubled times long gone. Along the walls were seated a similar group of smelly, grumpy old men sitting on wooden benches waiting their turn that I remembered so well. Two 'dentists' chairs filled the far side of the room, whilst two barbers in white coats cut, poked and prodded their victims' hair with large scissors. I made my excuses and swiftly fled to the nearest bar for a coffee and brandy.

Thinking about the new kid's salon in Las Palmas, with Carlos sitting in the fire engine and Maria on the horse eating sweets and listening to music that they liked, made me realise just how lucky they were. If I had been them, I would have chosen the shocking pink sports car!

You look well!

Many of us have words or phrases that make us cringe when we hear them. For me, it is usually the American misinterpretation of the English language, as I see it anyway. I often think that there is no such thing as American English, and that English used in the USA should simply be called 'American' and have done with it, leaving 'English' as the very distinct form of English spoken in England!

Although I love most Americans, maybe with the exception of George Bush and Sarah Palin, why use the word 'fall' when you mean 'Autumn', 'semester' when you simply mean 'term'? As for the use of the word 'cellphone', when we simply mean 'mobile', words fail me. For that matter, why do pupils in the USA 'graduate' and receive a cap, gown and diploma when they simply leave infant school? I could go on, but I won't!

When I make a rare visit to relatives back in Lincolnshire in the UK, I am usually greeted with the welcome "You look well!" How I hate this! It actually shows no concern whatsoever about my general state of health, or recognition of my healthy Canarian tan; it simply means, "You look fat" or "You've put on weight". I grit my teeth and smile a benign smile.

My well meaning and much-looked-forward-to visit tends to go rapidly downhill from that point onwards. Maybe it is the Lincolnshire equivalent of a deeply resonating "eeee" that many Canarians and Spanish utter when they are desperately trying to think of something to say when responding to a phone call, or the "errr" sound, much loved and used by the British, as a way of playing for time and before entering into meaningful conversation. I guess they are simply 'thinking sounds'.

I also detest the use of current expressions such as "growing a business", which, if you think about it, is complete nonsense, but fill many chapters of some of the American "How to succeed in business" management theory books. However, for me, one of the worst expressions used in recent times is the use of the word "product" when referring to some kind of financial service.

This is a very dangerous expression and is, in my view, one of the main reasons why we have entered into an economic downturn. I was taught at school that a product is "something that is produced by labour or effort". Over recent years, I have failed to see why the banks' latest packaging of an over-priced bank account or a new financial service, designed to ease away as much cash from my pocket as it can, could be in any way be seen as a product.

Maybe, over the years the use of the word 'product' has lulled us into a false sense of security: we think we are actually producing something, when in reality we are producing nothing at all. Maybe it is akin to the story of 'The Emperor's new clothes", when the little boy declared to the Emperor, who was busily flaunting his new gear, that actually he was naked and was wearing no clothes at all. Well, that is part of my explanation for the financial crash!

I am sure that we all have words and expressions that irritate us. If you have a favourite one, do please let me know.

It's an island thing

I have always loved islands. Maybe it was reading just too much Robinson Crusoe, Enid Blyton's 'Five on a Treasure Island' and other stories about islands that inspired me, but I always knew that one day I would live on an island.

Maybe it was that first glimpse of the magical and mysterious Brownsea Island pointed out to me by my elderly great aunt. We could only view it through binoculars from Poole Harbour in Dorset, because, in those days, as my great aunt explained, it was inhabited by an old witch and her elderly manservant, and they cooked and ate all newcomers to the island. Animals, birds and insects that lived there were special and unique to that special place. Indeed, the giant ants could eat people alive. As I discovered many years later whilst accompanying classes of schoolchildren to the island, she was partly right about the giant ants! Great Aunt Gertie did have a vivid imagination, but it was the stuff of inspiration.

For many years I thought that my eventual island destination would be the Isle of Wight. Career opportunities often seemed to lead me there, and on one occasion it was the dreadful realisation that I was about to be offered a job that I didn't really want, that made me flee the island at 5.00am one morning and well before the final interview, and I didn't return for many years.

We visited the Scilly Islands - a delightful destination, but I soon realised that the rusting bath tub, which the islanders call a ferry, was a nightmare, and after one terrible voyage with myself and other passengers vomiting for most of the journey, I flew back to the mainland by helicopter realising that I could never attempt that journey by boat ever again, let alone live there.

We spent many glorious summers exploring islands around the UK and beyond. We tasted delicious malt whiskies on the Isles of Skye and Islay, exploring the Outer Hebrides, avoiding tweed jackets in Harris and Lewis, as well as tasting the relative decadence of Orkney and Shetland.

Islands as diverse as Majorca, Cyprus, Ibiza and Madeira were also visited, but although wonderful in their own unique ways, none seemed to inspire me as a possible home for the future. That is until we visited the Canary Islands in general, and Gran Canaria in particular. I knew then that this would be home and found myself gripping the handrail and forcing myself up the steps of the plane going home at the end of our first visit. I was determined to return again one day.

So what is so special about islands? It is a difficult one to answer, because people are inspired in many different ways. Maybe it is the feeling of being part of a small community, never being far from the sea, or the reminder of a primitive form of survival instinct.

Maybe it is just that feeling of "Getting away from it all", although critics of this view will quickly point out that this can be difficult to achieve on islands such as Tenerife, and parts of Gran Canaria and Lanzarote! If you really do want to get away from it all, I suggest heading to El Hierro, La Gomera or La Palma instead!

An elderly friend visited a few days ago. "I could never live on an island," she declared loudly after critically peering out to sea. What do you do for shopping? You have only got one small shop," she asked.

"We have many good local shops nearby, and you can get anything in Las Palmas, the seventh largest city in Spain," I replied.

"It must be so difficult to get off the island in an emergency?" she frowned.

"Not really, after all Las Palmas airport is the third largest in Spain. Flights are always available, but the fares vary depending upon demand."

"I would need still need to be in Europe, because of the health service".

"The Canary Islands are part of Europe and offer some of the best medical treatment available anyway. Indeed, patients are often flown to Las Palmas from the Peninsular for specialist treatment."

"Hmm, well, I still wouldn't like to live in an island..." she mumbled.

Great, I thought. I am so pleased you are not going to move here. Intending islanders need to be committed to island life and be aware of the disadvantages, as well as the advantages. Islands are rather like Marmite, Blackpool or Benidorm. You either love them or hate them.

Tulip Heads and Cabbage Fields

Life in the Canary Islands and Spain always seems to be punctuated by amazing Carnivals and enthusiastic Fiestas. There are just so many, with each town and village having their own special patron saint and accompanying fiesta days (or weeks, in some cases!); sometimes it is hard to keep up with them. I love to see, hear and take part in them if I can. It is wonderful to see Canarian children dressed in traditional costume, singing and dancing, with their parents and friends enjoying the warmth of the day until late evening or, more usually, early morning. I am sure that these early experiences, traditions and social activities have a considerable influence upon the sense of belonging, community spirit and working together that is so important for a well-balanced life. During the recent fiesta in my own village, I began to reflect and contrast what I was seeing with some of my own childhood experiences.

I was born and grew up in fenland Lincolnshire which, to be frank, was never my favourite place. A landscape of endless fields growing the same crop in a tree-less and hedge-less landscape, without a hill in sight, and usually accompanied by a grey sky was simply not for me. I felt from a very early age that I was in the wrong place and I knew that one day I would have to escape. However, in fairness, I also know many people who, if not exactly loving it, tolerated it as a place where they grew up, have many happy memories, and I respect their views. However, sadly, that was not the case for me.

One overpowering memory that I still have, in more ways than one, is the overwhelming smell of rotting cabbages at certain times of the year, often combined with the sweet, sickly smell of sugar beet being processed in the local beet factory. It was a strange and heady combination if the wind was in the wrong direction. The fertile land of South Lincolnshire is, of course, where farmers grow much of the nation's crops, and a very good job they make of it too. However, endless fields of cabbages, cauliflowers and potatoes were never quite my thing, and I always seemed to be surrounded by fields emitting the bad stench of rotting cabbages and cauliflowers. How I longed to escape from that place. I guess this is when I started to dream about islands.

In contrast, some fields were dedicated to the growing of tulip bulbs. In springtime, the usual bland landscape that haunted me as a child would burst into life with thousands upon thousands of tulips. Each field would specialise in one particular variety and colour; sparkling yellows, vivid reds, variegated varieties, and even blood red or almost black varieties. On my journey to and from school each day, the school bus would weave its way through fields of colour, much like large patches of raw, vivid colour on an artist's palette. It lifted my spirits tremendously, and was such a change from cabbages.

The tulips were, of course, grown for their bulbs and not for their flowers, and so the time would come when all the flowers were beheaded and carted off in huge trucks to the nearest compost heap. This would allow the bulbs to grow, divide and make healthy profits for the farmers. Indeed, this part of Lincolnshire was called Holland, and was reclaimed land from the Wash with a flower and bulb industry similar to its neighbour, the Netherlands, which was just a short hop across the North Sea.

Fortunately, imaginative people began to realise that the tulip heads could in themselves still be quite useful, and the beginnings of a kind of Carnival began to grow in my home town of Spalding. Large floats, sponsored by local businesses and large companies, were decorated with tulip heads. Amazing, spectacular creations from tulip heads, now in the form of floats, arrived each year as local groups and businesses tried to outdo their rivals. A huge procession would take place through the town and 'The Tulip Parade' became known worldwide as a spectacular event, which was well worth including on the tourist map. There was even a 'Tulip Queen', suitably crowned, who rode through the town in her carriage of tulips. The floats would then be on show for the general public to admire for several days until the heads finally died and all would be forgotten for another year. For me, and others like me, those few days each year were heaven sent during a time when my world seemed to be full of cabbages.

Many years later, when I was working as a school inspector, I was dispatched to Lincolnshire for a week to inspect a school. I arrived at the motel late at night and so was unsure of my immediate surroundings. When I awoke the following morning, I was once again greeted with that familiar smell, the overpowering smell of rotting cabbages!

Faith, Politics and Belief

The Euro Game

It was a hot, sunny day and the boys and girls in the village school were enjoying their lunchtime games as usual in the schoolyard. However, today, tempers seemed a little more frayed than usual during this particular ball game. I watched the children closely for some time anticipating that the dinner lady who was supervising would have to step in and bring the game to an abrupt end, intervening with the usual talk about sporting behaviour and "it's not the winning, it's the playing" reminder that teachers and dinner ladies are so good at repeating.

I then noticed one girl from my class, Sally, was frowning and concentrating hard. Sally was a born leader; she had presence, and although not always liked by her classmates, she would be the one to lead and organise whenever anything needed doing. She was barking instructions to one very agile small boy, Peter, who seemed to pop up all over the playground at the same time from nowhere. Peter was a very happy little boy, friendly to everyone and always happy to help out, yet he had a quiet determination that could bring about revolution if he wished; such was his charisma. Sally and Peter working together brought about a special kind of teamwork, that initially seemed unlikely, but now appeared to be working. Although the shouting and arguments continued, there now seemed to be order and a plan in their game.

Suddenly, there was a cry from Charles. Charles looked angry as the ball bounced off his back. His face was red and he angrily dived towards the ball, which he grabbed and then stood glaring at the others. His teammates shouted for him to pass the ball. He looked defiant and his face was now filling with tears. Charles placed the ball under his arm, marched off the playground with the ball and back into the school building. He bit his bottom lip angrily and slammed the door behind him. For a few seconds, the rest of the children stood and watched with their mouths open, wondering what all the fuss was about.

Sally looked angry as she strode off the playground and found another ball in the sports shed. She returned to the playground and threw the ball to Peter who deftly caught it and threw it back into the game. The children cheered as the game continued at a pace that was faster and more focussed than before.

Before I returned into the school building, I caught a glimpse of Charles, his tear stained face watching the game alone from the classroom window.

The recent meeting of leaders in Paris, designed to discuss the future of the Euro and Britain's participation in amending its financial rules, reminded me of a children's game in a Dorset rural primary school some years ago.

Does one size fit all?

I still enjoy reading and listening to UK news. However, I do find it irritating to hear economists and financial 'experts' (In the UK they are usually anti EU and anti euro) including Portugal, Italy and Spain in any discussion about the euro crisis and Greece. I hear Spain condemned in similar terms as Greece in the same breath, almost as if it is an extension of the same problem.

Most UK financial 'experts' appear to be anti European and certainly anti euro, and the arrogance of the "we told you the euro would be a disaster" brigade is breathtaking, particularly as many of us remember those very same pundits recommending the UK's entry to the eurozone some years ago. Yes, hindsight is indeed a wonderful thing.

Spain's problems, and therefore the cure, are very different from those of Greece, as well as Italy, Ireland and Portugal. Spain has been an enthusiastic member of the European Union from its very beginning, and most Spanish people readily accept that the highly successful transition from the dictatorship of General Franco to a modern democratic state in a short period of time has been largely due to the support and encouragement from the EU.

Most of the eurozone's problems relate to excessive borrowing by governments who were ineffective in managing their economies. Greece, for instance, was unable to control its spending, and produced figures that were simply not true when applying to join the eurozone. Portugal spent and borrowed too much. Italy also had too much debt stemming from overspending in the 1970s and 1980s.

Believe it or not, Spain has been a model European state, very similar in approach to Germany. Germany had wisely insisted upon including a 'stability pact', which was designed to ensure that governments inside the eurozone would organise their finances sensibly. If a country wished to join the eurozone, a condition of entry was that their debts should be no more than 60% of their GDP. However, this condition was quietly forgotten at the beginning, because Germany would not have qualified for entry to the eurozone, because its debts were too high; this was the eurozone's first big mistake.

The stability pact itself was not implemented, because Germany broke the annual borrowing limit each year from 2002 to 2005. However, the Spanish government ran a balanced budget, with borrowing at zero every year until the 2008 financial crisis. Spain's debt ratio fell and its economy grew rapidly, whilst Germany's debt continued to rise. This was hardly a Greece scenario.

Spain now faces a difficult economic dilemma, because interest rates reduced to the lower levels operating in Germany when it joined the eurozone. Although the Spanish government resisted the temptation of low interest loans, most ordinary Spanish people did not, and the country enjoyed a long economic boom, accompanied by a housing bubble, as Spanish families obtained larger mortgages, encouraged by some banks with less than rigorous lending policies; a problem that was also echoed in the UK. House prices increased by 44% between 2004 and 2008, yet now have fallen.

Spanish workers earned more and spent more during the years of growth, which helped to increase the government's finances from taxation, yet also helped to increase Spanish wages to uncompetitive levels, when compared with workers in Germany. Its construction sector, which became bloated during the building boom, also collapsed.

Currently, households are attempting to reduce their spending, as they struggle to repay their mortgages and financial debts. Unemployment has increased rapidly, with 50 per cent of under 25-year-olds currently out of work.

Surprisingly, unlike Greece, the Spanish government has relatively little debt, but now has to borrow to cover the shortfall left by a collapse in tax revenues and a rise in unemployment benefits during the downturn. Banks too are exposed to the collapse of the housing market due to their mortgage debts, which makes financial markets cautious about lending to Spain.

It is also well worth remembering that, unlike Greece, Spain is the EU's fourth largest economy and the twelfth largest in the world. The country still maintains a large and strong industrial base; for example, it manufactures cars, heavy machinery, washing machines and refrigerators. Agricultural, fish and wine products continue to find a ready market within other countries of the EU, traditional links with South America, as well as newly established markets in China and India. Spain's tourism industry continues to boom and is still the largest within the European Union.

Spain has much going for it, and it has very different issues, as well as possibilities, to those of Greece and other eurozone economies. Wise economists, who have knowledge of the country, are slowly realising that Spain requires a different solution to its problems, and a gradual recognition that one size does not fit all. Spain can reform itself, but the support of its European partners is essential for it to succeed. The one common factor with Greece is that there is a limit to how much pain its people can take.

Bankers Go Bananas

I thought that I recognised the voice over the underground station's speaker system; it sounded familiar, but I couldn't quite place it. The doors slid silently to a close as I sat in the immaculate carriage and sped my way to Canary Wharf.

Many years had passed since I last made the journey to this centre of the UK's banking industry and I was curious to see how it had developed. It was a strange day to visit, as the Barclays interest rate scandal had just been announced, and it was clear that heads would soon roll.

I was also curious, since many years ago when the Thatcher government was busily telling UK citizens that they should all be shareholders, my building society account had been gobbled up by the bank that was now causing so much grief to Government and bankers alike, and was now based in Canary Wharf. It was a delicious form of irony, as it seemed that a number of wayward chickens were about to come home to roost.

I felt a special affinity to this part of London. The Canary Islands are now my home and I am well aware of the banana trade and the impact that it made upon Canary Wharf.

Bananas from the Canary Islands were once unloaded right in the centre of what is now London's vibrant financial district, which takes its name from the No. 10 Warehouse of the South Quay Import Dock, built in 1952 for the Canary Islands' fruit trade. This grey glass and steel paradise proudly retains the name Canary Wharf to this day.

The train slid into the bland and clinical station. I stepped out of the concrete, stainless steel and glass structure, relieved to smell relatively fresh air once again. It was a grey, depressing day and the grey steel, concrete and glass structures that loomed around me seemed to be more intimidating than the last time that I had visited. Apart from a few tourists holding their Union flag umbrellas, the place seemed abandoned. I wandered alongside the river for a while, marvelling at the huge number of sushi bars, coffee shops and fast food restaurants; most were empty.

At exactly midday, thousands of ant-like creatures appeared from the grey, glass and steel towers. I have never seen so many suits gathered in one place at one time before. The ant-like creatures swept into the sushi bars, coffee shops and fast food restaurants devouring anything in sight.

I wandered into one of the many high tech shopping centres; glass doors silently opening and closing behind me. Suit clad ants sped in all directions carrying what seemed to be an obligatory cup of coffee in a plastic mug in one hand, and a mobile phone clamped in the other. Expressionless faces swept by me as they darted around the high tech paradise.

I sat inside one of the many coffee shops sipping my coffee, watching these expressionless faces. Many were deep in conversation on their mobiles, or peering into the screens of laptops, mobiles and tablets; few were talking to each other.
The enormous screens in the coffee bar continued to beam endless streams of trading figures and financial statistics, and transfixed anxious faces by its magical, seductive power.

By mid afternoon, the 'ants' had all but disappeared back into their grey steel and glass towers, the anxious chattering into handsets silenced, busy cafe bars, restaurants and sushi bars emptied and the streets were deserted once again.

I returned to the station, anxious to return to what I regarded as civilisation. I was troubled by what I had seen and experienced. It was not a happy place; it reminded me of a book that I had read long ago, but couldn't quite remember. A familiar voice boomed around the station once again. It was slightly humorous, with a hint of self-deprecation, yet tinged with just a hint of a threat. Yes, the book was 1984 and I suddenly realised that I had briefly entered the Orwellian nightmare. I now recognised the voice of Big Brother - it was the voice of Boris Johnson, the Mayor of London.

Quakers in the Canaries

My mother warned me long ago not to talk about politics, sex or religion at the dinner table. I think to this, she would have added not talking about vegetarianism at a barbecue. All these subjects appear to be off limits in polite company, and maybe for good reason as outspoken, individual views may offend, lead to disagreement, argument or, indeed, revolution. In this chapter, I am going to break the rule about religion, not I might add because I wish to cause offence, but because I know that it is an issue that troubles many expats, as well as being an issue that I have only recently become aware of. If talking about God and faith isn't quite your thing, please accept my apologies and skip to the next chapter.

My personal faith is very simple. I believe in a loving God, Creator, or whatever you wish to call Him (or Her). I have a deep faith, but dislike organised religion. I don't feel the need for vicars, ministers, priests, Pope's, Imams and the like, because I wish to have a direct relationship with my God. I don't feel the need to use rosary beads, sing hymns and psalms, and chant meaningless phrases, because I believe that my God understands and tolerates me just as I am. I feel uncomfortable in extravagant cold and underused church buildings that often ignore the needs of their communities.

I dislike the hoarding and display of valuable paintings, gold and silver plate, cups and chalices, which I regard as fripperies and largely irrelevant. However, I do like stained glass windows, which make me think and deepen my faith. I don't like the smell of incense, which makes me sneeze, nor do I have the urge to listen to dozens of choirboys singing in their high pitched, yet beautiful, voices; I know that most would much rather be elsewhere on an early Sunday morning.

Despite my personal views, I fully accept that many people value and appreciate the traditions and trappings of organised religion. Many find priests, vicars and ministers invaluable and many dedicate their lives to giving high quality leadership, support and care to their parishioners. This is fair enough, as long as the views of the organised Church do not disrespect, disturb or ignore the values or rights of others. Much of this is, of course, about tolerance and recognition of the needs and views of others in a civilised society.

Many years ago, my partner and I became Quakers. Without going into too much detail here, Quakers hold simple beliefs based around simple truths. There are no priests, ministers and Popes. Church buildings (called Meeting Houses) are simple, welcoming places and are often used for other purposes by the local community.

There is no fixed order for the service; indeed, there is no service as such. There are usually no hymns, no prayer books or psalms. Quakers meet in silence for an hour; it is a time for peace and meditation and a time for people to relate to their own God. Occasionally, a member may share a thought or an idea with the meeting. These thoughts that are shared with the Meeting are often reflective and thoughtful, yet rarely dull.

Although Quaker meetings are held in silence, there is plenty of opportunity for laughter, discussion and gossip afterwards over coffee! After attending many churches over the years, I immediately felt comfortable when I walked through the door of a Meeting House in the UK. This is one of the things that I do miss as an expat.

Over time, I have come to realise that I can worship anywhere. The area by the sea where I walk Bella, our dog, each day is my Church. My God hears me when I talk and explain my problems, share my successes, ask for forgiveness and ask for advice. My silent prayers are accompanied by the sounds of an often, stormy sea or wind. My church has no walls, stained glass windows or ornate crosses - just a simple backdrop of a blue sky, a few fluffy white clouds, and some seabirds and lizards for company.

It is always good to go home. My partner, David, and myself experienced just that feeling recently when we visited our Bournemouth Quaker 'home'. For the last ten years, we have lived and worked in Spain's Costa Blanca and now the Canary Islands. Although we love our Canary Island's home, I guess nothing is ever perfect, and we do miss our friends and family in the UK and the opportunity to attend meeting.

There are relatively few Quakers in Spain, and none that we are aware of living on the island where we live. I occasionally receive emails and letters from visiting Quakers, usually from the USA, asking for a contact or meeting house in the country, and it is sometimes difficult to assist, as people change and move on. David and I often crave the opportunity to worship with like-minded people, but we have been fortunate in being welcomed in meeting houses in Dublin, Lincolnshire and Devon, whilst visiting family and friends.

The sun beamed through the tall windows of the meeting room. We had arrived early to make the most of our brief visit. As we sat in silence, Friends slipped into the room and sat down. Several who remembered us from ten years earlier, looked surprised and warmly acknowledged us, whilst others we had not seen before nodded and smiled. There were many new faces and it was good to see that the overall attendance seemed to have increased.

Superficially, some things had changed, the washroom had been refurbished, areas redecorated and floors looked even more highly polished than I recall. A candle replaced the fresh flowers that were usually placed on the central table, and there was now even an automatic door to the front entrance. However, the seats were still just as uncomfortable as I remember.

Despite the physical changes, the many new faces and the absence of many older friends, the atmosphere remained as supportive, warm and loving as we remembered. Although Quakers usually worship in silence, they certainly make up for it over coffee and can chatter with the best of them. We renewed acquaintance with many members from the past, as well as meeting many new members and attenders. It was a happy and emotional visit and our only regret was that we could not stay longer for lunch.

Even though we now live in the Canary Islands, we are still members of the Bournemouth Meeting. We receive the newsletter and other information each month, as we have for the last ten years, and this is always much appreciated. During difficult times we have received letters of support from Friends. David and I still worship most Sundays, at 10.30am to feel part of the Bournemouth Meeting, even though we are many miles away. We have our quiet hour, when sometimes David plays reflective music on the keyboard. Although we are usually only two, we recall these words of Jesus:

"For where two or three are gathered together in my name, there am I in the midst of them."

As usual, our time in the UK was a manic one. Visiting friends and family, book events and a school visit meant that our time was limited and we had to be on our way. Thank you Bournemouth Meeting; we hope it will not be too long before we visit again.

The Conservatory Government

Despite the seriousness of the current recession, I have been amused and irritated by the constant references to the relaxation of rules for the building of conservatories in the UK. Presumably the rules were originally introduced for a good reason and it seems a little unwise to many people to suddenly abandon them. It is as if suddenly allowing a huge conservatory to be built in the back garden of a semi in Huddersfield, without planning permission, will transform the nation's economy.

Now, I know it is easy to be cynical at such times, and I like conservatories as much as the next person, but maybe the emphasis upon conservatories may give the wrong idea about priorities to the struggling masses? It is just a thought.

We don't have the conservatory problem in the Canary Islands and much of Spain. If we are fortunate, our homes have a roof terrace to sit on, dry washing on, plant a few tubs, or maybe, if it is large enough, to have a barbecue.

It is often amusing to watch the newly arrived expat, when faced with a glorious roof terrace, to almost immediately have it covered with glazed roof panels! I can see that it will provide an additional room, as well as being a lovely garden room to sit in on the occasional cool, windy day, but such home improvements tend to ignore the intense heat that we enjoy for much of the year.

What originally seemed an excellent idea in providing additional covered space, quickly turns into a nightmare of searing heat, which becomes an oven if entering the room for more than half a minute.

Modifications are then made to the offending roof panels, ranging from shading, or expensive blinds, painting or covering the outside of the glass panels with reflective paint, installing electric opening or sliding roof panels, covering it with a solid roof, or removing the complete installation. How Canarian builders must snigger when they receive their next order from a well-intentioned expat to create a sun room!

Maybe the Conservatory Government should consider this possibility when developing recession busting policies; it would suddenly create huge additional demand for building work across the nation.

On a more serious note, Canarian and Spanish families traditionally look after the elderly members of their families. Unlike the UK, there are few private residential homes in the country, other than those run by holy orders, which may not be everyone's idea of having a good time in old age. It is therefore a Canarian's first priority, when moving into a new home with a terrace or balcony, to immediately build a solid roof and turn it into a bedroom for Granny, with or without planning permission.

As a result, some of the structures look rather strange and I feel for all the Grannies on the island when there is excessive wind or heavy rain. Granny, in turn, often will look after the kids, Mum and Dad can go out to work with no childcare concerns, and so all the family benefits from this system of in-house Granny care.

So my advice to the Conservatory Government and the Chancellor of the Exchequer in the UK, for what it is worth, is to allow the building of everything anywhere, with little or no planning permission, to create as many homes in as many nooks and crannies as possible, especially for the nation's Grannies. This will create jobs for builders, solve the Granny housing crisis, reduce the cost of care for Grannies, provide additional childcare, and allow all Mums and Dads to go out to work.

As a bonus, it will provide additional work for insurance companies and lawyers when dealing with insurance claims for collapsed roofs, as well as compensation for infringement of light and privacy claims from the folks next door. The nation's economy will boom and it will be the end of the recession. Only then will the UK have a true Conservatory Government.

Food, Drink and Health

A decent cup of coffee

In a previous 'Twitter' I referred to a high quality coffee grown in Gran Canaria and now marketed in a number of European countries as a premium product. Now it seems that another type of coffee, grown in the Canary Islands, will shortly enter the market and this time it is made from pistachio nuts.

A decent cup of coffee is, for me, an essential part of each morning. I don't think I have ever been disappointed with a cup of coffee in Spain and the Canary Islands. However, the soup bowls full of the stuff in the UK's many overpriced 'Costa Lottee' chains invariably make both my stomach and wallet churn.

Even though I like a cup of good coffee in the morning, I am careful not to drink too many and reluctantly settle for a cup of decaffeinated coffee later in the evening, although I am not that keen on the taste. I know that coffee with a high caffeine content significantly reduces the quality of sleep and is best avoided late at night; however, late evening meals and the desire for a good cup of coffee and a decent brandy to round off a good meal makes for a difficult choice, and I easily succumb to temptation.

Maybe the Canary Islands have an answer? It seems that coffee made from pistachio nuts can be used to make a healthier, caffeine-free alternative to coffee, as well as being a genuine alternative that actually tastes like coffee. Coffee manufacturers have been searching for a good stimulant-free alternative to coffee that maintains the flavour, but without the kick of real coffee.

The fruit of Pistacia terebinthus (terebinth and turpentine tree), a deciduous tree that grows to a height of more than 30 feet is native to the Canary Islands, as well as Morocco, Turkey and Greece, and produces red to black coloured fruit, and scientists claim that if these are carefully roasted they will produce a drink that has the same flavour as coffee, but without the high. One added bonus for producers is that this fruit is significantly cheaper than the real thing.

As well as producing a sap that is a source of turpentine, the tree produces a special type of pistachio nut that has the same chemical "signature" as real coffee, and with the same taste and aroma. When roasted, there is a change in the chemical profile similar to that when coffee beans are roasted.

Coffee experts report that the new "healthy coffee" is brewed in the same way as Turkish coffee, and produces a dark brown, rich coffee with a nutty and chocolate smell. However, the new product is not as successful in producing espresso coffee, which may restrict its marketing potential to the trendy coffee bars, because the roasted nuts turn into a less than attractive gunge that prevents water from running through the product.

It will be interesting to see what happens, but I hope that once again, it proves that when it comes to a decent cup of coffee, it is hard to beat the Canary Islands.

The World Cradle of Rum

Visitors to the Canary Islands may remember that at the end of a good meal in a local restaurant, and before the bill arrives, they are presented with a 'shot' - a small glass of liqueur to round off a good meal. This 'shot' is presented as a 'on the house' gesture of gratitude from the restaurant for visiting, with the hope that you will visit again, as well as remembering to leave a tip before you leave.

This 'shot' is often a local Canarian Honey Rum, known as Ron Miel, which is made from a centuries old tradition of blending aged rum and honey. It is a sweet drink, but not as sweet as you might at first think, and certainly not as sickly to the taste as some liqueurs. It also includes a remarkable 'kick' if you drink too many, and it may also be wise not to accept your 'shot' if you are the driver!

It is often forgotten that when you speak about rum, you are talking about the Canary Islands; the two are intertwined. Many rum connoisseurs describe the Canary Islands as the 'World Cradle of Rum', where this beautiful spirit is made by combining a centuries old tradition with the superb quality of locally produced raw materials. White rum, banana rum, toffee rum, chocolate cream, coco-pineapple and coffee rum are just some of the many varieties available although, personally, I am rather fond of the banana variety!

So how is Honey Rum made? Seven-year-old rum is blended with natural honey from the Canary Islands, which create a natural combination of flavour. It may be enjoyed on its own, or you can ruin it by mixing it into a range of mixed drinks and cocktails. Although mixing may not be for the rum connoisseur, it is fair to say that Honey Rum does an excellent job as a natural substitute for man-made sugars and liqueurs.

One company that produces honey rum is Distillery Arehucus, which has recently proudly announced that it is shipping and selling its traditional 'Ron Miel de Canarias' to the USA. **Distillery Arehucas is a fourth generation family owned business, which produces a range of world class rums and is the official supplier to the Spanish Royal family, so it can't be bad!** Traditional methods of production and quality are still used at the distillery, a local family business, which began rum production 125 years ago, and currently produces around 1.5 million litres each year. It is a fair bet that if you have already tried honey rum, or one of its sister flavours, it may well have been one produced by Distillery Arehucas, since they have around 50 per cent of the market share in honey rum on the islands and Europe.

The new export to the USA, as well as designed to tickle the American palette, also has an interesting history, with established links to the sugar cane industry, rum production and the USA.

All four voyages of Christopher Columbus, or Cristobal Colon as they like to call him over here, departed from the Canary Islands to the New World, and the first sugar canes planted in America left from the Canary islands bound for the West Indies in the second voyage of Christopher Columbus, in 1493. Very appropriately, the current stock of sugar cane currently growing in the West Indies is originally from the Canary Islands.

Personally, I am not a great lover of cocktails, and to use Ron Miel as a mixer in any drink would be, in my view, dangerously close to sacrilege. My personal favourite is the banana variety, and I am sure that you will have great enjoyment trying out the range of Ron Miel! Besides, it may also be regarded as almost medicinal, as it is great for soothing sore throats, so do keep a bottle in your medicine cabinet, just in case!

Pie in the Sky

Most expats will find themselves frequently travelling to and from their countries of origin. Whether it is visiting family and friends, or the occasional flight back to the UK for business or maybe a shopping trip, most expats will find themselves spending hours on the Internet attempting to find the best value flights.

The joy of finding a so called 'cheap flight' from one of the not so cheap low cost airlines is often tempered by a plethora of additional charges for luggage, taxes and credit card surcharges.

There is also a variety of other available options, such as a once in a lifetime opportunity to purchase a cabin bag that is guaranteed to be allowed on board, paying an optional charge for the joy of sitting together as a couple or family, extra leg room, or maybe for an in-flight meal.

How about insurance, a hotel room, or maybe car hire? By the time would-be travellers have booked their flights, most are just relieved to have reached the end of the process and no longer care about the detail!

I am one of those rare species of traveller who actually enjoys eating airline food. For years I have remained silent whilst my fellow travellers sneered and complained about the contents of the plastic food tray, lovingly presented to them by beaming and mostly efficient airline stewards and stewardesses.

Mostly, my fellow passengers consumed the offerings grudgingly, but a few trays remained uneaten. Incidentally, who remembers the days when the meal ended with the serving of a steaming hot damp cloth, delicately served with a pair of serving tongs from a silver tray? Nice touch, but a little pointless, I felt.

Some passengers would decline their meals with a meaningful grunt, and turn their backs upon the offending tray that was offered to them. They were making a statement about something or other, and anyway, they had a less than fresh ham and cheese sandwich stuffed somewhere about their person, which would offer them a modicum of comfort during the serving of these culinary delicacies. Meanwhile, the rest of us were enjoying the latest hot food offering, whilst flying at a height 30,000 odd feet, and very good it was too.

I could never understand the complaints, or the endless jokes that the in-flight meal caused. Indeed, the flying food tray became the butt of many aspiring comedians. Maybe I just didn't notice, had such a boring and unappetising diet in my out-of-the-air life, or maybe it was because I am a vegetarian and always ordered the vegetarian option. Whatever it was, my veggie meal often used to elicit admiring glances from fellow passengers or comments of "that looks tasty" as they peered into my Mediterranean casserole or mushroom omelette.

All this of course was when the airline meal was included in the price of the ticket. That, and the obligatory ancient cartoon on tiny screens were included as part of the package deal; there was simply no choice. The in-flight meal then became an easy target for many Brits, being a cynical lot at the best of times, to ridicule something that was actually rather good. How I missed its sudden demise!

The in-flight meal was replaced by a sad selection of filled rolls, designer paninis and expensive crisps, and the total outlay often cost far in excess of an in-flight meal. However, some of the more sensible airlines continued to offer in-flight meals, but usually only as an optional extra. In-flight meals then became the province of designer TV chefs to have their say, and produce meals worthy of launching or ending a holiday in the sun, rather than the product of ex-school cooks who couldn't quite hack it in airline catering departments, and were tucked away on an industrial estate somewhere.

Nowadays, I much prefer to book flights with airlines that offer this option, as well as a booked seat, as I prefer this to the gallop across the tarmac and the purchase of a packet of nuts from a certain Irish airline, with a "catch them out if we can" attitude on its website.

As I write this, I have just finished my in-flight meal. It was a delicious gnocchi with butternut squash, strawberry cheesecake, cheese and biscuits, coffee and a chocolate mint, and very good it was too. Interestingly, over half of the passengers on my flight had opted to purchase the in-flight meal, albeit I guess most opted for the beef or chicken options. The creator of this particular in-flight meal chef promised "Good satisfying comfort food, made with quality ingredients", which it certainly was.

It is now all about personal choice, which is fair enough as long as the choices remain. A decent in-flight meal certainly beats that packet of warm and curling ham and cheese sandwiches stuffed in coat pockets, I guess.

Don't do as I do, do as I say

"Three rashers, three sausages, two eggs, black pudding twice, fried bread twice and no tomatoes," boomed the voice in front of me in the queue. "Oh, and two rounds of toast and a large mug of coffee."

"Beans?" responded the unsmiling automaton in the white overall, a woman with no facial expression whatsoever.

"Goodness no, I'll have wind all day if I do," came the reply.

Wind is the least of your worries, I thought, as I watched the layers of cholesterol being piled onto a very large plate. I like a cooked breakfast as much as the next person (albeit the vegetarian variety) when I am on holiday, but I know enough about healthy eating to ensure that for most of the year, fresh fruit and muesli is the healthiest way to start my day at home.

"Yes?" snapped the automaton, looking vaguely in my direction.

"Do you have any fresh fruit, apples or bananas maybe?" I enquired hopefully.

"Bananas, no, but you may find some apples in the basket by the till. They may be a bit old though, there's not a lot of call for them in here. I may have got some tinned fruit in the back."

I turned and looked at the two forlorn apples in the basket by the till and decided to give them a miss.

"No, I'll leave that. Just two slices of toast please."

"Do you want them spreading?"

After having seen the thick layer of butter spread upon the previous customer's toast, I declined.

"Do you have some vegetable margarine?"

"Over by the till, but that costs extra."

"Just the toast then, please. No butter."

Whilst I was waiting for the toast, I attempted some conversation. I was curious to know the reasoning behind the massively unhealthy diet being served in the hospital's canteen for visitors. As with so many hospital facilities in the UK nowadays, the hospital restaurant had been privatised, and I was amused to see it being run by the same company that is involved in school inspections, as well as refuse collections in the UK.

The hospital restaurant was in one of the UK's large city hospitals and I had been visiting an elderly relative in its care. As is often the case with sick, elderly patients, they can only cope with short visits and so I decided to take a short coffee break before returning to the ward.

"Don't you think it is a little strange that you are serving such unhealthy food in a hospital restaurant?"
"I just does what I'm told. They decides what's to be served," was the snapped response, although now, at least, the face showed some expression and feeling, which was an encouraging development.

"Yes, I can see that, and I'm not blaming you," I protested, "but you are killing your customers. Maybe your previous customer could have been offered a healthier alternative? Surely it's a good opportunity to encourage visitors to consider healthy eating when they visit patients. Maybe some fruit? With a diet like that he'll soon be in here as a patient."

The woman snorted. "He's no visitor," she laughed. "He has that for breakfast most days, and he's a doctor here!"

I ate my toast slowly, with a mixture of disbelief, anger and amusement, but wondering if my elderly relative was receiving the most enlightened care in that hospital after all.

Dentists and Sweet Delights

Most expats will quickly discover that Spanish dentistry is very good. It is mostly private based, with no National Health Service support, and strongly supported by private medical insurance schemes. There has been considerable investment in dentistry over the years and many young people made dentistry their profession, and this led to a situation where there were too many qualified dentists in the country. Many newly qualified dentists subsequently moved to other parts of Europe, and particularly to the UK, where they established lucrative practices, and often in areas where there was no dental surgery, and offered treatment under the UK's National Health Service, which came as a relief to many patients.

Over time, dental care in Spain moved full circle and there became a shortage of Spanish dentists working in the country. This gap was filled with many dentists moving from South America, where Spain has many historical, cultural and trade links, and many dentists from Argentina and Cuba, particularly, established new practices in Spain and the Canary Islands.

I have visited a number of dental surgeries in Spain and the Canary Islands over the years and, with one notable exception with a Swedish dentist in the Costa Blanca, they have all been excellent. New treatments and specialisms are offered in Spain that are often unavailable in the UK.

One example of this is dental implants, which is now becoming more common, yet only two years ago, my dental surgery in the Canary Islands was one of the very few offering this specialist surgery in Spain and much of Europe. Indeed, it is now possible to have dental implants fitted in one day, and could be part of your holiday in the Canary Islands! Indeed, as with many other medical treatments, such as breast implants and cosmetic surgery, medical tourism is becoming very much part of the new tourist economy of the islands.

Back to the dental surgery business. I am sure that one of the reasons behind the growth of dental businesses in Spain is the Spanish love of sweets! I have rarely seen such emporiums of sweets elsewhere that I see over here. It certainly puts the old 'Pick and Mix' delights to shame. These sweet shops are usually full of customers, and the large bags of sweets that are carried out of these shops makes me wonder about the health of their teeth.

Most banks, lawyers, accountants, veterinary surgeries, hotels, restaurants and other businesses have a basket of boiled sweets on their counters, or in their waiting rooms, to tempt customers as they pay their bills, or carry out other business. Adults and children alike grab handfuls of these tempting offerings, sucking and chewing as they leave the establishment. My dentist too has a basket of boiled sweets on his counter. No wonder the dental business is doing so well over here!

Expat life, Sport and Community

Helping Hands

I try to see good things coming out of the bad experiences in life, and good usually defeating evil. Maybe it is all about the fight between good and evil that is often so vividly portrayed in movies, as well as in video games. Some will possible consider this to be a naive view and take a much more pessimistic view of life. For me, it is not particularly a religious thing, although I do believe that the human experience has to be essentially one of optimism, because without it what would be the point of it all?

We often hear about the 'Wartime Spirit' that prevailed in the UK and other countries during both World Wars, and at other times of national difficulty. Although many of us are too young to remember, it is clear that desperate times often called for desperate measures. The Canary Islands are not immune from the current financial crisis and many of us have witnessed friends and neighbours losing their jobs, relationships falling apart, and with many returning to their countries of origin.

For the Canary Islanders themselves, times are currently very difficult, with this Spanish autonomous region having one of the highest unemployment statistics in all of Spain. It is heartbreaking to see so many of last year's school leavers without a job. Many young people are just hanging around with their friends in village and town squares, with little to do and a bleak future ahead of them. What an appalling waste of resources, energy and talent!

Many families, as well as individuals fall through the Spanish Social Security net too. Unlike the UK, there is no automatic right to benefits. There is also the problem of illegal immigrants, with many people not being registered as living on the island. We may not approve of their illegal entry, but they and their families still have to be fed and cared for. A society that does not look after its weakest members is no society at all.

It was heartening to see a group of ladies collecting food for people in distressed circumstances at my local supermarket last week. As customers entered the store they were simply asked to purchase one additional food item to give to the local charity, which supported the needy in all parts of the island. The supermarket would then double the quantities of all items purchased from them to help to feed those in need. Items such as flour, rice, pasta, tinned sardines, fruit and vegetables were all items that were welcome. It was good to see so many people giving generously and the collection point outside the store was soon filled with items of generous donations from Saturday shoppers. I guess this scheme is not unique to the Canary Islands, and I do hope that there are similar ventures operating in all parts of Spain.

As I reached the checkout, the gum chewing, tattooed, teenage checkout girl set about her business of swiping all the items in my basket. She suddenly stopped her work as she saw an elderly and poorly looking woman standing in the queue.

She beckoned her towards the till, but the old lady just nodded and smiled. "No, come over here, you can sit here", insisted the young woman, leaping out of her seat by the till, lowering to the height of the small woman and pushed it towards her. "You sit here and rest." She then stood and resumed swiping the items in my basket.

"That was very kind of you," I commented. The young woman smiled, "Well, we will all be old one day."

I left the store with a warm glow, feeling humbled by the actions of this carefree, gum chewing teenager that I had such brief contact with. I had witnessed many examples of people thinking of others. Maybe that "Wartime Spirit" that I had heard so much about from my grandfather was not in the past after all.

A Letter from George

A few days ago, I received a letter from an elderly reader, who has occasionally written to me over the years, either to congratulate or to disagree with one of my 'Twitters'. Although I have never met George, I feel that I know him, as he has told me quite a lot about his life as an expat in Spain, and much of it has been very interesting and, on occasions, very helpful. I had suspected for some time that George was a habitual complainer and one of the "my glass is half full brigade". Still, it takes all sorts to make an expat world, but I find that a naturally positive outlook is always the best advice for would-be expats.

George, who originated from Preston, had lived and worked in Spain for many years. As is the case with many expats, George had assumed that Spain would be his home for life. However, suddenly, he had decided to return to the UK for health reasons, as well as intending to resume contact with an ever-diminishing group of family and friends, whom he began to miss even more as he grew older.

The return to the UK was a mistake, and George quickly became disenchanted with the weather, which meant that he had to spend much of his day in a small, cold and expensive apartment. This, together with the realisation that an adequate pension that had meant a comfortable life in Spain would now hardly pay the essential bills, led George to realise that he had made a grave mistake.

Although he had done his homework thoroughly before moving to Spain some thirty years earlier, he had failed to complete this process in reverse. He was totally unprepared for the many changes that he had to face living in what now seemed a foreign country, and not the "return home" that he had expected.

As George was getting older, he needed his home to be warm, and his first gas bill came as a tremendous shock. He also quickly realised that after living for many years in Spain, his life in the UK, family and friends had moved on. Some had died, others had moved away, and those who had previously kept in contact a few times a year were busy with their own hectic lives, and they had little time left for George. It was not the homecoming that he had expected, and he began to long for his home, climate and life in Spain.

It was a sad letter, and there were points that helped me to understand some of the many issues that many expats face if they decide to make the return trip to their countries of origin. George went on to say that he was considering returning to Spain once again; after six months he already had enough of the UK, and this time he was considering moving to Gran Canaria. He identified the wonderful climate as the main reason, and would I help him to find somewhere suitable to live?

George then went on to tell me that he didn't want to live on either the east or the west coasts of the island. He was opposed to the west of the island, because of the "heavy Atlantic rain" and the strong winds on the east coast.

He was also totally opposed to living in "the fleshpots of the south", because he loathed the tourist industry, and wanted to live well away from tourist beaches and other tourist centres. As George also suffers badly from travel sickness, he would not wish to live anywhere that involved a journey up a twisting mountain road!

I was now wondering exactly where I could suggest as a new home for George. I briefly considered Las Palmas, but realised that based on other correspondence, George didn't like cities either. Residents of Gran Canaria, and visitors who know the island well, will by now recognise my dilemma. I wanted to be helpful, but other than Galdar or maybe, Sardina on the north coast, there really was nowhere in Gran Canaria for George to live. Gran Canaria is often called a continent in miniature", and with very good reason, yet I could suggest nowhere really suitable for George.

If any readers do have (polite) suggestions of where they think George would be happy, do please let me know. However, I also suspect that if I did suggest anywhere, George would be the kind of person who would complain for years, and blame me for the suggestion! I give up! I have come to the conclusion that I will suggest that George moves to Tenerife, and let the good people of Tenerife deal with the problem.

Blisters and sore bums

It is rowing across the Atlantic time again! Why anyone would choose to row across the Atlantic Ocean in a small boat is beyond me, and particularly when there are some very pleasant liners that follow the same route, and with at least three decent meals a day thrown in! I simply don't feel the need to climb a mountain or row across an ocean simply because "It is there." I do, however, have respect for those who take the view that mountains and oceans have no meaning by themselves and that their very presence inspires a dream of pitting our puny strength against their might, and to conquer not them, but ourselves. Rowers row across the Atlantic for the same reasons that mountaineers climb mountains. They like a good stiff challenge, and conditions of adversity tend to bring out the best in them. Indeed, it is as much about psychological strength as it is physical.

The Canary Islands are an ideal launching point for east to west ocean rows, being situated at the base of the Trade Wind Belt. It is 3000 miles from the Canaries to the Caribbean. Although the route begins and ends on islands, it is considered to be a complete Atlantic crossing, and takes advantage of the ideal weather conditions and currents.

December is the time when the races start, and is chosen to coincide with the end of the hurricane season and to get the most benefit from the easterly trade winds and Atlantic currents expected at this time of year.

Rowers who are fortunate to experience favourable current and trade winds can make the trip in as little as two months. Those with bad luck can take three or four months to cover the same distance. This race follows the most favoured route across the Atlantic seeking the Trade Winds and taking in the warm seas and spectacular wildlife of the mid Atlantic.

Teams from all over the world are attracted to take part in the Atlantic Ocean Rowing Race, which provides ordinary people from a wide variety of ages, abilities and backgrounds with the extraordinary opportunity to take on a once in a lifetime challenge and push themselves beyond their mental and physical limits. For most, it is a life changing experience.

Rowers become all too familiar with extreme temperatures, sore bottoms and blisters, powerful storms, 30-foot waves, non-friendly wildlife and hazardous shipping. There is no room on board for home comforts, no bathroom facilities, limited cooking ability and a diet of high calorie expedition foods and desalinated water. Modern rowing boats may not have many amenities, but many are high tech with a wind generator and solar panels to provide power for GPS, reading and navigation lights, radios and the obligatory satellite phone.

Many rowers undertake this challenge as a way of raising money for charity. For me, a soldier who lost both legs in a bomb blast in Iraq and who is to compete the 3,000 mile rowing race across the Atlantic represents the spirit of this competition.

Lieutenant Neil Heritage, from Poole in Dorset (UK) will spend up to 70 days at sea with five crewmembers when he departs from the Canary Islands in December. Neil will take part in the race without prosthetic limbs and will rely totally on his upper-body strength throughout the race. The six-man team includes four soldiers who were injured in Iraq and Afghanistan. The men will be raising money for Row2Recovery, a charity that supports servicemen and women wounded in action (further details on my website); I wish them well.

Rowing across the Atlantic may not be for everyone, and neither is climbing Everest. However, for the right person with the right attitude, it could be a dream come true.

Extreme sport or natural selection?

There have been a number of very sad cases recently of mostly British tourists falling off hotel balconies to their deaths in Spain, the Balearic and the Canary Islands. A recent tragic case of a 22-year-old British man plunging 50ft to his death from the balcony of a holiday apartment in Gran Canaria spurred me on to ask a few more questions about what appears to be a growing phenomena in holiday resorts.

I began to wonder if hotel balconies in Spain, the Balearic and Canary Islands were somehow more dangerous than others. I have stayed in quite a few hotels with balconies in Spain over the years and thought they were no worse than those in Greece, Italy, Portugal or, indeed, the UK. Maybe ancient hotel and apartment buildings, poorly converted in previous years, were to blame? Maybe they are poorly maintained or lack basic safety features?

It seemed strange that so many of these lethal falls from balconies related to older teenagers and young people in their twenties, yet thankfully very rarely to unsupervised toddlers and very young children, which would be easier to understand in some ways. Surely, if balconies were so dangerous, there would have been more accidents relating to this younger age group? Yet, I can hardly remember the last time such an accident involving young children occurred in any Spanish resort. Maybe I was missing something and there were other reasons to be considered, which I had overlooked.

The answer to my questions came in the form of a conversation with a friendly police officer whom I was talking to recently. He drew my attention to another factor that I had never previously considered. It seems that young, mainly British, holidaymakers when staying in hotels with a swimming pool, have invented a new and dangerous 'sport'. This game is referred to as 'balconing' by the Spanish, and is the name given to a relatively new and dangerous activity.

This new game is usually played by young holidaymakers, who have left their brains behind at Gatwick Airport, encouraged by their friends, and often high on alcohol and drugs, who decide to scramble up the sides of high buildings and then proceed to jump from one balcony to another at hotels and apartments. Some of the successful attempts are even filmed and proudly displayed on YouTube and other social media sites. Some even deliberately jump from very high hotel balconies in attempts to land in the swimming pool below, rather in the style of Batman, but with much less purpose. This temporary euphoria often ends in disaster, as the youngsters forget all sense of reality, and as they realise too late that they are not Batman, usually fail to hit the intended spot, and lose their lives, or are permanently injured, as a result.

Young Swedes, Irish and Germans are now also getting in on the act, but it is the Brits who, so far, hold the dubious gold medal in foolishness. In the good old days, it used to be young British men, affectionately referred to worldwide as 'lager louts'.
These lovingly named young people were famed for their binge drinking, colourful language and challenging behaviour. Their charming lack of social awareness and lack of academic prowess made such a fascinating, yet unforgettable impression on holidaymakers in the past. Now it seems that we have merely moved on to a more modern phase, where some young holidaymakers merely leave holidaymakers with memories of a nasty mess in and around the swimming pool. How very inconsiderate.

Some cultures have rituals and traditions for their young men before they pass into adulthood. These 'rights of passage' are often dangerous, life threatening activities designed to test the strength and 'gene worthiness' of members of the species. It is a process by which the weakest and more intellectually challenged members of the species are weeded out. So is 'balconing' an extreme sport or just a basic form of natural selection?

Look, no lights!

I occasionally hear horror stories from expats, as well as from those who have a holiday home in Spain, who suddenly find that their electricity, telephone or water supply has suddenly been disconnected, without warning and with no reason given.

In some cases, and particularly for those who live in another country and only occasionally visit their holiday home, it is often because their direct debit has been bounced by the bank, because of lack of funds in the bank account. This is often a simple explanation where maybe there has been some additional expenditure, and overseas bank accounts are infrequently checked and it can be easy to forget to top up an account to meet regular bills for a holiday home in another country.

However, more seriously, I am hearing more frequent occasions when this is not the case. Some friends recently visiting Gran Canaria were shocked to find that on arrival at their holiday apartment, there was no electricity. There had been sufficient funds in their bank account, yet the direct debit had never been presented to the bank, resulting in disconnection. This situation took several days of their holiday to rectify, and not always easy if you don't happen to speak the language, and in this case involved employing a translator to telephone and later to visit the electricity company.

Eventually, our friends' electricity supply was reconnected, but without the help of the manager of the apartment block, who arranged for a temporary power line to be installed, the first week of a two-week holiday would have been ruined.

We had similar problems with our telephone line with Telefonica some years ago, which was suddenly disconnected for no apparent reason. The bank assured me that there had been sufficient funds in the account, but that no direct debit had been presented. They also advised me that similar problems had affected other bank customers and suggested that this was during the transition period when Telefonica were in the process of changing their name to Movistar.

Despite considerable argument and representations, Telefonica were totally unsympathetic to the problem, and insisted that I pay a reconnection fee before they restored my telephone line. As a result, I transferred the line away from 'The Big Beast', as it is often called, to Vodafone, which offered me a much better service, enhanced facilities and at a lower price.

Last week, I became concerned that I had not received or paid an electricity bill for nearly three months. Even though all my essential bills are paid by direct debit, I have learned not to rely upon this and began to fear that I would, like other expats, find myself without electricity. I checked with my bank, which assured me that no direct debit had been submitted in the last three months.

I called the electricity company and, after several calls, the helpful representative confirmed that it was merely a change in their billing arrangements from monthly to bi-monthly. Anyway, excuses included August was within the billing period, and little happens in August due to the holidays, and bills are delayed...

The August holiday blip and bi-monthly billing I could understand, but bearing in mind that the change to bi-monthly billing had been announced last year, with the company later reverting to monthly bills a couple of months later, I was totally confused.

The customer support representative finally managed to reassure me that they had once again reverted to bi-monthly billing, confirmed that my account was in order and that I wouldn't be disconnected. However, this still didn't explain the gap of three months in their billing.

As is often the case, all is not always as it seems when living as an expat in a new country, and particularly in August. Fingers crossed that I will keep my electricity supply, but I will let you know what happens if it is disconnected!

Where should I move to?

I often receive emails from readers in different countries telling me of their experiences, or asking for advice. Although I cannot always reply to everyone, I am happy to assist whenever I can. However, one email from a middle-aged couple, Sue and Bill, a few days ago set me thinking. The email was along the lines of "We know we want to move away from the UK; the Canary Islands sound ideal, so where do you suggest we move to?"

This message was, in many ways, a strange one. Usually, my correspondents know exactly where they want to move to, or who are already there; their questions usually relate to how to make it possible. This message was different; these writers were completely open-minded, were looking at a blank sheet of paper and could move wherever they wanted to. For me, it was a unique and enviable situation, with the open-minded and fearless attitude common in many idealistic young people, who want to explore the world with only a spare pair of shorts and a toothbrush for company.

My immediate reaction was Gran Canaria, a purely subjective response, of course, because I happen to live here. Why would I recommend somewhere else? However, I tried to point out that it is always a good idea to visit what would-be expats perceive as their ideal destination first.

The ideal way is during holidays over a number of years, until you begin to feel that a certain place is your second home. Of course, I know this is often not possible. Emergency situations, illness or a new job may mean that the ideal method of visiting an intended new country over time, and at different times of the year, may not always be possible. Be it the South of France, Slovakia, the Netherlands or the Canary islands, the seasons bring with it different challenges that may either be a delight or an anathema to the intending expat. So my first piece of advice has to be, try to visit your intended destination at different times of the year and, ideally, over a number of years.

Secondly, different regions of a country, or in my case, the different islands that make up the Canary Islands, are often very different. In the case of the Canary Islands, I adore Gran Canaria because of its 'live and let live' attitude to culture, colour, sexuality, race and religion. It just doesn't matter what you do, within reason, just as long as it doesn't hurt anyone else.

I am also very fond of Fuerteventura, where we will often take a weekend break. The white sands, brilliant blue sea and an uncompromising landscape always refresh me, as does the very different volcanic landscape of its neighbouring island, Lanzarote.

The smaller western Canary Islands, La Palma, La Gomera, and El Hierro, with their lush forests, small, tight knit communities and lack of modern day facilities is like stepping back in time. However, could the would-be expat cope without a regular bus service, a decent broadband connection and large well-equipped hospitals to cope with all possible emergencies? I guess what I am trying to say, is that it is 'horses for courses' and you always need to try it out before you commit.

I have known many expats who have sold up in their birth country and immediately purchased a new home in their newly adopted country. This is usually a great mistake, as we all need time to explore and get used to new communities, people and places.

Renting an apartment for a year or two is my best advice. Only then will the newly arrived expat be sure that what was thought to be perfect, really is. If not, it is best move on again, but now just a little wiser.

So, to Sue and Bill, I would also add two further pieces of advice. If you are intending to move to a non-English speaking country, learn the language! Some expats, sadly, never bother, remain in expat enclaves for the remainder of their expat lives and never fully experience the joy of truly living in another country. Not only should you make an effort to learn the language out of general courtesy to your new neighbours, but in doing so, the door to a new cultural experience opens and genuine expat living begins.

Finally, an essential piece of advice that my first neighbours gave to me when I arrived in Spain, was never believe what you hear in bar gossip or read on some expat blogging sites, where the information given may be selective at best or misleading at worst; always try find out for yourself. Laws, both local and national, tend to change frequently in Mediterranean countries, and particularly during these times of recession when hard-pressed governments are desperately trying to reign in expenditure.

Invariably, the full facts have often been omitted and some bloggers, in my experience, tend to have a distorted view of cultural, financial and political reality. Bad news and panic make good headlines, and attract many followers, but are rarely completely true.

Try to find out for yourself from a reliable expat newspaper, check with your local consulate, trusted lawyer or new neighbours; they will usually know best, or tell you how to find out.

Christmas

The Poinsettia

This is the time when many Town Halls on the island plant out displays of poinsettia for the festive season. Many roundabouts are planted with a wonderful display of these brilliant red plants. In the city of Las Palmas, particularly, the display of these cheerful plants, with their bright red foliage and fresh green leaves, make a very attractive and colourful display for the Christmas and New Year season, and last for many weeks.

I enjoy looking at them and remember that when we lived in the UK, we used to buy one for the Christmas season. However, despite my best efforts of careful watering and positioning, after just a few days the plant would drop its leaves, shrivel and die. Over here, they are treated almost as weeds.

The Flor de Pascua, or poinsettia, is an essential part of Christmas in the Canary Islands and they grow wild, mostly on the northern slopes of the island, but are native to Central America. The Aztecs put the plant to practical, as well as decorative, use and from its bracts they extracted a purplish dye for use in textiles and cosmetics. The milky white sap, today called latex, was made into a preparation to treat fevers.

The poinsettia may have remained a plant native to Mexico for many years had it not been for the efforts of Joel Roberts Poinsett, the son of a French physician. Poinsett was appointed as the first United States Ambassador to Mexico in 1825. Although Poinsett had attended medical school, his real love was botany.

He maintained his own greenhouses on his South Carolina plantations, and while visiting Mexico he became enchanted by the brilliant red blooms that he saw there. He sent some of the plants back to South Carolina, where he began propagating the plants and sending them to friends and botanical gardens.

The poinsettia is also known by a number of other names including, 'Mexican Flame Leaf', 'Christmas Star' and 'Winter Rose'. My favourite name is 'The Flower of the Holy Night', which has a story that goes like this:

There was once a brother and sister who were very poor, and whose names were Maria and Pablo. At Christmas, parties, festivities and parades were held in the village that excited all the children. A large Nativity scene was set up in the village church, and all the children were eager to visit the Baby Jesus and to give him a present. Maria and Pablo also wanted to give a present to the Holy Child, but they had no money and had nothing to give.

On Christmas Eve, Maria and Pablo set out for church a little earlier than the others to attend the service. Since they had nothing to give to the child, they picked some weeds from the roadside to make a soft bed for Baby Jesus and to decorate his crib. While they were still decorating the crib, other children arrived and teased and made fun of them. Maria and Pablo were in tears for their shame and helplessness, but then a miracle occurred.

Suddenly, the weeds burst into bright red petals that looked like stars and were so beautiful that everyone was in awe of their beauty. Everyone then realised that a gift of love is dearer to Jesus than the most expensive presents that money could buy.

I like this story, because it reminds us that expensive gifts are not what Christmas is really about. A Happy Christmas and Festive Season to you all.

Sandcastles at Christmas

I love watching children playing in sand and building sandcastles on the beach. As they grow older, most children quickly become aware that it is only a question of time before the tide comes in, and just one wave destroys all their hard work. I guess it is experiences such as this that helps children to learn that the joy is in the creation and that nothing lasts forever.

In the Canary Islands, we are fortunate that we can all build sandcastles at any time of the year that we wish, and that the Christmas period is no exception. For me, the Christmas season begins during my visit to the amazing sand sculpture on Las Canteras beach in Las Palmas.

Now in its sixth year, these amazing sculptures are created by a team of international artists at the beginning of December and remain for visitors to enjoy until they are bulldozed away on 8 January. Thousands of tonnes of sand, water, as well as the skills of eight of the best sand sculpture artists in the world come together to create 'a Belen', a scene that tells the timeless story of the first Christmas.

This year has a particularly interesting and unusual theme, because it merges features of the Canary Islands with Bethlehem, the town where Jesus was born. Scenes representing Roque Nublo, cliffs, Maspalomas dunes and other aspects of Canarian life co-exist with traditional Bethlehem scenes creating a fascinating and relevant glimpse into Biblical times, which merge with scenes that are so familiar to residents and visitors who know Gran Canaria well.

Artists taking part in this year's 'Arena Bethlehem' are from the Czech Republic, Ireland, Russia, Portugal and Denmark who were given just twenty days to create this year's spectacular scene. Not only does this annual creation help to promote tourism to Gran Canaria, but also adds a very spiritual dimension that is, for many, the start of the Christmas season. Visitors to the sand sculpture are asked to give a donation, which this year will be given to CARITAS (Catholic agency for overseas aid and development), which operates in 200 countries.

The Christmas season can bring with it so many pressures. Buying and paying for presents, particularly in these troubled financial times, food, drink, and entertaining visitors all take their toll. Visitors and residents can give the manic Christmas shopping a miss for a couple of hours and take a stroll in the sunshine along Las Canteras beach. There are plenty of traditional bars and restaurants to enjoy and the scenery is spectacular.

These few minutes help people to enjoy and reflect upon the nativity scene created by the hands of these skilful artists and wonder at the story it tells. Hopefully, the pressures of the Christmas season will begin to ebb away and visitors can begin to enjoy a truly happy and peaceful Christmas.

Roundabouts, Girls and Prickly Cactus

Roundabouts are interesting phenomena in Spain and the Canary Islands. They are a relatively new idea for the country, and it takes time, patience and understanding for most expats to understand the local customs of how to deal with a roundabout. Most of the locals living near me approach a roundabout as fast as they possibly can, and if anything is likely to hit or obstruct them, they slam on their brakes as hard as possible. Great fun!

I approach a roundabout in the boring, studied way that I was taught, and according to the rules of the British Highway Code, i.e. slowing down, approaching the roundabout with caution etc. Needless to say, the result is that I am usually hooted at in a very aggressive way from the vehicle behind. Initially, I thought it was because they were admiring my driving skills, but sadly no. Why is it I that too have not learned that roundabouts in Spain are meant to be an exciting daredevil experience of who dares survives the experience?

Have I mentioned the Brits? Well, although the Spanish and Canary Islanders really do take some beating for shear foolhardiness when behind a wheel, British expat drivers really do win the gold medal. Firstly, they will not accept that it is not normal to drive on the 'wrong' side of the road. By that I mean on the left hand side, when most of the world drives on the right.

Despite many years living in Spain, it is amazing how many British drivers suddenly forget that they are living in Spain, and insist upon driving on the left hand side of the road. Needless to say, this does tend to cause a few problems for other drivers, and I have witnessed a number of occasions when a car approaches a roundabout at speed, and then proceeds to drive the wrong way around it. It can be a very troubling experience to witness.

When I lived in the Costa Blanca, we had roundabouts adorned with pretty, scantily dressed young women, usually of Eastern European origin, clearly looking for someone to take care of them, offer them warmth and shelter and a cup of soup (this is a family publication, after all!). After each mayoral election, the roundabout girls would disappear, only to reappear again a few weeks later. A new mayor always meant a temporary slowdown in business, and time for a much-needed break, that's all.

By contrast, roundabouts in the Canary Islands are adorned with spectacular creative masterpieces, real works of art created by local artists and, in the poorer municipalities, many giant prickly, vicious looking cactus. Yes, you can easily judge the status and wealth of a municipality just by looking at the quality of its roundabouts. It has simply nothing to do with art, but the size of the balance sheet and the influence of the mayor.

A few years ago, our local roundabout was suddenly adorned with a huge and very attractive Christmas tree, appropriately decorated and lit for the Christmas season.

It looked wonderful and, no doubt, added considerable festive pleasure for anyone approaching it. A few evenings before Christmas, a driver headed towards our roundabout and instead of driving around it, decided to head straight for the Christmas tree. I suspect that he was trying to take his place at the top of the tree. Needless to say, he didn't quite manage it, and the car, driver and Christmas tree were badly injured.

That was the end of Christmas for our roundabout and, since that time, no Christmas tree has appeared during the festive season. Mind you, we do have a wonderful display of prickly cactus, so any drivers considering driving over the roundabout to save time - just beware. Prickly cactus hurt!

Final Thought

Although sending messages in a bottle is a very romantic idea from a bygone age, and could always still be useful, if seriously stranded; nowadays we have much more effective means of communication. Fax, Emails, text messages, Facebook, Twitter, WhatsApp and iMessages are all new forms of communication that many of us regularly embrace.

What message would you send in a bottle, or by text message, if it could only be a few words? Maybe it would be your very last words, or just a few words of advice that would make all the difference to the reader in another time and another place…

Printed in Great Britain
by Amazon.co.uk, Ltd.,
Marston Gate.